Developing
A Market
Orientation

About the Marketing Science Institute

The Marketing Science Institute (MSI) was established in 1961 as a not-for-profit institute with the goal of bringing together business leaders and academics to create knowledge that will improve business performance. The primary mission was to provide intellectual leadership in marketing and its allied fields. Throughout the years, MSI's global network of scholars from leading graduate schools of management and thought leaders from sponsoring corporations has expanded to encompass multiple business functions and disciplines. Issues of key importance to business performance are identified by the board of trustees, which represents MSI corporations and the academic community. MSI supports studies by academics on these issues and disseminates the results through conferences and workshops as well as through its publications series.

Developing A Market Orientation

Rohit Deshpandé
Editor

SAGE Publications
International Educational and Professional Publisher
Thousand Oaks   London   New Delhi

For information:

SAGE Publications, Inc.
2455 Teller Road
Thousand Oaks, California 91320
E-mail: order@sagepub.com

SAGE Publications Ltd.
6 Bonhill Street
London EC2A 4PU
United Kingdom

SAGE Publications India Pvt. Ltd.
M-32 Market
Greater Kailash I
New Delhi 110 048 India

Printed in the United States of America

Library of Congress Cataloging-in-Publication Data

Developing a market orientation / edited by Rohit Deshpandé
    p.   cm.
    Papers originally published as Marketing Science Institute working papers.
    Includes bibliographical references and index.
    ISBN 0-7619-1692-X (acid-free paper)
    ISBN 0-7619-1693-8 (pbk.: acid-free paper)
    1. Marketing research. 2. Customer services. 3. Corporate culture. 4. Organization. 5. Competition. I. Deshpandé, Rohit. II. Marketing Science Institute.
    HF5415.2 .D44   1999
    658.8′3dc21   98-40184

99   00   01   02   03   04   05   7   6   5   4   3   2   1

Acquiring Editor: Harry Briggs
Editorial Assistant: MaryAnn Vail
Production Editor: Diana E. Axelsen
Editorial Assistant: Nevair Kabakain
Typesetter/Designer: Christina M. Hill
Cover Designer: Candice Harman
Indexer: Mary Mortensen

Contents

Acknowledgments

This book is truly a collaborative effort. Clearly it represents the efforts of its authors but also, importantly, the behind-the-scenes efforts of the MSI staff. Particular credit goes to Paul Root, president of MSI from 1990 to 1998, to whom this book is dedicated; Katherine Jocz, vice president of research operations, who developed the idea of this book; Marni Clippinger, vice president of MSI member company relations, who has worked tirelessly to identify companies with an interest in this research; Susan Keane, editorial director, whose work on the working papers and on the book itself brought this project to fruition; Michele Kennedy Rainforth, communications and systems manager, who organized the research database for the working papers; and Harry Briggs, acquisitions editor at Sage Publications.

Introduction

Rohit Deshpandé

The History: How Did It Happen?

Terms such as *market-oriented, customer-focused, market-driven,* and *customer-centric* have become synonymous with proactive business strategy in firms worldwide. The notion that the customer needs to be at the origin of business planning processes seems a very contemporary one. In fact, however, the idea of organizing the firm's activities around a deep understanding of customer needs is not recent. Many management theorists cite Peter Drucker's (1954) statement that marketing is not a specialized functional activity but rather "the whole business seen from the point of view of its final result, that is, from the customer's point of view" (p. 39) as an early exemplar of the thinking needed to drive the "marketing concept" through organizational planning. Programmatic scholarly research focusing on the essence of being market driven can be traced to more recent history, however—specifically to three significant events.

In April 1987, the Marketing Science Institute (MSI) organized a conference in Cambridge, Massachusetts, on the topic "Developing a Marketing

Orientation." The purpose of the forum was both to showcase some early learning from market orientation implementation and, more important, to articulate the need for strong, scholarly research to better define, measure, and model the construct. Interestingly, the four speakers at this conference were not academics but executives from leading companies (Borg-Warner Chemicals, GTE, Leo Burnett Advertising, and Ryder). In facilitating the post-presentation group discussion at this conference, then MSI executive director John Farley noted three themes that have continued to represent the bulk of the empirical work in the 10 years since: (a) a need for measurement of the level of a firm's market orientation; (b) a need for understanding whether there is an optimal level of market orientation, given the strategic context of a firm and its industry; and (c) a need for thinking of market orientation as a basis of, rather than a substitute for, innovation in a company.

The second major development that accelerated market orientation research was an MSI conference in September 1990. In contrast to the conference in 1987, this conference featured both academics and practitioners. The latter, including representatives from GE, Du Pont, McKinsey, and USWest, summarized their companies' experiences with instilling a market orientation. Academic speakers framed their remarks within the context of understanding organizational change and included management theorists (Andrew Van de Ven) and marketing scholars (John Mullins, Robert Ruekert, Orville Walker, and Barton Weitz). In a session devoted to reporting findings from recently initiated (and MSI-funded) empirical studies on market orientation, three teams of researchers spoke of the antecedents and consequences of market orientation (Bernard Jaworski and Ajay Kohli), customer orientation in major Japanese companies (Rohit Deshpandé, John Farley, and Frederick E. Webster, Jr.), and strategies for increasing market orientation (John Narver and Stanley Slater). At this conference, two additional themes surfaced: (a) a need for understanding what causes a high market orientation in a company and its impact on business profitability and (b) a need for understanding market orientation at multiple levels, including those of a corporate culture and a strategic orientation. (For a conference summary, see Swartz [1990].)

The final historical development came with the establishment of research on market orientation as a "capital research topic" or highest research priority for funding by MSI (1994-1996 MSI Research Priorities). This designation ensured that future generations of scholars would continue to examine this topic and would submit research proposals to MSI. In fact, market orientation research quickly became a popular area for dissertation thesis research in part because of MSI's showcasing of the strategic importance of the topic for its member firms and MSI's support of the annual Alden G. Clayton doctoral dissertation proposal competition.

Hence, MSI has been the key research organization shepherding the growing body of scholarship on market orientation and continues to provide an important source of funding on the topic as well as a sounding board for generating research ideas relating to market orientation. MSI has served as an intellectual bridge between academic and practitioner communities, surfacing research ideas based on corporate interest, marshalling a group of scholars who would work in this area, and providing a mechanism for diffusing the research knowledge generated to both practitioner and scholarly communities.

This book attempts to capture most of the key contributions to the scholarship on market orientation. All the chapters in this book were originally published as MSI working papers, and most represent research that MSI supported through a variety of financial and nonfinancial means.

The Research: What Is It All About?

Borrowing from past executive director Donald Lehmann's paper, "Market Orientation: State of the Area" (1994), I summarize the scholarship on market orientation as revolving around four questions: What is market orientation? How does market orientation fit in the firm? How do you get it? (i.e., what are its antecedents?) and What impact does it have? (what are its consequences?)

Market orientation was originally defined as an organization-level culture (Deshpandé & Webster, 1987)—a set of shared values and beliefs about putting the customer first in business planning. Recently, market orientation has been defined, and hence measured, as a set of activities or behaviors relating to market intelligence gathering, market intelligence dissemination cross-functionally within a firm, and the action responses based on this intelligence (see Chapter 2). It has also been suggested that market orientation involves an external or outward-looking perspective from a firm—that is, a focus not only on customers but also on competitors (see Chapter 3).

As the previous definitions suggest, there is a strong knowledge or market-related information aspect to market orientation. Hence, its fit within a firm is related to the ability of that firm to effectively manage its market research and intelligence system. Furthermore, market orientation relates to the translation of market knowledge into strategic capabilities (competence) that become disseminated organizationwide. In this sense, market orientation is related to the notion of a learning organization. Also, market orientation provides the basis for a corporate strategy that focuses on serving actual and potential customers. Hence, the fit of market orientation within a firm is three-fold: as part of a market knowledge management system, as part of the development of strategic competence as a learning organization, and as a foundation for corporate strategy.

There continues to be much work on the antecedents of a market orientation. Both top management support for a market orientation and the establishment of appropriate reward systems to make it work are critical (see Chapters 2 and 5; Day, 1991). Furthermore, market orientations flourish in corporate environments in which continuous learning and improvement are encouraged (see Chapter 10) and in which risk taking and innovation are paramount (see Chapter 4).

Finally, as would be expected, there has been much documentation of the positive impact of market orientation on business performance. The latter has been measured in a variety of ways, including organizational commitment and esprit de corps (see Chapter 5), profit impact of market share types of relative market share and profitability measures (see Chapter 4), and sales growth and return on assets (see Chapter 3). This should not be surprising because, due to its external focus, a market-oriented firm has a competitive advantage in both speed and effectiveness in responding to opportunities and threats in its environment (Webster, 1991).

The Themes: What Have We Learned and Where Do We Go Now?

If we recap the themes from the MSI conferences of 1987 and 1990, we can briefly assess how far we have traveled and where we need to go. The five themes are as follows:

1. A need for measurement of the level of a firm's market orientation
2. A need for understanding whether there is an optimal level of market orientation given the strategic context of a firm and its industry

3. A need for thinking of market orientation as a basis of, rather than a substitute for, innovation in a company
4. A need for understanding what causes a high market orientation in a company and its impact on business profitability
5. A need for understanding market orientation at multiple levels, including those of a corporate culture and a strategic orientation

In 1994, Lehmann stated, "We need to refine and integrate existing survey-based measures of market orientation and to develop readily observable measures of it." This was the explicit purpose of the research that culminated in the 1996 working paper by Deshpandé and Farley (Chapter 9) that presents a short 10-item scale measuring market orientation based on a factor analysis of three of the most widely used survey-based measurements (see Chapters 3-5 for these measures).

Lehmann (1994) also stated as research desiderata the

> need to further understand under which conditions market orientation is most crucial . . . and what leads to market orientation. More specifically, we need to develop an understanding of what change mechanisms/interventions can be used to increase market orientation in firms with a low level of it and maintain market orientation in firms with a high level of it.

Here also we have made significant headway. Starting with initial work on the antecedents and consequences of market orientation (see Chapter 5) and progressing to work on market orientation in a learning organization (see Chapter 10), within small firms (see Chapter 7) and within a marketing channel relationship (see Chapter 11), there has been significant progress in answering the questions "How do you get it?" and "What impact does it have?"

Themes 2, 3, and 5 from the previous list need work. First, thinking of optimal levels of market orientation within a contingency framework would be helpful. Perhaps there are diminishing returns to scale in building a market orientation, and we should be thinking of its relationship to business performance as being inverted U shaped rather than linear. Second, most of the empirical work on market orientation has not examined alternative strategic levers of business performance. One MSI-supported research project discovered that, although market orientation is important, organizational innovativeness might be even more important in impacting business profitability (Deshpandé, Farley, & Webster, 1997). Hence, the relationship between a market orientation and a firm's ability to innovate must be researched further. Third, although market orientation was initially defined in terms of a corporate culture, recent work operationalized the construct as a series of activities and behaviors. Clearly, it is both. In fact, we might think of market orientation as operating at three levels: as a *culture* (the shared set of values and beliefs regarding putting customers first), as a *strategy* (creating continuously superior value for a firm's customers), and as *tactics* (the set of cross-functional processes and activities directed at creating and satisfying customers). As will be shown in the chapters in this book, most market orientation measurement has been at the tactical level; hence, we need to better define and measure the construct as a culture and a strategy.

Conclusion

This book documents the MSI research program on market orientation. Although, as noted earlier, MSI can take much credit for having given birth to and nurtured research on this topic, there has been and continues to be much independently conducted scholarship on this strategically vital area. Hence, the chapters in this book provide the conceptual and empirical foundations for this body of work, but we cannot hope to be comprehensive because there is much work in progress, especially in non-U.S. contexts.

References

Day, G. S. (1991). *Learning about marketing* (Report No. 91-117). Cambridge, MA: Marketing Science Institute.

Deshpandé, R., Farley, J. U., & Webster, F. E., Jr. (1997). *Factors affecting organizational performance: A five-country comparison* (Report No. 97-108). Cambridge, MA: Marketing Science Institute.

Deshpandé, R., & Webster, F. E., Jr. (1987). *Organizational culture and marketing: Defining the research agenda* (Report No. 87-106). Cambridge, MA: Marketing Science Institute.

Drucker, P. F. (1954). *The practice of management.* New York: Harper & Row.

Lehmann, D. (1994). *Market orientation: State of the area.* Unpublished executive overview, Marketing Science Institute, Cambridge, MA.

Swartz, G. S. (1990). *Organizing to become market driven* (Report No. 90-123). Cambridge, MA: Marketing Science Institute.

Webster, F. E., Jr. (1991). *The changing role of marketing in the corporation* (Report No. 91-127). Cambridge, MA: Marketing Science Institute.

Market Orientation

The Construct, Research Propositions, and Managerial Implications

Ajay K. Kohli
Bernard J. Jaworski

The authors propose that market orientation may be defined as the organizationwide generation of market intelligence, or information on customers' current and future customer needs, dissemination of that information across departments, and organizationwide responsiveness to it. In essence, market orientation refers to the way that an organization implements the marketing concept.

This three-component view of market orientation (generation of, dissemination of, and responsiveness to market intelligence) makes it possible to diagnose an organization's level of market orientation, pinpoint specific deficiencies, and design interventions tailored to the particular needs of an organization.

Market orientation involves taking concrete actions in response to market intelligence. These actions relate to targeting select market segments and designing new products and programs or modifying existing ones to meet customer needs. It is important to emphasize that a market orientation is not

7

the exclusive responsibility of marketing departments but rather is an organizationwide mode of operation.

The authors contend that a market orientation is likely to lead to higher (a) customer satisfaction and repeat business; (b) esprit de corps, job satisfaction, and employee commitment; and (c) business performance. A market orientation is likely to be more strongly related to performance under conditions of high market turbulence, technological stability, strong competition, and weak economic conditions.

In implementing a market orientation, top managers should first assess the extent to which it is important for their organizations to be market oriented. The impetus for change must come from top managers, who should demonstrate their commitment to customers and a market orientation both in speech and in deed. Top managers should seriously consider promoting a change-oriented attitude, encouraging considered risk taking, supporting mixed-department training programs to foster interdepartmental harmony, instituting integrative mechanisms such as communication networks, and reevaluating performance evaluation criteria so that rewards (compensation and appreciation) are based partly on employees' effort to make the organization market oriented.

The literature reflects remarkably little effort directed toward developing a framework for understanding the implementation of the marketing concept. The purpose of this chapter is to synthesize extant knowledge on the subject and stimulate future research by clarifying the construct's domain, developing research propositions, and constructing an integrating framework that includes antecedents and consequences of a market orientation.

We draw on the occasional writings on the subject during the past 35 years in marketing literature, work in related disciplines, and 62 field interviews with managers in diverse functions and organizations. Managerial implications of this research are discussed. Although the marketing concept represents a cornerstone of the discipline, very little attention has been focused on its implementation. It is important to note that the marketing concept is essentially a business philosophy, an ideal, or a policy statement (Barksdale & Darden, 1971; McNamara, 1972).

The business philosophy may be contrasted with its implementation, as reflected in the activities and behaviors of an organization. In keeping with tradition (McCarthy & Perreault, 1984, p. 36), we use the term *market orientation* to mean the implementation of the marketing concept. Thus, a market-oriented organization is one whose actions are consistent with the marketing concept.

In the past decade, there has been a strong resurgence of academic and practitioner interest in the marketing concept and its implementation (Deshpandé & Webster, 1989; Houston, 1986; Olson, 1987; Webster, 1988). We seek to further these efforts by providing a foundation for the systematic development of a theory of market orientation.

Given its widely acknowledged importance, one might imagine that the concept has a clear meaning, a rich tradition of theory development, and a related body of empirical findings. On the contrary, a close examination of the literature reveals a lack of clear definition, little careful attention to measurement issues, and virtually no empirically based theory. Furthermore, there is little discussion in the literature of the contextual factors that may make a market orientation either more or less appropriate for a particular business. In this chapter, we attempt to delineate the domain of the market orientation construct, provide an operational definition, develop a propositional inventory, and construct a comprehensive framework for directing future research.

We first describe the method employed to attain our objectives. Essentially, we draw on the literature in marketing and related disciplines and supplement it with data from field interviews with managers in diverse functions, hierarchical levels, and organizations. Our discovery-oriented approach (Deshpandé, 1983; Mahrer, 1988) is similar to the qualitative, practitioner-based approach employed by Parasuraman, Zeithaml, and Berry (1985) and is designed to tap the cause-and-effect maps of managers (Zaltman, Duncan, LeMasters, & Heffring, 1982).

Next, we compare and contrast the alternative conceptualizations in the literature with the results of the field data and provide a synthesis. We then develop a series of research propositions developed in such diverse areas as sales management (Walker, Gilbert, Churchill, & Ford, 1977; Weitz, 1981), organization of marketing activities (Ruekert, Walker, & Roering, 1985), diffusion of technology (Robertson & Gatignon, 1986), information processing (Alba & Hutchinson, 1987), and marketing control systems (Jaworski, 1988).

These literature- and field-based propositions are synthesized in an integrative framework that provides for a parsimonious conceptualization of the overarching factors of interest. Finally, we conclude with a discussion that alerts managers to important issues involved in modifying business orientations.

Method

Literature Review

A review of the literature from the past 35 years reveals that relatively little attention has been given to the marketing concept. The limited research primarily comprises (a) descriptive work concerning the extent to which organizations have adopted the concept (Barksdale & Darden, 1971; Hise, 1965; Lusch, Udell, & Laczniak, 1976; McNamara, 1972); (b) essays extolling the virtues of the business philosophy ("Marketing Men," 1950; McKitterick, 1957; Viebranz, 1967); (c) work on the limits of the concept (Houston, 1986; Levitt, 1969; Tauber, 1974); and, to a lesser extent, (d) discussions of factors that facilitate or hamper the implementation of the marketing concept (Felton, 1959; Lear, 1963; Webster, 1988). We draw on these limited writings, especially the last category, and also on related literature in the management discipline.

Field Data

The field research consisted of in-depth interviews with 62 managers in four U.S. cities. Because the purpose of the study was theory construction (i.e., elicitation of constructs and propositions), it was important to ensure that a wide range of experiences and perspectives were tapped in the course of data collection. Therefore, a purposive theoretical sampling plan (Glaser & Strauss, 1967) was used to ensure that the sample included marketing and nonmarketing managers from industrial, consumer, and service industries. Care was also taken to sample large and small organizations.

Of the 62 individuals interviewed, 33 held marketing positions, 15 held nonmarketing positions, and 14 held senior management positions. A total of 47 organizations were included in the sample, and multiple individuals were interviewed in certain organizations. Eighteen interviewees worked for organizations that marketed consumer products, 26 worked for companies that marketed industrial products, and 18 worked for companies that marketed services. In terms of size, the organizations ranged from four employees to several tens of thousands. The sample thus reflects a diverse set of organizations, departments, and positions and hence provides a rich sampling of ideas and insights.

In addition to managers, 10 business academics at two large U.S. universities were also interviewed. The purpose of these interviews was to tap insights that might not emerge from the literature review and the field interviews.

The interviewers generally followed a standard format for the interviews. After a brief description of the research project, each interviewee was asked the following questions:

1. What does the term *market* or *marketing orientation* mean to you? What kinds of things does a market- or marketing-oriented company do?
2. What organizational factors foster or hinder this orientation?
3. What are the positive and negative consequences of this orientation?
4. Can you think of business situations in which this orientation may not be very important?

Although these questions provided a structure for each interview, it was often necessary to explain and clarify some of the questions to elicit examples and illustrations. The personal interviews typically lasted approximately 45 minutes and were audiotaped except when interviewees requested otherwise. The data obtained from these interviews offer novel insights into the meaning, causes, and consequences of a market orientation.

Market Orientation: The Construct

Comparing Literature and Field Perspectives

A review of the literature reveals many diverse definitions of the marketing concept. Felton (1959) defines the marketing concept as "a corporate state of mind that insists on the integration and coordination of all the marketing functions which, in turn, are melded with all other corporate functions, for the basic purpose of producing maximum long-range corporate profits" (p. 55). In contrast, McNamara (1972) takes a broader view and defines the concept as "a philosophy of business management, based upon a company-wide acceptance of the need for customer orientation, profit orientation, and recognition of the important role of marketing in communicating the needs of the market to all major corporate departments" (p. 51). One or another variant of these ideas is offered by Lavidge (1966), Levitt (1969), Konopa and Calabro (1971), Bell and Emory (1971), and Stampfl (1978).

It is important to note that there are three core themes or pillars in these ad hoc definitions: (a) customer focus, (b) coordinated marketing, and (c) profitability (Kotler, 1988). Barksdale and Darden (1971) point out, however, that these idealistic policy statements represented by the marketing concept are of severely limited practical value, and they assert that "the major challenge is the development of operational definitions for the marketing concept" (p. 36).

Thus, although the literature sheds some light on the philosophy represented by the marketing concept, it is unclear on the specific activities that translate the philosophy into practice. Even so, it appears reasonable to conclude that the literature suggests that a market-oriented organization is one in which the three pillars of the marketing concept (customer focus, coordinated marketing, and profitability) are operationally manifest.

The view of market orientation that emerges from the field data is consistent with the received view in the literature, although certain differences are also evident. Importantly, the field data provide a significantly clearer idea of the construct's domain and enable us to offer a more precise definition. This precision facilitates theory development, construct measurement, and eventually theory testing. In the following discussion, we compare the field-based view of market orientation with the received view along its three commonly accepted pillars—customer focus, coordinated marketing, and profitability—and then elaborate on the elements of the field-based view of the construct.

Customer Focus

Without exception, the managers interviewed for this research believed that a customer focus is the central element of a market orientation. Although they agreed with the traditional view that a customer focus involves obtaining information from customers about their needs and preferences, several executives emphasized that it goes far beyond customer research. The field data suggest that being customer oriented involves taking actions based on market intelligence rather than verbalized customer opinions alone. Market intelligence is a broader concept that includes consideration of exogenous market factors (e.g., competition and regulation) that affect customer needs and preferences and current as well as future customer needs. It is important to recognize that these extensions do not challenge the spirit of the first pillar (customer focus); rather, they reflect practitioners' broader, more strategic concerns related to customers.

Coordinated Marketing

Although few interviewees explicitly mentioned coordinated marketing in the discussions, the majority emphasized that a market orientation is not the sole responsibility of a marketing department. The executives also emphasized that it is critical for a variety of departments to be cognizant of customer needs (i.e., aware of market intelligence) and responsive to them.

Thus, the interviewees stressed the importance of concerted action by the various departments of an organization. Importantly, the field data limit the domain of the second pillar of market orientation to coordination with respect to market intelligence. This focused view of coordination is important because it facilitates operationalizing the construct by clearly specifying the type of coordination that is relevant.

Profitability

In sharp contrast to the received view, the idea that profitability is a component of market orientation was conspicuous by its absence in the field data. Without exception, interviewees viewed profitability as a consequence of a market orientation rather than a part of it. This finding is consistent with Levitt's (1969) strong objection to viewing profitability as a component of a market orientation, which he asserts is "like saying that the goal of human life is eating" (p. 236).

Thus, the meaning of the market orientation construct in the field is essentially a more precise and operational view of the first two pillars of the marketing concept—customer focus and coordination. The field data suggest that a market orientation entails (a) one or more departments engaging in activities geared toward developing an understanding of customers' current and future needs and the factors affecting them, (b) a sharing of this understanding across departments, and (c) the various departments engaging in activities designed to meet select customer needs. In other words, a market orientation refers to the organizationwide generation of, dissemination of, and responsiveness to market intelligence. Furthermore, although the term *marketing orientation* has been employed in previous writings, it appears that the label "market orientation" is preferable for three reasons.

First, as Shapiro (1988) suggests, market orientation clarifies that it is not exclusively a concern of the marketing function but that a variety of departments participate in generating market intelligence, disseminating it, and taking action in response to it. Hence, labeling the construct as marketing orientation is both restrictive and misleading.

Second, market orientation is less politically charged in that it does not inflate the importance of the marketing function in an organization. The label takes the province of the construct away from the marketing department and makes it the responsibility of all the departments in an organization. As such, the orientation is more likely to be embraced by nonmarketing departments.

Third, the label focuses attention on markets (that include customers and forces affecting them), which is consistent with the broader management of market orientation proposed by Park and Zaltman (1987, p. 7) for addressing limitations in currently embraced paradigms. Each of the three elements of a market orientation (intelligence generation, dissemination, and responsiveness) is discussed more completely in the following section.

Explicating the Market Orientation Construct

Intelligence Generation

The starting point of a market orientation is market intelligence. Market intelligence includes customers' verbalized needs and preferences as well as an analysis of exogenous factors that influence those needs and preferences. For example, several managers indicated that a market orientation includes monitoring factors such as government regulations and competition that influence the needs and preferences of their customers. Several interviewees who catered to organizational customers emphasized that a market orientation includes an analysis of changing conditions in customers' industries and their impact on the needs and wants of customers. Likewise, the importance of monitoring competitor actions and how these might affect customer preferences emerged in the course of the interviews. (See Day and Wensley [1983], who point out the limitations of focusing on customers to the exclusion of competitors.) Thus, although market intelligence pertains to customer needs and preferences, it includes an analysis of how these may be affected by exogenous factors such as government regulation, technology, competitors, and other environmental forces. As such, environmental scanning activities are subsumed under market intelligence generation.

An important idea expressed by several executives was that effective market intelligence pertains not just to current needs but also to future needs. This idea echoes Houston's (1986) assertion and reflects a departure from conventional views (e.g., find a need and fill it) in that it urges organizations to anticipate customer needs and initiate steps to meet them. The notion that market intelligence includes anticipating customer needs is important because it often takes years for an organization to develop a new product offering.

A senior vice president of a large industrial services company observed,

> [When] should [our company] enter the [certain services] area? Is there a market there yet? Probably not. But there's going to be one in, 1990, '91, '92, '96. And you don't want to be too late because it's going to take you a couple of years getting up to speed, getting your reputation established. So you've really got to jump into it two years before you think [the market for it is going to develop].

Although assessment of customer needs is the cornerstone of a market orientation, defining customers is not simple. In some cases, businesses may have consumers (i.e., end-users of products and services) and clients (i.e., organizations that may dictate or influence the choices of end-users). For example, executives from several packaged goods companies indicated that it is critical for their organizations to understand the needs and preferences of both end-customers and retailers through whom their products are sold. This sentiment reflects the growing power of retailers over manufacturers owing to the consolidation of the former, retailers' access to scanner data, and increased competition among manufacturers because of the proliferation of brands. One executive indicated that it was important for him to keep retailers satisfied to ensure that they carried and promoted his products, which in turn enabled him to cater to the needs of his end-customers.

It is interesting to note that in the 1920s and 1930s, the term *customer* primarily referred to distributors who purchased goods and made payments (McKitterick, 1957). Starting in approximately the 1950s, the focus shifted away from distributors to end-consumers and their needs and wants. Today, the appropriate focus appears to be the market, which includes end-users and distributors as well as exogenous forces that affect their needs and preferences.

Identifying who an organization's customers are has lent additional complexity in instances in which service is provided to one party but payments are received from another. For example, the manager for a health care organization recalled,

> In the past we asked patients what they wanted for services, how they wanted the service delivered. Now the patient is no longer making those decisions. [It is] more complicated. [We define] our customers today as those paying for the patients' care.

The generation of market intelligence relies not only on customer surveys but also on a host of complementary mechanisms. Intelligence may be generated through a variety of formal and informal means (e.g., informal discussions with trade partners) and may involve collecting primary data or consulting secondary sources. These mechanisms include meetings and discussions with customers and trade partners (e.g., distributors), analysis of sales reports and worldwide customer databases, and formal market research, such as customer attitude surveys and sales response in test markets. The following statement by a director of marketing at a high-tech industrial products company illustrates the information collection and analysis activity:

> We do a lot of visiting with customers, talking with customers on the phone, we read the trade press—it is full of good information about what our competitors are doing. We always want to position relative to competitors. A lot of marketing is information gathering.

Intelligence generation is not the exclusive responsibility of a marketing department. For example, R&D engineers may obtain information at scientific conferences, and senior executives might uncover trends reported in trade journals. Managers in several industrial products companies indicated that it was a routine affair for their R&D personnel to interact directly with customers to assess their needs and problems and develop new business targeted at satisfying those needs. One company we interviewed goes to extreme lengths to encourage the exchange of information between nonmarketing employees and customers. For its annual "open house," invitations to customers are hand-delivered by manufacturing rather than marketing personnel. Customers visit the plant and interact with shop floor personnel and white-collar employees. This enables manufacturing personnel to understand better the purchase motivations of customers and helps customers better appreciate the limits and constraints of the processes involved in manufacturing items they required. The president of this company stated,

> [The open house] does two things for you. First, it impresses the customers that the people in manufacturing are interested in your business, and the other thing is that it impresses on the people in manufacturing that there are people who buy the product—real, live-bodied, walking-around people. Our people learn, but our customers are educated at the same time.

To help it anticipate customer needs accurately, one blue-chip industrial products company has individuals devoted exclusively to studying trends and forces in the industries to which major customer groups belong (see related discussion in Lenz & Engledow [1986]). This company goes so far as to identify future customer needs and plan future offerings jointly with customers. The important point is that the generation of market intelligence does not stop at obtaining customer opinions, but it also involves careful analysis and subsequent interpretation of the forces at work on customer needs and preferences. Equally important, the field data suggest that the generation of market intelligence is not, and probably cannot be, the exclusive responsibility of a marketing department (Webster, 1988). Rather, market intelligence is generated collectively by individuals and departments throughout an organization. As such, it is important that mechanisms are in place for intelligence generated at one location to be effectively disseminated to other parts of an organization.

Intelligence Dissemination

As the interviews progressed, it became increasingly clear that effectively responding to a market need requires the participation of virtually all departments in an organization—R&D to design and develop a new product, manufacturing to gear up and produce it, purchasing to develop vendors for new parts and materials, finance to fund activities, and so on. Several managers noted that for an organization to adapt to market needs, market intelligence needs to be communicated, disseminated, and perhaps even sold to relevant departments and individuals in an organization.

Marketing managers in two consumer products companies developed and circulated periodic newsletters to disseminate market intelligence. These activities echo suggestions in the literature that organizational direction is a result of marketing, educating, and communicating with other management functions (Levitt, 1969), and that marketers' most important role may be one of selling within the firm (Anderson, 1982). As noted earlier, however, market intelligence need not always be disseminated by the marketing department to other departments. The direction of the intelligence flows may be reversed depending on where it is generated. Effective dissemination of market intelligence is important because it provides a shared basis for concerted actions by different departments. An executive recounted the intelligence dissemination process for a new product required by a customer as follows: "I get engineering involved. Engineering gets production involved. We have management lunches and informal forums. Call reports circulate. By the time you design, [you have] engineering, production, and purchasing involved early in the process."

Although a formal intelligence dissemination procedure is obviously important, it became clear from the discussions with managers that informal conversations are an extremely powerful tool for keeping employees tuned to customers and their needs. Despite sparse treatments of the effects of informal information dissemination in virtually any literature (for a rare exception, see Aguilar [1967]), managers recognize its importance and tap it extensively. For example, the vice president of a manufacturing firm indicated that customer information is disseminated in her organization by telling stories about customers, their needs, their personality characteristics, and even their families. The idea is to have the secretaries, engineers, and production personnel "get to know" customers. She described her informal intelligence dissemination as follows:

> One goal when I took over was to know everything about customers: [whether] they liked cats . . . [their] wives' names, favorite pet peeve about our products. Our sales reps need to know this. . . . I do a lot of storytelling. Later, [I] developed software to computerize all this. Everyone in the organization has access to this database.

The emphasis on intelligence dissemination parallels recent acknowledgment of the important role of "horizontal communication" in service organizations (Zeithaml, Berry, & Parasuraman, 1988). Horizontal communication refers to the lateral flow that occurs both within and between departments (Daft & Steers, 1985) and serves to coordinate people and departments to attain overall organizational goals. In the current context, the horizontal communication of market intelligence represents one form of intelligence dissemination within an organization.

Responsiveness

The third element of a market orientation is responsiveness to market intelligence. An organization can generate intelligence and disseminate it internally; unless it responds to market needs, however, very little is accomplished. Responsiveness refers to the actions taken after intelligence is generated and disseminated. The following quote from an account executive in a service organization describes this type of responsiveness: "We are driven by what the customer wants. We try to gather data, do research, put together new products based on this research, and then promote them."

The field data indicate that responsiveness to market intelligence takes the form of selecting target markets, designing and offering products and services for catering to their current and anticipated needs, and producing, distributing, and promoting the products in a manner that elicits favorable end-customer response. As noted earlier, virtually all departments—not just marketing—participate in responding to market trends in a market-oriented company.

Synthesis and Commentary

On the basis of the preceding discussion, we offer a formal definition of market orientation as the organizationwide generation of market intelligence pertaining to current and future customer needs, dissemination of the intelligence across departments, and organizationwide responsiveness to it. Defining market orientation as the organizationwide generation of, dissemination of, and responsiveness to market intelligence addresses the concerns of Barksdale and Darden (1971) by focusing on specific activities rather than philosophical notions, thereby facilitating the operationalization of the marketing concept.

Interestingly, it appears to be more appropriate to view a market orientation as a continuous rather than a dichotomous, either-or construct. A sales manager for an industrial products company noted, "The first thing to recognize is that there is no absolute, that there are many shades of gray." In other words, organizations vary in the extent to which they generate market intelligence, disseminate it internally, and take action based on the intelligence. It is therefore more appropriate to conceptualize the market orientation of an organization as one of degree that lies on a continuum rather than as either present or absent. This conceptualization facilitates measurement by avoiding certain difficulties inherent in asking informants to indicate whether their organization is market oriented (e.g., what if it is somewhat market oriented?). The proposed definition suggests that a measure of market orientation need only assess the degree to which a company is market oriented—that is, generates intelligence, disseminates it, and takes actions. Relatedly, the appropriate unit of analysis appears to be the strategic business unit (SBU) rather than the corporation because it is likely that the different SBUs of a corporation may be market oriented to different degrees.

Next, we discuss antecedents and consequences of a market orientation and moderators of the linkage between market orientation and business performance. We draw on the marketing and management literatures and field data for developing research propositions.

Research Propositions

A conceptual framework is provided in Figure 2.1 for guiding the following discussion. Briefly, the framework is composed of four factors: (a) antecedent conditions that foster or hinder a market orientation, (b) the market orientation construct, (c) consequences of a market orientation, and (d) moderator variables that either strengthen or weaken the relationship between market orientation and business performance. In turn, we discuss each of the four factors and develop propositions based on the literature and the field data.

Antecedents to a Market Orientation

Antecedents to a market orientation refer to the organizational factors that enhance or impede the implementation of the business philosophy represented by the marketing concept. Our examination of the literature and the insights from the field interviews reveal three hierarchically ordered catego-

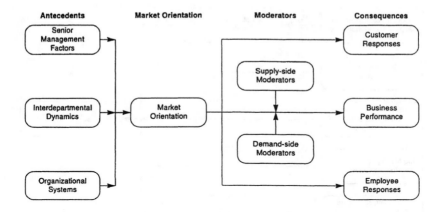

Figure 2.1. Antecedents to and Consequences of a Market Orientation

ries of antecedents to a market orientation: individual, intergroup, and organizationwide factors. We label these senior management factors, interdepartmental dynamics, and organizational systems.

Senior Management Factors

The role of senior management emerged as one of the most important
factors in fostering a market orientation (Figure 2.2). Interviewees repeatedly
emphasized the powerful impact that top management has on an organization.
The following quotes are representative of the ideas that surfaced in the
course of the interviews:

> We'll do almost a $100 million [worth of sales] this year. We have a cus-
> tomer that bought [a mere] $10,000 worth of services. [He] calls the presi-
> dent, [and launches into a long tirade of complaints]. [The president]
> writes down what he says and responds to him in writing. He investigates
> the difficulty. He gets back to him. In that process, if you are a junior
> engineer who just worked on a $10,000 project and the president calls you
> up and says, "Let's talk about this and work out some kind of response to
> him," the word spreads throughout the base of the company [that] we're
> a customer-oriented company, we're marketplace-oriented, we want to
> satisfy customer needs.
>
> *—Senior vice president, industrial services company*

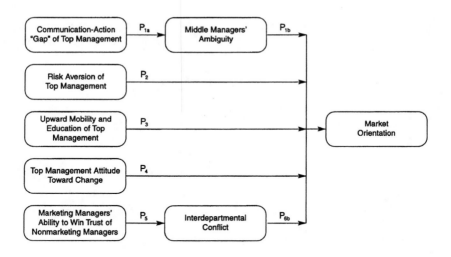

Figure 2.2. Senior Management Factors and Market Orientation

> The founder of this organization is a salesman. His shortcoming is that he does not know what marketing is. We reflect the leader.
>   —*Marketing manager, service organization*

The critical role of top management in fostering a market orientation is also reflected in the literature. For example, Webster (1988) asserts that a market orientation originates with top management, and that "customer-oriented values and beliefs are uniquely the responsibility of top management" (p. 37). Likewise, Felton (1959) believes that the most important ingredient of a market orientation is an appropriate state of mind, and that this is attainable only if "the board of directors, chief executive, and top-echelon executives appreciate the need to develop this marketing state of mind" (p. 55). In other words, the commitment of top management is an essential prerequisite to a market orientation.

In addition, Levitt (1969) argues that one of the factors that facilitates the implementation of the marketing concept is the presence of "the right signals from the chief operating officer to the entire corporation regarding its continuing commitment to the marketing concept" (p. 244). In a similar vein, Webster (1988) suggests that "CEOs must give clear signals and establish clear values and beliefs about serving the customer" (p. 37). Thus, these scholars assert that in addition to being committed to a market orientation, top management must clearly communicate its commitment to all concerned in an organization.

Interestingly, the management literature goes a step further to provide novel insights. Argyris (1966) argues that a key factor affecting junior managers is the gap between what top managers say and what they do (e.g., they say "be market oriented" but cut back market research funds and discourage changes). Argyris examined 265 decision-making meetings with senior executives and concluded that the actual behavior of managers does not conform to what they espouse. It may be argued, however, that if the gap is consistent over time, junior managers may be able to infer what top management truly wants. In contrast, if the size and direction of the gap are inconsistent over time, junior managers are unlikely to be able to infer top management's actual preferences. Such variability in gaps in the current context is likely to lead to ambiguity on the part of junior managers about the amount of effort and resources they should allocate to market-oriented tasks, thereby leading to lower market orientation. Thus,

P_{1a}: The greater the variability over time in the gap between top managers' communications and actions concerning a market orientation, the greater the junior managers' ambiguity concerning the organization's desire to be market oriented.

P_{1b}: The greater the junior managers' ambiguity concerning the organization's desire to be market oriented, the lower the market orientation of the organization.

A market orientation involves being responsive to market intelligence. Changing market needs call for the introduction of innovative products and services to match evolving needs. The introduction of new or modified offerings and programs, however, is inherently risky in that the new offerings may fail. A marketing director of a service organization noted, "Hospitals cannot survive unless they are innovative throughout the organization. It means taking risks, doing some real concrete things with customers," and a president of an industrial services company stated,

> To be marketing oriented is not to be safe because you're running a risk. You have to invest in your ideas. To not be marketing oriented is to be safe.

[It means doing] the same old [thing]. You're not investing in your business, not (taking) risks.

In the course of the discussion with the latter executive, it became clear that top management's response to innovative programs that do not succeed sends clear signals to junior employees in an organization. If management demonstrates a willingness to take risks and accept occasional failures as natural, junior managers are more likely to propose and introduce new offerings in response to changes in customer needs. In contrast, if top management is risk averse and intolerant of failures, subordinates are less likely to be responsive to changes in customer needs. Thus,

P_2: The greater the risk aversion of top management, the lower the market orientation of the organization.

As noted previously, a market orientation involves being responsive to changing customer and client needs with innovative marketing programs and strategies, and therefore it may be viewed as a continuous innovative behavior. Hambrick and Mason (1984) suggest that organizations headed by top managers who are young, have extensive formal education, and have low socioeconomic origins (and, by implication, have demonstrated upward social mobility) are more likely to pursue risky and innovative strategies. In the diffusion-of-innovation literature, formal education and upward mobility are reported as being consistently related to innovative behavior (Rogers, 1983, Chapter 7).

The age variable, however, does not produce consistent findings across studies. Taken together, these findings suggest that the market orientation of an organization may be a function of the formal education of its senior managers and the extent to which they are upwardly mobile. More formally,

P_3: The greater the senior managers' educational attainment and upward mobility, the greater the market orientation of the organization.

A positive attitude toward change has been consistently linked to individual willingness to innovate. In a comprehensive review, Rogers (1983, p. 260) reports that 43 of 57 studies found a positive relationship between these two constructs. As noted earlier, willingness to adapt and change marketing programs based on analyses of consumer and market trends is a hallmark of a market-oriented firm. Thus, top management's openness to new ideas and acceptance of the view that change is a critical component of organizational success is likely to facilitate a market orientation. That is,

> P_4: The more positive the senior managers' attitude toward change, the greater the market orientation of the organization.

Certain characteristics of department managers and the nature of interactions among them appear likely to affect an organization's market orientation through their impact on interdepartmental conflict (Figure 2.2). Interdepartmental conflict refers to tension between two or more departments that arises from incompatibility of actual or desired responses (Gaski, 1984; Raven & Kruglanski, 1970, p. 70). Felton (1959) and Levitt (1969) suggest that it is critical for a marketing vice president to be able to win the confidence and cooperation of his or her corporate peers to minimize conflict and engender a market orientation. The authors, however, do not elaborate on the factors that engender this ability. Nevertheless, this suggests the following:

> P_5: The greater the ability of top marketing managers to win the confidence of senior nonmarketing managers, the lower the interdepartmental conflict.

Interdepartmental Dynamics

Interdepartmental dynamics refer to the formal and informal interactions and relationships among an organization's departments. In Proposition 5, we introduced the first interdepartmental construct, "conflict." In this section we discuss the linkage between interdepartmental conflict and market orientation and additional interdepartmental dynamics (Figure 2.3). Levitt (1969), Lusch et al. (1976), and Felton (1959) suggest that interdepartmental conflict may be detrimental to the implementation of the marketing concept. Interdepartmental conflict may stem from natural desires of individual departments to be more important or powerful or may even be inherent in the charters of the various departments. For example, Levitt (1969) argues that the job of a manufacturing vice president is to run an efficient plant. As such, it is natural for the vice president to oppose costly endeavors that might be called for by a market orientation. Recent research (Ruekert & Walker, 1987)

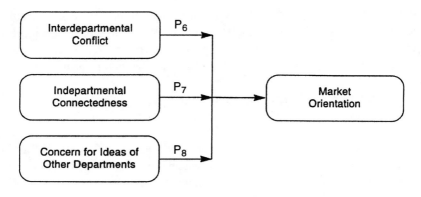

Figure 2.3. Interdepartmental Dynamics and Market Orientation

suggests that interdepartmental conflict inhibits communication across departments. In the current context, therefore, it appears likely that interdepartmental conflict inhibits market intelligence dissemination, which is an integral component of a market orientation. In addition, tension among departments is likely to inhibit concerted response by the departments to market needs, also a component of market orientation. We therefore expect the following:

P_6: The greater the interdepartmental conflict, the lower the market orientation of the organization.

A second interdepartmental dynamic that emerged in several interviews as an antecedent of a market orientation is interdepartmental connectedness. This variable refers to the degree of direct formal and informal contact among employees across departments. For example, one executive noted that to improve its market orientation, her organization opened up communication channels across departments—in stark contrast to the previous practice of departments operating independently of one another, coordinated only by top management. One interviewee indicated that her organization formally required periodic meetings of employees from different departments, thereby facilitating the sharing of market intelligence. The importance of interdepartmental connectedness in facilitating the dissemination and responsiveness to market intelligence is supported by the evaluation literature (Cronbach et al.,

1981) and the marketing literature (Deshpandé & Zaltman, 1982). Indeed, the key predictors of research information utilization in program evaluation settings are the extent and quality of interaction between the evaluators and the program personnel (Patton, 1978). The preceding discussion of the field data and the literature suggests the following:

P_7: The greater the interdepartmental connectedness, the greater the market orientation of the organization.

As Figure 2.3 illustrates, an additional construct pertaining to interdepartmental dynamics suggested by the literature on group dynamics is concern for others' ideas (Argyris, 1965, 1966) or interest in the suggestions and proposals of other individuals or groups. In a study on decision making, Argyris (1966) observes that low levels of concern are directly related to restricted information flows, distrust, and antagonism, which result in ineffective group processes.

In the current context, therefore, it may be argued that low levels of concern for the ideas of individuals in other departments impede the dissemination of market intelligence across departments and the responsiveness of individuals to intelligence generated in other departments. Thus,

P_8: The greater the concern for ideas of employees in other departments, the greater the market orientation of the organization.

Organizational Systems

The third set of antecedents to a market orientation relate to organizationwide characteristics and are therefore labeled "organizational systems" (Figure 2.4). A set of barriers to a market orientation briefly discussed in the marketing literature concerns the structural form of organizations. Lundstrom (1976) and Levitt (1969) discuss departmentalization or specialization as a barrier to communication (and hence intelligence dissemination). In addition, Stampfl (1978) argues that greater formalization and centralization make organizations less adaptive to marketplace and environmental changes.

These references to organizational structure have their roots in the organizational sciences literature. *Formalization* refers to the degree to which rules define roles, authority relations, communications, norms and sanctions,

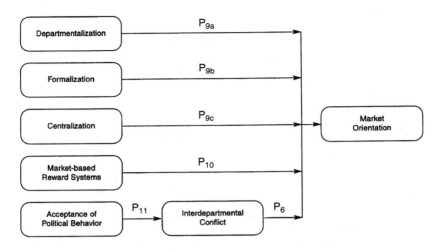

Figure 2.4. Organizational Systems and Market Orientation

and procedures (Hall, Haas, & Johnson, 1967). *Centralization* is defined as the delegation of decision-making authority throughout an organization and the extent of participation by organizational members in decision making (Aiken & Hage, 1968). Historically, both formalization and centralization have been inversely related to information utilization (Deshpandé & Zaltman, 1982; Hage & Aiken, 1970; Zaltman, Duncan, & Holbek, 1973). In the current context, information utilization corresponds to being responsive to market intelligence. Thus, the literature suggests that structural characteristics of an organization can influence its market orientation.

Interestingly, there is reason to believe that the organizational structure may not affect the three components of a market orientation in a like fashion. As noted earlier, because a market orientation essentially involves doing something new or different in response to market conditions, it may be viewed as a form of innovative behavior. Zaltman et al. (1973, p. 62) characterize innovative behavior as being composed of two stages: initiation (i.e., awareness and decision-making stage) and implementation (i.e., carrying out the decision). In the current context, the initiation stage corresponds to intelligence generation, dissemination, and the design of organizational response, whereas the implementation stage corresponds to the actual organizational response. Zaltman et al. (1973) draw on numerous studies to argue that organizational dimensions, such as departmentalization, formalization, and centralization, may have opposite effects on the two stages of the innovative behavior. In particular, they indicate that although these variables may hinder the initiation stage of innovative behavior, the same variables may actually facilitate the implementation stage of innovative behavior. This suggests that departmentalization, formalization, and centralization may be inversely related to intelligence generation, dissemination, and response design but positively related to response implementation. Thus,

$P_{9a:}$ The greater the departmentalization, (a) the lower the intelligence generation, dissemination, and response design and (b) the greater the response implementation.

$P_{9b:}$ The greater the formalization, (a) the lower the intelligence generation, dissemination, and response design and (b) the greater the response implementation.

$P_{9c:}$ The greater the centralization, (a) the lower the intelligence generation, dissemination, and response design and (b) the greater the response implementation.

The management literature reflects a rich history of work on measurement and reward systems and their effects on the attitudes and behavior of employees (Hopwood, 1974; Lawler & Rhode, 1976). Recent research in marketing builds on this work by emphasizing the importance of measurement and reward systems in shaping both desirable and undesirable behaviors (Anderson & Chambers, 1985; Jaworski, 1988). Webster (1988) argues that "the key to developing a market-driven, customer-oriented business lies in how managers are evaluated and rewarded" (p. 38). He observes that if managers are primarily evaluated based on short-term profitability and sales, they are likely to focus on these criteria and neglect market factors, such as customer satisfaction, that ensure the long-term health of an organization.

Webster's (1988) observations are supported by the practices of several organizations included in the study. Only one organization in the sample measure appeared to have tied compensation to market-oriented performance. If rewards are more broadly construed to include appreciation, recognition, and approval, however, many organizations measure and reward market-based performance. For example, several organizations made it a point to single out and recognize employees who were identified by customers as being particularly helpful. Other organizations instituted one or more variations of the "employee of the month" theme. There is considerable variance in the ex-

extent to which organizations measure and reward market-based performance, however.

One marketing manager described a system in which employees are
rewarded for short-term financial performance (i.e., units sold). She noted
that this system worked against a long-run market orientation and any long-
run strategic orientation that the organization may wish to take. A sales manager in an industrial firm made a similar observation, noting that his sales
representatives may lead the company astray because their reward systems are
based on sales in the short run. Currently, there is no system in place to encourage them to think strategically. The preceding discussion suggests the
following:

> $P_{10:}$ The greater the reliance on market-based factors for evaluating
> and rewarding managers, the greater the market orientation of
> the organization.

All the previously discussed organizationwide characteristics refer to
formal systems within organizations. Recent writings in the management literature reflect an increasing recognition of the important role of looser, less
formal systems in shaping organizational activities (Feldman & March, 1981;
Ouchi, 1979; Ouchi & Wilkens, 1985; Pettigrew, 1979; Smircich, 1983).
Recently, these informal characteristics have gained the attention of marketing academics (Deshpandé & Webster, 1989; Jaworski, 1988). Although
many concepts can be identified, an informal organizational characteristic
that appears to be particularly relevant as a determinant of a market orientation is political norm structure, a variable discussed in detail by Porter, Allen,
and Angel (1981). *Political behavior* refers to individuals' attempts to promote self-interests and threaten others' interests (Porter et al., 1981). *Political
norm structure* is an informal system that refers to the extent to which members of an organization view political behavior in the organization as being
acceptable. As discussed earlier, a market orientation calls for a concerted
response by the various departments of an organization to market intelligence. A highly politicized system, however, has the potential for engendering interdepartmental conflict (thereby inhibiting a market orientation). Thus,

> $P_{11:}$ The greater the acceptance of political behavior in an
> organization, the greater the interdepartmental conflict.

Linkages Among the Market Orientation Components

As discussed earlier, a market orientation may be characterized as comprising the following three elements: generation of, dissemination of, and responsiveness to market intelligence. Although we have not considered linkages among these, there exists literature suggesting that the three elements may be interrelated. For example, the literature on source credibility (Petty & Cacioppo, 1986; Zaltman, Duncan, & Moorman, 1988) suggests that individuals in an organization are likely to be more responsive to intelligence that is generated by an individual(s) who is regarded as having a high amount of expertise and trustworthiness. That is, responsiveness to market intelligence is likely to be a function of the characteristics of the source that generates the intelligence. Furthermore, the literature on research utilization (Deshpandé & Zaltman, 1982) suggests that responsiveness may be a function of factors such as the political acceptability of intelligence and the extent to which it challenges the status quo. Similarly, it may be argued that the extent to which intelligence is disseminated within an organization may depend on the political acceptability of intelligence and the challenge posed to the status quo.

The preceding discussion suggests that the source of market intelligence and the very nature of intelligence may affect its dissemination and utilization (i.e., responsiveness). More formally,

P_{12a}: The greater the perceived expertise of the source generating market intelligence, the greater the organization's responsiveness to it.

P_{12b}: The greater the perceived trustworthiness of the source generating market intelligence, the greater the responsiveness to it by the organization.

P_{12c}: The smaller the challenge to the status quo posed by market intelligence, the greater (a) its dissemination and (b) the responsiveness to it by the organization.

P_{12d}: The greater the political acceptability of market intelligence, the greater (a) its dissemination and (b) the responsiveness to it by the organization.

Consequences of a Market Orientation

We now discuss the insights obtained from the field interviews and the literature concerning the consequences of a market orientation. The interviews uncovered an interesting and important consequence of a market orientation. A sales manager of a European industrial products company indicated the following: "[Market orientation leads to a] cohesive product focus, clear leadership, better coordination of sales activities, much better job reviewing products from a worldwide basis, help in terms of differentiation."

In essence, the executive suggests that a market orientation facilitates clarity of focus and vision in an organization's strategy. This benefit corresponds to consistency, the first of Rumelt's (1981) four criteria (consistency, frame, competence, and workability) for evaluating strategies. *Consistency* refers to the extent to which a strategy reflects mutually consistent goals, objectives, and policies. Although strategies formulated by a single individual seldom suffer from internal inconsistencies, the likelihood of inconsistencies is enhanced when strategies emerge from the interactions and negotiations among individuals from different parts of an organization. A market orientation appears to provide a unifying focus for the efforts and projects of individuals and departments within the organization, thereby leading to superior performance. Not surprisingly, virtually all the executives interviewed noted that a market orientation enhances the performance of an organization. The typical response to our question concerning positive consequences was a "laundry list" of favorable business performance indicators, such as return on investment, profits, sales volume, market share, and sales growth. Preliminary support for some of these consequences is reported by Narver and Slater (1988). Hence,

P_{13}: The greater the market orientation of an organization, the higher its business performance.

The second set of consequences that emerged from the interviews relate to the effects of a market orientation on employees. Interestingly, these effects are not addressed in the extant literature. Many executives noted that a market orientation provides a number of psychological and social benefits to employees. Several respondents noted that a market orientation leads to a sense of pride in belonging to an organization in which all departments and individuals work toward the common goal of serving customers.

Accomplishing this objective results in employees sharing a feeling of worthwhile contribution and stronger feelings of job satisfaction and commitment to the organization. A vice president of a consumer products company described some of these consequences as follows: "better esprit de corps. [You get the feeling] that what you are doing is satisfying. I think people feel the need to contribute, to help individuals, the society, to make a contribution."

This idea has received some attention in the management literature (Jones & James, 1979) and is very similar to the teamwork construct identified by Zeithaml et al. (1988) in a services marketing context. They suggest that this variable is instrumental in reducing the gap between service quality specifications and actual delivery, thereby improving consumers' perceptions of service quality. Interestingly, our findings suggest that the esprit de corps within an organization may be improved by a market orientation. On the basis of the previous discussion, we propose the following:

P_{14}: The greater the market orientation, the greater the esprit de corps, job satisfaction, and organizational commitment.

The third set of consequences of a market orientation identified by the respondents focused on customer attitudes and behavior. They indicated that a market orientation leads to satisfied customers who both spread the good word to other potential customers and return to the organization. The following quotes illustrate these ideas: an executive vice president of a consumer products company noted, "[C]ustomer satisfaction, [positive] word of mouth, repeat business is enhanced. Customer retention is better for us; [it is] much less expensive," and a vice president of an industrial products company stated, "[A customer orientation] develops firm reputation, happy customers. Coming through when a customer is in a jam helps [our] reputation."

These ideas also reflect Kotler's (1988) assertions that a market orientation is likely to lead to greater customer satisfaction and repeat business. Thus,

P_{15}: The greater the market orientation, the greater the customer satisfaction and the greater the repeat business from customers.

The literature reflects few empirical studies of the consequences of a market orientation. Most studies focus primarily on the extent to which the marketing concept has been adopted by organizations rather than its specific consequences. One noteworthy exception is the Lawton and Parasuraman (1980) study. The authors found that the adoption of the marketing concept had no apparent effect on the sources of new product ideas, the use of marketing research in new product planning, and the innovativeness of new product offerings. In a sense, these findings run counter to the assertions of authors such as Bennett and Cooper (1981), Kaldor (1971), and Tauber (1974), who argue that the adoption of the marketing concept inhibits organizations from developing true innovations. Lawton and Parasuraman (1980), however, caution that additional research using new measures is needed before any firm conclusions can be drawn.

Environmental Moderators of the Market Orientation Business Performance

With few exceptions, writings in the literature tend to describe the marketing concept as a universally relevant philosophy. In contrast, the field data suggest that certain environmental contingencies moderate the strength of the relationship between market orientation and business performance. In the following discussion, we consider four such contingencies or moderator variables. One moderator that surfaced in the course of the interviews was market turbulence or changes in the composition of customers and their preferences. This variable is more focused than the widely studied environmental turbulence construct. The role of market turbulence in influencing the desirability of a market orientation was highlighted by the experience of two consumer (food) products companies that marketed their products in a specific region in the United States. The population in this region remained unchanged for years, and the preferences of the customers were known and stable. Neither company did much market research.

During the past few years, however, the region witnessed a tremendous influx of population from other parts of the country. Both companies were forced to initiate research to assess the needs and preferences of the new potential customers and develop new products. These experiences suggest that when an organization caters to a fixed set of customers with stable preferences, a market orientation is likely to result in little difference in performance. This is because little adjustment to a marketing mix is required to cater effectively to the stable preferences of a given set of customers. In contrast, if the customer sets or their preferences are less stable, there is a greater likelihood that the company's offerings will become mismatched with customers' needs over a period of time. Therefore,

$P_{16:}$ The greater the market turbulence, the stronger the relationship between a market orientation and business performance.

Several authors (Bennett & Cooper, 1981; Houston, 1986; Kaldor, 1971; Tauber, 1974) point out that many generic product class innovations do not evolve from consumer research. Rather, these innovations are developed by R&D personnel who are often outside the industries in which the innovations eventually assimilate. Similar notions emerged in our interviews. A sales manager of an industrial products company indicated that "[it is important to] recognize that new products do not always originate from the customer, [particularly] in the high-tech industry. [An organization needs] to balance R&D-[initiated] projects as well as customer-/market-driven products." Also, a marketing manager of a service organization noted,

> Let me explain why we are not marketing oriented. We are a complex business, the industry is changing dramatically. Some of our products did not exist three years ago. The technology is changing. Everyone is getting wrapped up in production and operations.

In industries characterized by rapidly changing technology (note that firms in such industries often sell to other firms), a market orientation may not be as important as it is in technologically stable industries. *Technology* here refers to the entire process of transforming inputs to output and the delivery of these outputs to the end-customer. It should be noted that the proposition is not that a market orientation is unimportant in technologically turbulent industries but rather that it is less important. Thus,

$P_{17:}$ The greater the technological turbulence, the weaker the relationship between a market orientation and business performance.

Several executives noted that the intensity of competition in an industry has a direct bearing on the importance of a market orientation. Strong competition leads to multiple choices for customers. As such, an organization must monitor and respond to customers' changing needs and preferences to ensure that customers select its offerings over competing alternatives. Two executives indicated the following:

> Historically, [we] were a technically driven company. In the early years it was a successful approach. If we had a better mousetrap, customers would search [us] out. However, as more companies come up with more solutions, we had to become more market oriented. Find out what solution [the] customer is looking for, and try to solve it. In the past little time was spent with customers. Now coordinate with customer, solution for him, try to utilize that development energy to provide solution for segment.
> —*Sales manager, industrial product firm*

> One thing is that marketing and advertising change so much. What worked last year may not work this year. A lot of it has to do with the competitive nature that you're in at the time because people's needs change. . . . If you don't have competition, you don't need it as much.
> —*Marketing director, service organization*

Thus, an organization with a monopoly in a market may perform well regardless of whether or not it modifies its offerings to suit changing customer preferences (Houston, 1986, p. 84). A service executive noted, "If one has a patent or lock on the product, it may not be efficient to allocate resources to marketing." In other words, the benefits afforded by a market orientation are greater for organizations in a competitive industry compared with organizations operating in less competitive industries. Thus,

P_{18}: The greater the competition, the stronger the relationship between a market orientation and business performance.

Several executives indicated that in strong economies characterized by strong demand, an organization may be able to "get away with" a minimal amount of market orientation. Customers in a weak economy, however, are likely to be very value conscious, thereby resulting in a greater need for organizations to be in tune with and responsive to customer needs to offer good value for money. The paradox, however, is that marketing seems to require more resources precisely at a time when the organization may be short of resources due to weak business conditions. An academic noted,

> I think in weak economies, on the one hand [there is a] need to be more marketing oriented [because] consumers might need better inducements;

their dollar has to go farther. On the other hand, to be marketing oriented requires greater amounts of money that they may not be able to provide at that point.

These observations suggest the following:

$P_{19:}$ The weaker the general economy, the stronger the relationship between a market orientation and business performance.

Our 19 research propositions fit in the broad framework depicted in Figure 2.1. It may be noted that the moderator variables discussed previously are labeled supply-side and demand-side moderators. The latter relate to the nature of demand in an industry (e.g., customer preferences and value consciousness), whereas supply-side moderators refer to the nature of competition among suppliers and the technology employed by them. The framework shown in Figure 2.1 facilitates parsimonious conceptualization and, more important, offers the potential for extending research by identifying additional constructs that may fall into each of the broad categories of senior management factors, interdepartmental dynamics, and so on.

Managerial Implications

The propositions developed in this research have direct managerial implications. First, our research suggests that a market orientation may or may not be very desirable for a business depending on the nature of its supply- and demand-side factors. Second, this research clearly delineates the factors that may be expected to foster or hinder a market orientation. These factors are largely controllable by managers and therefore may be altered by them so as to improve the market orientation of their organizations. Overall, this research provides managers with a comprehensive view of a market orientation, possible ways in which it may be attained, and its likely consequences.

To Be or Not to Be Market Oriented

This study suggests that although a market orientation is likely to be related to business performance in general, there exist certain conditions under which it may not be particularly critical. It is important to bear in mind that a market orientation requires the commitment of resources. The orientation is useful only when the benefits afforded by it exceed the cost of these resources. Thus, under conditions of limited competition, stable market preferences, technologically turbulent industries, and booming economies, a market orientation may not be particularly strongly related to business performance. Managers responsible for businesses operating under these conditions would therefore be advised to pay close attention to the cost-benefit ratio of a market orientation.

Implementing a Market Orientation

This research provides very specific suggestions concerning the factors that foster or hinder a market orientation in organizations. The factors identified in this research are controllable by senior managers and hence permit the deliberate engendering of a market orientation. For example, this research suggests that senior managers must be convinced of the value of a market orientation and communicate this commitment to junior employees. Although annual reports and public interviews proclaiming a market orientation are helpful, junior employees also need to witness behaviors and resource allocations that reflect a commitment to a market orientation.

Senior managers also need to develop positive attitudes toward change and a willingness to take calculated risks. A market orientation is almost certain to lead to a few projects or programs that at times may not succeed. Supportive reaction to failures, however, is critical for engendering a change-oriented philosophy represented by the marketing concept.

This research also identifies many interdepartmental dynamics that can be managed through appropriate in-house efforts. It is clear that interdepartmental variables (conflict and connectedness) play a key role in influencing the dissemination and responsiveness to market intelligence. The following are inexpensive ways to manage these two antecedents: (a) interdepartmental lunches, (b) sports leagues that require mixed department teams, and (c) newsletters that "poke fun" at various interdepartmental relations. More advanced efforts include (a) exchange of employees across departments, (b) cross-department training programs, and (c) senior department managers spending time with executives in other departments. Such efforts appear to foster an understanding of the personalities of managers in other departments, their culture, and particular perspectives. The third set of variables that senior management might alter for fostering a market orientation concern the organizationwide systems. The impact of structural factors, such as formalization and centralization, is unclear because although they appear to inhibit the generation and dissemination of market intelligence, these factors are likely to help an organization respond effectively to market intelligence. Thus, it appears that an organization should structure itself differently depending on the activity involved. It is clear, however, that senior managers can help foster a market orientation by changing reward systems from being completely finance based (e.g., sales and profits) to being at least partly market based (e.g., customer satisfaction and intelligence obtained). Simultaneously, informal norms such as the acceptability of political behavior in the organization also need to be changed to facilitate a concerted response by the departments to market developments.

The Pace and Dynamics of Change

It is important to bear in mind that a change in orientation takes place slowly. We were apprised of certain organizations that were actively involved in becoming more market oriented and planned on completing the change process only over a period of approximately 4 years. In describing a change to a market focus, an executive director noted that there is always a "pull and tug between a new idea and old ways of doing things." It appears especially difficult to "carry" employees who may be concerned that a movement toward market orientation might jeopardize their power in the organization or expose other inadequacies related to their jobs.

Furthermore, it is important to recognize that the balance of power across departments must be managed carefully in any efforts directed at becoming more market oriented. Although a market orientation involves the efforts of virtually all departments in an organization, the marketing department typically tends to have a larger role by virtue of its contact with customers and the market. As such, there is a danger of individuals in marketing departments trying to relegate other departments to a secondary status.

One health care administrator recounted a story in which the organization had recently emphasized a market philosophy and had started treating marketing personnel as the "blue-eyed boys" of the organization. Within a very short period of time, other departments resented this and raised questions with the chief executive such as "What are you doing for us?" It is also instructive to note that for any change to take place, an organization must first perceive a gap between its current and preferred orientation. We were apprised of several instances in which members of an organization believed they were very customer oriented but in fact were hardly so. An executive narrated the example of a service organization's employees who believed they were very responsive to customer needs. When the interactions of these employees with customers (hospital patients) were videotaped and played back to the employees, however, they were horrified at the callous manner in which they found themselves treating customers. As Weick (1979) notes, it is the perceptions of situations that are the triggers of action.

The Quality of Market Orientation

In general, organizations that develop market intelligence and respond to it are likely to perform better and have more satisfied customers and employees. There are important differences between simply engaging in market-oriented activities and the quality of these activities, however. Thus, the quality of market intelligence may be suspect, and the quality of execution of marketing programs designed in response to the intelligence may be poor. For example, to meet a customer's needs, one industrial products company went to extreme lengths to customize small batches of products for the customer, resulting in poor financial performance. Similarly, one executive noted that a company's efforts may raise customer expectations concerning product quality and response time so high that the result is either uneconomical operations or dissatisfied customers. This parallels the problem posed by over-promising in service settings discussed by Zeithaml et al. (1988).

We have not addressed the issue of variations in the quality of market intelligence, its dissemination, and organizational response. These variations are important and worthy of consideration by managers and researchers.

Conclusion

In this chapter, we attempted to clarify the domain of the market orientation construct and provide a working definition and a foundation for developing a measure of the construct. In addition, we identified three classes of factors affecting a market orientation and interrelationships among the elements of market orientation. Furthermore, we have highlighted its impact on an organization's strategy, employee dispositions, and customer attitudes and behavior. Finally, in a significant departure from previous work, we introduced supply- and demand-side factors as potential moderators of the impact of market orientation on business performance. The propositional inventory and the integrative framework developed in this research represent efforts directed at building a foundation for the systematic development of a theory of market orientation. It is important to note, however, that the objective of the current research effort is theory construction rather than testing. Considerable work remains to be done to develop a suitable measure of market orientation and empirically test the propositions advanced in this chapter.

In recent years, considerable interest has focused on the organizational resources and positions that represent sustainable competitive advantages (Day & Wensley, 1988). Much less attention has focused on the organizational processes, such as market orientation, that represent a long-term advantage. Because a market orientation is not easily installed, it may be of value to consider it as an additional and distinct form of sustainable competitive advantage.

References

Aguilar, F. (1967). *Scanning business environments.* New York: Macmillan.

Aiken, M., & Hage, J. (1968). Organizational independence and intraorganizational structure. *American Sociological Review, 33,* 912-930.

Alba, J. W., & Hutchinson, J. Wesley (1987, March). Dimensions of consumer expertise. *Journal of Consumer Research, 12,* 411-454.

Anderson, P. (1982). Marketing, strategic planning, and the theory of the firm. *Journal of Marketing, 46*(2), 15-26.

Anderson, P., & Chambers, T. (1985). A reward/measurement model of organizational buying behavior. *Journal of Marketing, 49*(2), 7-23.

Argyris, C. (1965). *Organization and innovation.* Homewood, IL: Irwin.

Argyris, C. (1966, March/April). Interpersonal barriers to decision making. *Harvard Business Review, 44,* 84-97.

Barksdale, H. C., & Darden, B. (1971). Marketers' attitude toward the marketing concept. *Journal of Marketing, 35*(4), 29-36.

Bell, M. L., & Emory, C. W. (1971). The faltering marketing concept. *Journal of Marketing, 35*(4), 37-42.

Bennett, R., & Cooper, R. (1981, June). Beyond the marketing concept. *Business Horizons, 22,* 76-83.

Cronbach, L. J., Ambron, S.-A. R., Dornbusch, S. M., Hess, R. D., Hornik, R. C., Phillips, D. C., Walker, D. F., & Weiner, S. S. (1981). *Toward reform in program evaluation.* San Francisco: Jossey-Bass.

Daft, R. L., & Steers, R. (1985). *Organizations: A micro/macro approach.* Glenview, IL: Scott, Foresman.

Day, G. S., & Wensley, R. (1983). Marketing theory with a strategic orientation. *Journal of Marketing, 47*(4), 79-89.

Day, G. S., & Wensley, R. (1988). Assessing advantage: A framework for diagnosing competitive superiority. *Journal of Marketing, 52*(2), 1-20.

Deshpandé, R. (1983). "Paradigms lost": On theory and method in research in marketing. *Journal of Marketing, 47*(4), 101-110.

Deshpandé, R., & Webster, F. E., Jr. (1989). Organizational culture and marketing: Defining the research agenda. *Journal of Marketing, 53*(1), 3-15.

Deshpandé, R., & Zaltman, G. (1982, February). Factors affecting the use of market research information: A path analysis. *Journal of Marketing Research, 19*, 14-31.

Feldman, M. S., & March, J. G. (1981, June). Information in organizations as symbols and signals. *Administrative Science Quarterly, 26*, 171-186.

Felton, A. P. (1959, July/August). Making the marketing concept work. *Harvard Business Review, 37*, 55-65.

Gaski, J. F. (1984). The theory of power and conflict in channels of distribution. *Journal of Marketing, 48*(3), 9-29.

Glaser, B., & Strauss, A. (1967). *The discovery of grounded theory.* Chicago: Aldine.

Hage, J., & Aiken, M. (1970). *Social change in complex organizations.* New York: Random House.

Hall, R. H., Haas, J. E., & Johnson, N. J. (1967, December). Organizational size, complexity, and formalization. *American Sociological Review, 32*, 903-911.

Hambrick, D. C., & Mason, P. A. (1984). Upper echelons: The organization as a reflection of its top managers. *Academy of Management Review, 9*(2), 193-206.

Hise, R. T. (1965). Have manufacturing firms adopted the marketing concept? *Journal of Marketing, 29*(3), 9-12.

Hopwood, A. (1974). *Accounting and human behavior.* London: Haymarket.

Houston, F. S. (1986). The marketing concept: What it is, what it is not. *Journal of Marketing, 50*(2), 81-87.

Jaworski, B. J. (1988). Toward a theory of marketing control: Environmental context, control types, and consequences. *Journal of Marketing, 52*(3), 23-39.

Jones, A. P., & James, L. R. (1979). Psychological climate: Dimensions and relationships of individual and aggregate work environment perceptions. *Organization Behavior and Human Performance, 23*, 201-250.

Kaldor, A. G. (1971). Imbricative marketing. *Journal of Marketing, 35*(2), 19-25.

Konopa, L. J., & Calabro, P. J. (1971, Spring). Adoption of the marketing concept by large northeastern Ohio manufacturers. *Akron Business and Economic Review, 2*, 9-13.

Kotler, P. (1988). *Marketing management.* Englewood Cliffs, NJ: Prentice Hall.

Lavidge, R. J. (1966, October). Marketing concept often gets only lip service. *Advertising Age, 37*, 52.

Lawler, E. E., & Rhode, J. G. (1976). *Information and control in organizations.* Pacific Palisades, CA: Goodyear.

Lawton, L., & Parasuraman, A. (1980). The impact of the marketing concept on new product planning. *Journal of Marketing, 44*(1), 19-25.

Lear, R. W. (1963, September/October). No easy road to market orientation. *Harvard Business Review*, 53-60.

Lenz, R. T., & Engledow, J. L. (1986). Environmental analysis units and strategic decision making: A field study of selected leading edge corporations. *Strategic Management Journal, 7*, 69-89.

Levitt, T. (1969). *The marketing mode.* New York: McGraw-Hill.

Lundstrom, W. J. (1976, Fall). The marketing concept: The ultimate in bait and switch. *Marquette Business Review, 20,* 214-230.

Lusch, R. F., Udell, J. G., & Laczniak, G. R. (1976, December). The practice of business. *Business Horizons, 19,* 65-74.

Mahrer, A. R. (1988, September). Discovery-oriented psychotherapy research. *American Psychologist, 43,* 694-702.

Marketing men take over GE units. (1950, June 24). *U.S. Business Week,* 30-36.

McCarthy, E. J., & Perreault, W. D., Jr. (1984). *Basic marketing* (8th ed.). Homewood, IL: Irwin.

McKitterick, J. B. (1957). What is the marketing management concept? In F. M. Bass (Ed.), *The frontiers of marketing thought and science* (pp. 71-92). Chicago: American Marketing Association.

McNamara, C. P. (1972). The present status of the marketing concept. *Journal of Marketing, 36*(1), 50-57.

Narver, J. C., & Slater, S. F. (1988, September). *Market orientation: Construct measurement and analysis of effects on performance.* Paper presented at the Marketing Science Institute conference, Boston.

Olson, D. (1987, April). *When consumer firms develop a marketing orientation.* Paper presented at the Marketing Science Institute conference, Cambridge, MA.

Ouchi, W. G. (1979, September). A conceptual framework for the design of organizational control mechanisms. *Management Science, 25,* 833-847.

Ouchi, W. G., & Wilkens, A. C. (1985). Organizational culture. *Annual Review of Sociology, 11,* 457-483.

Parasuraman, A., Zeithaml, V. A., & Berry, L. L. (1985). A conceptual model of service quality and its implications for future research. *Journal of Marketing, 49*(4), 41-50.

Park, C. W., & Zaltman, G. (1987). *Marketing management.* Chicago: Dryden.

Patton, M. Q. (1978). *Utilization focused evaluation.* Beverly Hills, CA: Sage.

Pettigrew, A. M. (1979, December). On studying organizational cultures. *Administrative Science Quarterly, 24,* 570-581.

Petty, R. E., & Cacioppo, J. T. (1986). *On communication and persuasion: Central and peripheral routes to attitude change.* New York: Springer-Verlag.

Porter, L. W., Allen, R. W., & Angel, H. (1981). The politics of upward influence in organizations. In B. Staw & L. Cummings (Eds.), *Research in organizational behavior* (Vol. 3). Greenwich, CT: JAI.

Raven, B. H., & Kruglanski, A. W. (1970). Conflict and power. In P. Swingle (Ed.), *The structure of conflict* (pp. 69-109). New York: Academic Press.

Robertson, T. S., & Gatignon, H. (1986). Competitive effects on technology diffusion. *Journal of Marketing, 50*(3), 1-12.

Rogers, E. M. (1983). *Diffusion of innovations* (3rd ed.). New York: Free Press.

Ruekert, R., & Walker, O. (1987). Marketing's interaction with other functional units: A conceptual framework and empirical evidence. *Journal of Marketing, 51*(1), 1-19.

Ruekert, R., Walker, O., & Roering, K. J. (1985). The organization of marketing activities: A contingency theory of structure and performance. *Journal of Marketing, 49*(1), 13-25.

Rumelt, R. P. (1981). Evaluation of strategy: Theory and models. In D. E. Schendel & C. W. Hofer (Eds.), *Strategic management: A new view of business policy and planning* (pp. 196-212). Boston: Little, Brown.

Shapiro, B. P. (1988, November/December). What the hell is "market oriented"? *Harvard Business Review, 66,* 119-125.

Smircich, L. (1983, September). Concepts of culture and organizational analysis. *Administrative Science Quarterly, 28,* 339-358.

Stampfl, R. W. (1978, Spring). Structural constraints, consumerism, and the marketing concept. *MSU Business Topics, 26,* 5-16.

Tauber, E. M. (1974, June). How marketing discourages major innovation. *Business Horizons, 17,* 22-26.

Viebranz, A. C. (1967, Autumn). Marketing's role in company growth. *MSU Business Topics, 15,* 45-49.

Walker, O., Jr., Gilbert, C., Churchill, A., Jr., & Ford, N. M. (1977, May). Motivation and performance in industrial selling: Present knowledge and needed research. *Journal of Marketing Research, 14,* 156-168.

Webster, F. E., Jr. (1988, May/June). Rediscovering the marketing concept. *Business Horizons, 31,* 29-39.

Weick, K. (1979). *The social psychology of organizing* (2nd ed.). Reading, MA: Addison-Wesley.

Weitz, B. A. (1981). Effectiveness in sales interactions: A contingency framework. *Journal of Marketing, 45,* 85-103.

Zaltman, G., Duncan, R., & Holbek, J. (1973). *Innovations and organizations.* New York: John Wiley.

Zaltman, G., Duncan, R., LeMasters, K., & Heffring, M. (1982). *Theory construction in marketing.* New York: John Wiley.

Zaltman, G., Duncan, R., & Moorman, C. (1988, October/November). The importance of personal trust in the use of research. *Journal of Advertising Research, 28,* 16-24.

Zeithaml, V. A., Berry, L. L., & Parasuraman, A. (1988). Communication and control processes in the delivery of service quality. *Journal of Marketing, 52*(2), 35-48.

The Effect of Market Orientation on Business Profitability

John C. Narver
Stanley F. Slater

It is a well-accepted maxim in the strategy literature that superior performance is the result of building a sustainable competitive advantage. Competitive advantage exists when a business creates value for its buyers in excess of the value of any competitor's offering (value being the difference between the perceived worth of the benefits of an offering and the perceived costs of acquiring and using the offering). There are two routes to competitive advantage, which may be pursued separately or in combination: differentiation, which focuses on buyer benefits, and lowest delivered cost, which focuses on buyer acquisition and use costs.

Competitive advantage requires that a business have an understanding of buyers' needs, competitors' offerings and capabilities, buyers' perceptions of the business's value relative to that of competitors, and appropriate interfunctional coordinating mechanisms for creating value for buyers. This can best be attained in a business with a market-oriented culture that makes the creation of buyer value its ultimate mission.

On the basis of an extensive review of the literature, authors Narver and Slater deduce that market orientation has three fundamental behavioral components: customer orientation, competitor orientation, and interfunctional coordination. Customer orientation is the sufficient understanding of the buyer's value chain within end-use segments such that the business continuously focuses on activities that will either increase benefits or decrease costs to the buyer. Competitor orientation is the ongoing assessment of the value of the business's offerings and capabilities relative to those of the competition. Interfunctional coordination means that information on buyers and competitors is shared throughout the business, decisions are made interfunctionally, and all functions contribute to the creation of buyer value. The behavioral activities are constrained by a long-run focus and a profit objective.

Although the logic linking market orientation and competitive advantage is intuitively sound, support for this relationship has been primarily anecdotal. Some scholars have argued that in some environments, the costs of the activities associated with maintaining a market orientation (e.g., scanning, development, coordination, and adaptation) offset the advantages from increased sales or improved price realization. Thus, the purpose of this study was to develop a valid measure of market orientation and test its relationship with business profitability, after controlling for important business-level and market-level variables.

The authors developed multiple items that characterize the three behavioral components and the two business-objective components of market orientation. These were reviewed by two panels of academics, and the items that passed these screens were pretested with current or former strategic business unit (SBU) managers. The final questionnaire was sent to the members of the top management teams of 140 SBUs of a major corporation.

Scales for the behavioral components of market orientation were found to be reliable. These scales also passed tests for discriminant validity, convergent validity, and concurrent validity, thus providing strong support for the construct validity of the behavioral core of market orientation.

In both commodity and noncommodity businesses, the magnitude of market orientation was determined to be strongly related to profitability, after controlling for important business-level and market-level factors.

This study is an important step in validating a basic tenet of marketing management—namely, that for a company to experience sustained success, it must have an external orientation and must coordinate all its activities around meeting the needs of its buyers. It also raises significant questions about market orientation for future research: How does a company create and sustain a market orientation? Is balance among the components of market orientation associated with profitability? What is the relationship between market orientation and innovative behavior?

A business that adopts a market orientation will improve its market performance. This observation has been offered by both marketing academics and practitioners for more than three decades; to date, however, there has been no valid measure of market orientation nor, therefore, any systematic analysis of its effect on a business's performance. This study reports the development of a valid measure of market orientation and the analysis of its effect on a business's profitability. Using a sample of 140 strategic business units consisting of commodity businesses, specialty-products businesses, and wholesale-distribution businesses, the study finds that a market orientation has a substantial, positive effect on the profitability of both the commodity and the noncommodity businesses.

A business that moves from an internal orientation to a market orientation will substantially improve its market performance. This proclamation has been issued regularly by both marketing academics and marketing managers for more than 30 years (Kotler, 1984; Kotler & Andreasen, 1987; Levitt, 1960; Webster, 1988). The "superiority" of a market orientation over an internal orientation commands a central place in the teaching and practice of marketing management.

Nevertheless, during the three decades that this conviction has persisted, two fundamental questions have remained unanswered: What precisely is a market orientation? and What are its effects on a business's performance? The strong belief in the superiority of a market orientation has been based solely on intuition and casual evidence (Kotler, 1984; Peters & Waterman, 1982). Without a valid measure of the market orientation construct, there can be no systematic investigation of the effect of a market orientation on business performance.

Not only are there no valid measures of the dimensions of market orientation but also attempts to measure its closest relative, the marketing concept, offer few insights. The several efforts to measure the marketing concept (Hise, 1965; Lawton & Parasuraman, 1980; Lusch, Udell, & Laczniak, 1976; McNamara, 1972; Morris & Paul, 1987) have consistently failed to provide evidence of the reliability of their measures, not to mention evidence of construct validity.

This chapter reports an exploratory study that develops a valid measure of market orientation and analyzes the effect of market orientation on business performance. We first discuss the concept of market orientation and its expected effect on performance. We then discuss the development of a valid measure of the construct. Finally, we discuss the analysis of its effect on business profitability.

Market Orientation and Performance: The Conceptual Model

For an organization consistently to achieve above-normal market performance it must achieve sustainable competitive advantage (Aaker, 1989, p. 91; Porter, 1985, p. xv). Sustainable competitive advantage (SCA) is the result of continuously creating superior value for customers.

The logic of SCA (its analytical roots are found in Chamberlin [1933/ 1962] and Alderson [1957]) is that for a buyer to purchase offering X, the buyer must perceive that the expected value to the buyer of that offering exceeds the expected value to the buyer of any alternative offering. The value of a seller's offering to a buyer is the difference between what the buyer perceives as the offering's expected benefits and what the buyer perceives as its expected total acquisition and use costs (Zeithaml, 1988). A seller—any seller—has numerous alternative opportunities for creating additional buyer value through increasing a buyer's benefits or decreasing a buyer's total acquisition and use costs (Forbis & Mehta, 1981).

The desire to create value for customers and attain SCA drives a business unit to create and maintain the business culture that will produce the necessary behaviors and activities. Market orientation is the organizational culture and climate (Deshpandé & Webster, 1989) that most effectively encourages the behaviors that are necessary for the creation of superior value for buyers and, thus, continuous superior profit for the business (Aaker, 1988; Kotler, 1984; Kotler & Andreasen, 1987; Peters & Austin, 1985; Peters & Waterman, 1982; Shapiro, 1988; Webster, 1988).

A market-oriented seller understands that, through the numerous means of creating additional benefits for buyers and the numerous types of reductions in the buyers' total acquisition and use costs, there are many potential sources of SCA (Aaker, 1988; Hall, 1980; Porter, 1985). Thus, the market-oriented business continuously examines how, from among these alternative sources of SCA, it can most effectively create sustainable superior value for its current and future target buyers. To maximize its long-run performance, the business knows it must build and maintain a long-run, mutually beneficial relationship with its buyers. Accordingly, the market-oriented seller decides

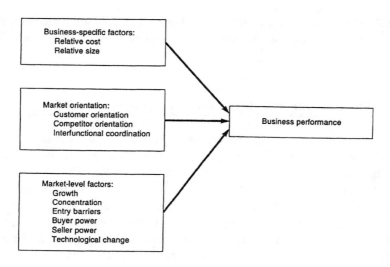

Figure 3.1. Independent Effects Model of the Relationship Between Business-Specific Factors, Market Orientation, Market-Level Factors, and Performance

how best to share with its buyers the superior value it creates for them (Forbis & Mehta, 1981; Hanan, 1985; Jackson, 1985).

Some scholars (Hrebeniak & Joyce, 1985; McKee, Varadarajan, & Pride, 1989; Miles & Snow, 1978) argue that in some environments the costs of the activities associated with maintaining a market orientation (e.g., scanning, development, coordination, and adaptation) offset the advantages accruing from the increased sales and increased price realization. This assertion, however, is inconsistent with the perspective of a true market-oriented business. By being externally focused, market-oriented businesses are prepared to recognize when the expected incremental costs of creating buyer value exceed the expected incremental benefits and, thus, when to cease pursuing a given market opportunity.

The primary elements in the theory of market orientation—the components of market orientation, business-level and market-level variables, and performance—are shown in the independent effects model (Boal & Bryson, 1987) in Figure 3.1. In this chapter, we describe the development of a valid measure of market orientation and the analysis of its relationship with business performance. We hypothesize that there is a significant positive relationship between the degree to which a business is market oriented and the business's profitability after controlling for business-level and market-level variables.

The Components of Market Orientation

We reviewed the major conceptual literature on both SCA and market orientation (Aaker, 1988; Anderson, 1982; Day, 1984; Kotler, 1977, 1984; Levitt, 1960, 1980; Ohmae, 1982; Peters & Waterman, 1982; Porter, 1980, 1985). From this review, we infer three behavioral components and two decision criteria in a seller's ability to create continuously superior value for buyers at a profit: customer orientation, competitor orientation, and interfunctional coordination. Continuous innovation is implicit in each of these components. The two decision criteria are a long-term focus and profitability. We discuss each in turn.

Customer orientation is the sufficient understanding of one's target buyers and, therefrom, the sufficient response to their needs, through which, other things being equal, one continuously creates superior value for the buyers (or, per Levitt [1980], continuously creates an augmented product). A customer orientation requires, in part, that a seller understand a buyer's entire value chain (Day & Wensley, 1988) not only as it is today but also as it will evolve over time subject to internal and market dynamics. There are only two ways a seller creates value for a buyer: by increasing benefits to the buyer relative to the buyer's costs or by decreasing the buyer's costs relative to the buyer's benefits. A seller must understand not only the cost and revenue dynamics of its immediate target buyer firms but also the cost and revenue dynamics facing the buyers' buyers, from whose demand the demand in the immediate market is derived. To understand the cost and revenue dynamics of one's buyers, and the cost and revenue dynamics of their buyers, requires a seller to understand the economic and political constraints at all levels in the channel. Only with such a comprehensive framework can a seller understand who its potential customers are at present and who they may be in the future, what they want now and what they may want in the future, and what they perceive now and what they may perceive in the future, as relevant to the satisfaction of their needs.

Competitor orientation is the second of the three behavioral components in creating superior value for buyers. To create value for buyers that is greater than that created by its competitors, a seller must understand the short-term strengths and weaknesses and long-term capabilities and strategies of both the key current competitors and the key potential competitors (Aaker, 1988; Day & Wensley, 1988; Porter, 1980, 1985). Paralleling customer analysis, the analysis of principal current and potential competitors must incorporate the entire set of technologies capable of satisfying the needs of the seller's target buyers. This will ensure an analysis that is sufficiently comprehensive to identify all potential satisfiers of the buyers' current and expected needs.

The third behavioral component in creating superior customer value is the interfunctional coordination of company resources. Any point in the buyer's value chain constitutes an opportunity for a seller to create value for the buyer firm. Thus, any individual in any function in a seller firm can potentially contribute to the creation of value for buyers (Porter, 1985). Creating value for buyers is much more than a marketing function; rather, a seller's creation of value for buyers is analogous to a symphony orchestra, in which the contribution of each subgroup is tailored and integrated by a conductor—with a synergistic effect. A seller must draw on and integrate effectively, as well as adapt as necessary, its entire human and other capital resources in its continuous effort to create superior value for buyers. Creating superior value for customers is thus the proper focus of the entire business and not merely that of a single department in it (Webster, 1988).

The literature suggests that businesses, on average, have the objective of maximizing their profits (or wealth) in the long term. A short-run focus on profits is not inconsistent with long-run profit performance. The relationship between short-run and long-run profits is as follows: At all times a business attempts to create superior value for buyers. As competitors respond and diminish a business's buyer-value superiority, the business discovers and implements additional value for its customers (i.e., it augments its product [Levitt, 1980]), thereby maintaining its buyer-value superiority. This continuous competitive short-term coping requires both short-term expenditures and strategic investments. It is through this continuous creation of superior customer value and, therefrom, satisfactory short-run profit performance, that a business creates its long-run superior profit performance.

Hypothesis of the Content of Market Orientation

We hypothesize that market orientation is a one-dimension construct consisting of five components: customer orientation, competitor orientation,

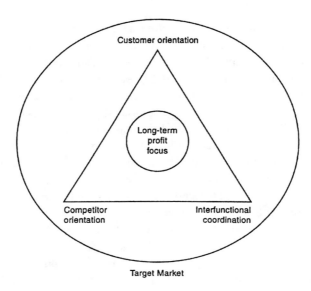

Figure 3.2. Market Orientation

interfunctional coordination, a long-run focus, and a profit objective. We hypothesize a one-dimension construct because the five components are conceptually highly related. For a business to maximize its long-run profits, it must continuously create superior value for its target customers. To create continuous superior value for customers, it must be customer oriented, competitor oriented, and interfunctionally coordinated (Figure 3.2).

From the literature review, we infer that the three behavioral components (customer orientation, competitor orientation, and interfunctional coordination) are, on average, of equal importance; hence, in Figure 3.2 they comprise an equilateral triangle.

On Developing a Valid Measure of Market Orientation

Face Validity

We developed multiple items that characterize the hypothesized five components of market orientation. We submitted these items to a panel of three academics who are recognized authorities on strategic marketing. They rated each item for its consistency with market orientation and also recommended additional items for inclusion. We submitted items that received a high rating or were suggested by a first-round panelist to a second panel of three academics who are similarly recognized as authorities on strategic marketing. The items that the second panel considered to have a high consistency with market orientation were included in the instrument.

Items were phrased to describe both favorable and unfavorable practices to offset any affirmation or negation response bias. Responses were recorded on a Likert-type scale of 1 to 7, with a 1 indicating that the business unit does not engage in that practice at all and a 7 indicating that it engages in it to a great extent.

The preliminary questionnaire was then pretested with six current or former strategic business unit (SBU) managers from the corporation from which our sample would be drawn. We debriefed the six managers regarding their perception of the ambiguity and interpretation of selected items and their perception of the likelihood of any statements inducing socially or professionally desirable responses. On the basis of their comments, we refined some items and developed the final instrument.

The Sample

The sampling units in the study are 140 SBUs of a major Western corporation. The SBUs are all in the forest products division of the corporation.

An SBU is defined as an organizational unit with a defined business strategy and a manager with sales and profit responsibility (Aaker, 1988). Within each SBU, the top management team (TMT) was identified by the responsible group executive. Each member of the TMT received a questionnaire titled "Business Practices Survey" that had questions relating to the competitive practices and strategies, competitive environment, and performance of the SBU in its principal served market. We assured respondents of their anonymity. We also used a coding scheme that precluded both us and the company management from identifying the response of any specific individual. Heneman (1974) has shown that subjects are more likely to give unbiased responses when their anonymity is ensured.

Of 440 questionnaires sent, 371 usable questionnaires were returned (an 84% response rate). There was a total of 113 SBUs (81%) with no missing data, and they consisted of 36 commodity businesses, 23 specialty products businesses, 51 distribution businesses, and 3 export businesses. The types of businesses that composed the sample are described as follows:

> *Commodity businesses:* These businesses sell physical products, such as dimension lumber, plywood, wood chips, and logs, all of which are essentially identical in quality and performance to those of the competitors. In trying to create superior value for buyers, these businesses are usually unable to adapt their generic product (Levitt, 1980) or, if they do, their effort seldom produces a long-lasting superior value for a buyer. Thus, to create superior value for buyers, they typically must add various customer-benefit services to the generic product. Their customers are the corporation's wholesale distributors and outside retailers, both domestic and foreign.
>
> *Noncommodity businesses:* A noncommodity business is one that, in trying to create superior value for buyers, can both adapt somewhat its generic product (or service) and add customer-benefit services to its generic product. There are two types of noncommodity businesses in the sample: specialty-products businesses and distribution businesses.
>
> - Examples of products of specialty businesses are hardwood cabinets, laminated doors, oriented strand board, particle board, and roof-truss systems. Their customers are national retailers, remanufacturers in the building industries, furniture manufacturers, and the corporation's own wholesale distributors.
> - Distribution businesses are merchant-wholesaler businesses within the corporation that buy products primarily from within the corporation and sell them to building-supply retailers, contractors, and exporters.

Reliability Analysis

We randomly divided the data into two samples before assessing reliability and validity (Churchill, 1979). We conducted reliability analyses on the first sample, replicated these analyses on the second sample, and conducted tests for construct validity.

The scale reliabilities (alpha coefficient) and item-to-total correlations are reported in Table 3.1. Reliabilities for the customer orientation, competitor orientation, and interfunctional coordination scales exceeded .7, which is the threshold Nunnally (1978, p. 245) recommends for exploratory research. The long-term orientation and profit objective measures, however, did not meet this criterion.

We hypothesized a five-component, one-dimensional construct of market orientation but found that only the three behavioral components' scales

Table 3.1 Reliability Analysis

Item	Sample 1 (N = 190) Cronbach's Alpha	Item-to-Total Correlations	Sample 2 (N = 175) Cronbach's Alpha
Customer orientation	.8547		.8675
Customer commitment		.7021	
Create customer value		.6580	
Understand customer needs		.6717	
Customer satisfaction objectives		.6517	
Measure customer satisfaction		.6342	
Products based on customer ideas		.5794	
Competitor orientation	.7164		.7271
Salespeople share competitor information		.5466	
Respond rapidly to competitors' actions		.5908	
Top management discusses competitors' strategies		.5421	
Target opportunities for competitive advantage		.3612	
Interfunctional coordination	.7112		.7348
Interfunctional customer calls		.4090	
Information shared among functions		.4775	
Functional integration in strategy		.6618	
All functions contribute to customer value		.5060	
Share resources with other business units		.3171	
Long-term horizon	.4775		.4080
Quarterly profits are primary objective		.3382	
Require rapid payback		.3020	
Positive margin in long term		.2613	
Profit emphasis	.1398		.0038
Profit performance measured market by market		.1021	
Top management emphasizes market performance		.1366	
All products must be profitable		−.3463	

met the reliability criterion. This may have been due to insufficient or inappropriate items representing the long-term focus and a profit objective so that they do not load on the same dimension as the other three components. It is possible, of course, that long-term and profit focus constitute a second dimension of market orientation. Currently, we can determine that long-term focus and profit objective appear not to be in the same dimension as customer orientation, competitor orientation, and interfunctional coordination. Whether they are in fact two components of a one-dimension construct, two components of a second dimension, or neither is an important question—one that we must leave for future research.

Because long-term focus and profit objective have only a low correlation with the other three components, we can eliminate them and still obtain unbiased estimates of the other three components. Therefore, in the following discussion of the tests of construct validity we consider only customer orientation, competitor orientation, and interfunctional coordination—the three behavioral core components of market orientation. As mentioned previously, given the equal conceptual importance of each of the three components, a business's market orientation score is the simple average of the scores of the three components.

With respect to these three components and to market orientation and the performance variable (return on assets [ROA]), the interrater reliability is satisfactory. (The interrater reliability is measured by the average standard deviation by TMT, which indicates the extent of dispersion in responses.) For all businesses in the sample, the average standard deviations by TMT (7-point scale) are as follows: customer orientation (Custo), .360; competitor orientation (Compo), .402; interfunctional coordination (Coord), .321; market orientation (MKTOR), .280; and ROA, .705.

Construct Validity

Evidence of construct validity exists when the pattern of correlations among variables conforms to what is predicted by theory (Cronbach, 1970, p. 143; Kerlinger, 1973, p. 463). We examined with simple correlation and factor analysis the relationships among the behavioral-core market orientation components Custo, Compo, and Coord and their relationships with three other management policy variables that are conceptually linked to market orientation. In testing for significant differences between correlations, we used the procedure described by Cohen and Cohen (1975, p. 53). The management policy variables are human resources management policy (HRM), differentiation-based competitive advantage (Diff), and low-cost-based competitive advantage (Locost). The reliabilities and item-to-total correlations for these scales are reported in Table 3.2. Three predictions were made regarding the theoretical relationships among the variables.

Table 3.2 Scale Descriptions for Management Policy Variables

	Total Sample	
Item	*Cronbach's Alpha*	*Item-to-Total Correlation*
Human resources management policy	.8122	
Effective personnel policies		.6034
Optimize turnover		.5029
Improve attitudes		.6774
Reward creativity		.5164
Effective grievance procedures		.5366
Stimulate employee education		.6332
Differentiation-based competitive advantage	.8259	
Introduce new products		.7203
Differentiate products		.6665
Offer broad product line		.6022
Utilize marketing research		.6181
Low-cost-based competitive advantage	.7624	
Lower manufacturing costs		.5636
Modernize manufacturing		.4301
Improve plant layout		.5100
Increase capacity utilization		.6352
Perform raw material value analyses		.4632
Improve raw material access		.4817

Convergent Validity. There will be a strong correlation among the three components of market orientation. A strong correlation among the three components of market orientation indicates that they are converging on a common construct, thereby providing evidence of convergent validity. All the correlations exceed .65 and are significant at $p < .001$ (Table 3.3). Convergent validity is further suggested by the high Cronbach's alpha (.8810) attained when the scores on the three scales are combined into one scale and by the one-factor solution in an exploratory factor analysis (eigenvalue = 7.2; 44.8% of the variance explained).

Discriminant Validity. The correlation between Coord and HRM will be substantially less than the correlations between Coord and the other market orientation components. To assess discriminant validity, we included in the questionnaire a scale for measuring HRM (Hitt & Ireland, 1986). This scale

Table 3.3 Correlation Analysis of Market Orientation, Management Policy, and ROA Scales

	Custo	Compo	Coord	MKTOR	HRM	Diff	Locost	ROA
Custo	—							
Compo	.7353***	—						
Coord	.7210***	.6564***	—					
MKTOR	.9120***	.9047***	.8699***	—				
HRM	.4366***	.2686**	.5308***	.4561***	—			
Diff	.4424***	.4482***	.3261***	.4540***	.1630*	—		
Locost	.2676**	.1766*	.3243***	.2767**	.5704***	.2276**	—	
ROA	.3029***	.3892***	.2287**	.3454***	.0321	.1677*	.0856	—

NOTE: Compo, competitor orientation; Coord, interfunctional coordination; Custo, customer orientation; Diff, differentiation-based competitive advantage; HRM, human resources management; Locost, low-cost-based competitive advantage; MKTOR, market orientation; ROA, return on assets.
$*p < .05; **p < .01; ***p < .001.$

was developed to assess the importance that a business organization attaches to policies and activities for recruiting, motivating, and rewarding employees. HRM and Coord are both people-management policies. To be confident that Custo, Compo, and Coord are measuring market orientation instead of some general halo describing good management, the correlation between HRM and Coord should be substantially less than the correlations between Coord and Custo and between Coord and Compo.

The results of the test for significant differences between dependent correlations shown in Table 3.4 demonstrate that the correlation between HRM and Coord is significantly less than the correlations between Coord and Custo and between Coord and Compo. These results provide support for the discriminant validity of the three-component market orientation construct.

Concurrent Validity. The correlations between the market orientation components and Diff will exceed their correlations with Locost. Porter (1980) characterizes the sources of competitive advantage as low cost or differentiation. In practice, at any time, businesses may emphasize either or both of these (Hall, 1980). In the Porter (1980, p. 37) conception, approaches to differentiation (which we interpret to be additional product benefits) can take many forms, including brand image, product features, customer service, dealer network, and technology. These differentiation effects are essentially external— that is, each is an attempt to shift a business's demand curve outward. In contrast, low cost advantage (which we interpret as internal efficiencies that

Table 3.4 *t* Test of the Significance of Differences Between Dependent Correlation Coefficients

Variable	*r*	*t*[a]	*p (one-tailed)*
HRM-Coord	.5308	−1.749 ($n = 126$)	< .05
Compo-Coord	.6564		
HRM-Coord	.5308	−3.045 ($n = 125$)	< .005
Custo-Coord	.7210		
Diff-MKTOR	.4540	1.790 ($n = 123$)	< .05
Locost-MKTOR	.2767		

a. The *t* statistic is computed according to a formula in Cohen and Cohen (1975, p. 53).

may be passed on to buyers as lower acquisition and use costs) relies on economies of scale, volume, and scope resulting in cost reductions in such activities as research and development, production, service, sales force, and advertising. When passed on to buyers, the low MD+INMD+INMDNM cost advantage moves a business down its existing demand curve.

It seems reasonable that an SBU with a strong market orientation differentiation strategy would be more likely to pursue a differentiation strategy than a low cost strategy, which does not necessarily have an external emphasis. A higher correlation between the market orientation components and Diff than between them and Locost would provide support for the concurrent validity of the market orientation construct.

Previous studies have identified activities associated with differentiation and low cost bases of competitive advantage (Dess & Davis, 1984; Galbraith & Schendel, 1983). On the basis of the activities identified in these studies, we developed scales to measure the extent to which these two strategies are used. Respondents were asked to rate the importance of competitive activities on a Likert-type scale of 1 to 7. Reliabilities for the scales exceeded .75, and their intercorrelation was .304 ($p < .001$). The correlation of market orientation with Diff is .45, and the correlation with Locost is .28. The difference between the correlations is significant at $p < .05$ (Table 3.4). The results support the concurrent validity of the three-component market orientation construct.

In summary, we find evidence of convergent validity, discriminant validity, and concurrent validity, and thus we find support for the construct validity of the three-component model of market orientation. We next examine the relationship of the three-component market orientation construct with business performance.

The Effect of Market Orientation on Business Performance

Measurement of Market Orientation and Profitability

As mentioned previously, a balance among the components of a market orientation is believed to be important (Day & Wensley, 1988, p. 2). Thus, we compute an SBU's score for market orientation as the simple average of the sum of scores of the responses of its top management team on the three components: customer orientation, competitor orientation, and interfunctional coordination. This, of course, gives an equal weighting to the three components.

An SBU's profitability is measured as the TMT's assessment of the SBU's ROA relative to all other competitors in the SBU's principal served market during the past year. Relative performance was used to control for performance differences among the SBU's different industries and served markets. Subjective measures of performance are commonly used in research on private companies or on business units of large companies. Previous studies have found a strong correlation between subjective assessments and their objective counterparts (Dess & Robinson, 1984; Pearce, Robbins, & Robinson, 1987). Respondents were asked to consider return on investment, ROA, and return on net assets as equivalent.

Expected Relationships Between Market Orientation and Profitability

We hypothesize that the greater a business's market orientation, the greater the business's profitability will be, other things being equal. In particular, we expect to find a general positive relationship between market orientation and business profitability within all three types of businesses in the sample (commodity, distribution, and specialty businesses). We do not expect to find, however, the same form of the relationship among the three types of businesses.

A monotonically increasing relationship between market orientation and business profitability is most likely for the distribution and specialty businesses and least likely for the commodity businesses. It is much easier for the distribution and specialty businesses to adapt their generic product or service than it is for the commodity businesses. Also, on average, it is easier for them to add buyer value-enhancing benefits to their generic product or service than it is for the commodity businesses. Thus, we expect distribution and specialty businesses to be able to adapt and implement a market orientation as a continuous process, thereby achieving approximately proportionate gains in ROA.

A commodity business, however, especially in a tradition-bound industry such as forest products, may easily have and maintain an internally oriented perspective of itself rather than a market-oriented perspective—that is, seeing itself to be in the business of selling lumber rather than in the business of identifying and satisfying buyers' needs. The tendency toward an internal orientation is reinforced by the fact that the commodity businesses in this company sell the vast majority of their products by telephone, either at a central sales office that comprises the sales arm of most of the lumber and plywood mills or at other commodity business locations. Thus, by selling remotely as they do, commodity businesses, in contrast to distribution and specialty businesses, are not easily positioned to create superior value for buyers by helping the buyers discover and solve problems of which they are not yet fully aware.

Moreover, in contrast to the person-to-person selling approach, the telephone approach to selling tends, unintentionally, to increase the price sensitivity of buyers because, without the opportunity for the seller to demonstrate and explain fully the total benefits and total transaction costs, and thereby the total value to the buyer, the tag price is taken out of the context of the buyer's value equation. As a result, tag price receives excessive attention. Therefore, given the sales- and price-oriented context that reinforces the traditional perspective of commodity businesses, we would expect them to have a lower mean score on market orientation and a lower mean score on each of the three components of market orientation than either the specialty or distribution businesses.

The data in Table 3.5 are consistent with this expectation. Table 3.5 also aggregates the specialty and distribution businesses into total noncommodity businesses. It shows the results of a *t* test for differences in means between

Table 3.5 Means and Ranges by Type of Business (1-7 Scale)

	Business			
Variable	Commodity	Specialty	Distribution	Noncommodity Means[a]
Custo	4.53 (2.8-5.8)	5.05 (3.7-6.0)	4.99 (3.4-6.1)	5.01**
Compo	4.06 (2.8-5.3)	5.71 (3.3-5.8)	4.92 (3.4-6.6)	4.85**
Coord	4.25 (2.6-5.4)	4.53 (3.2-5.7)	4.38 (3.3-5.8)	4.43*
MKTOR	4.28 (2.7-5.4)	4.77 (3.4-5.7)	4.76 (3.4-6.0)	4.76**
ROA	4.0 (1.0-6.5)	4.65 (1.0-7.0)	4.71 (1.0-7.0)	4.69**

a. Specialty and distribution businesses combined. The p value is based on t test of differences in means between commodity and noncommodity businesses.
$*p \leq .10; **p \leq .01$.

the three market orientation components, MKTOR, and ROA for the commodity and noncommodity businesses. All the differences are significant at $p \leq .10$ or higher.

Among the commodity businesses, we expect those that have the lowest mean market orientation score to include many of the largest businesses, for whom changing to a radically different business culture (namely, market orientation) would be the most costly and thus unattractive strategy, at least in the short run. To make the change successfully, a commodity business (or any business) must be consistent and pervasive in adapting all its systems to be customer and competitor oriented and be effective in coordinating interfunctional efforts to create customer value. It is likely that some of the commodity businesses will get "stuck in the middle." That is, they will be tentative in adopting a market orientation. They will initiate some of the appropriate steps but not in sufficient magnitude or with sufficient persistence or quality to create a truly different culture, and thus they will give mixed messages both internally and externally.

The implication is that for commodity businesses the relationship between market orientation and profitability may well be U-shaped, with the low and high market orientation businesses showing a higher profitability than the businesses in the midrange of market orientation. In particular, we expect the businesses with the highest level of market orientation to have the highest profitability and those with the lowest level of market orientation to have the second highest profitability. The explanation for this seeming paradox is that the businesses lowest in market orientation—that is, the most internally oriented businesses—may be very consistent (and efficient) in what they do. As a result, they may be able to survive through a low cost strategy and achieve some profit success, though never the profit success of the businesses that consistently and persistently adopt a market orientation.

The commodity businesses within the corporation use a sales-center approach proportionately more than any of their major competitors. The most effective means for a seller to discover various ways to create superior value for a buyer on a continuous basis is for the seller to understand thoroughly the buyer's business. This requires the seller to frequently visit the buyer's business and customers. Thus, the commodity businesses, in relying primarily on a sales-center or telephone approach, are at a disadvantage relative to their competitors in creating superior value for customers. The commodity businesses will also be less able to achieve SCA relative to the specialty and distribution businesses within their own company (neither of which uses a sales center). For these two reasons, we expect the commodity businesses to have a lower average relative profitability than either the specialty or distribution businesses. The data in Table 3.5 suggest the expected relationships exist.

The Relationship of the Control Variables to Business Profitability

The industrial organization and marketing management literature places considerable emphasis on eight situational variables that may affect a business's profitability. These situational variables must be controlled in analyzing the effect of a market orientation on a business's profitability.

The first variable is buyer power (Porter, 1980; Scherer, 1980), which is the degree to which a buyer can negotiate lower prices or, in general, a higher value from a seller. The traditional point of view is that buyers and sellers are opponents, and each buyer, like each seller, attempts to extract from the other a maximum contribution to its own profit. Thus, following the traditional perspective and other things being equal, we hypothesize a negative relation between buyer power and a business's profitability.

Supplier power (Porter, 1980; Scherer, 1980), the second control variable, is the degree to which a supplier can negotiate higher prices or, in general, a higher value from a buyer. Following the traditional perspective that buyers and sellers are opponents and that every seller wishes to extract from every buyer the maximum possible contribution to the seller's profits, we hypothesize a negative relation between supplier power and a business's profitability.

The third control variable is seller concentration (Bain, 1959; Scherer, 1980). Seller concentration, conventionally, is the degree to which sales in a market are accounted for by the four or eight firms with the largest sales. Two unrelated reasons are advanced as to why seller concentration, especially at high levels, may be associated with high profitability. First, a high concentration of sellers may encourage tacit or explicit joint-maximizing monopoly behavior. A business that is not among the four largest sellers can benefit from the profit umbrella that is created if the four largest firms behave in accordance with this first explanation (Demsetz, 1974). Second, high seller concentration may be a proxy for the firms with the largest sales capturing substantial scale and volume economies. In this perspective, seller concentration implies benefits to a business only if the business is among the four largest sellers. (This is an accurate assumption for the businesses in our sample.) Implying either or both of these explanations, we hypothesize a positive relation between seller concentration and a business's profitability.

Ease of entry of new competitors (new sellers) into the market is the fourth control variable (Bain, 1959; Porter, 1980; Scherer, 1980), which is defined as the unique incremental costs required of a firm to enter and become competitively viable in the market. The greater the ease of entry, the greater the competitive pressure on extant competitors from both current and new competitors. We hypothesize a negative relation between ease of entry and a business's profitability.

Rate of market growth is the fifth control variable (Scherer, 1980). When market demand is growing, it is, in principle, easier for all sellers to acquire and retain customers and earn profits. There are four reasons why a business may not profit from short-run demand growth, however. First, some of the short-term demand change is unexpected; thus, a business may be unprepared to respond. Second, a considerable amount of a business's production and marketing capacity in the short term may be fixed in quantity and quality; thus, adjustments to demand changes are slow. Third, if there is easy entry by new sellers, then when market demand increases, new competitors will easily enter, capture some of the profits, and drive profitability to a negative level. If exit barriers are also low, the new competitors depart when the market demand decreases, only to enter once again upon the next increase in market demand. Finally, a business may choose to capture its gains from short-run demand increases in the form of increased sales at current prices, which will increase short-run ROA less than if it raised its prices, as it could do in the face of a demand increase.

Thus, the relationship between short-run market growth and ROA is conjectural. We follow convention, however, and hypothesize a positive relationship between market growth and a business's profitability.

Rate of technological change is the sixth control variable (Scherer, 1980). On the one hand, the greater the technological change in a market, the more diverse will be the opportunities to create value for buyers. On the other hand, the required investment for successful R&D and implementation of a new technology may be substantial and, in the short term, may produce negative profits. We expect the latter to outweigh the former in the short run; thus, we hypothesize a negative relation between short-term technological change and profitability.

The seventh control variable is the size of a business relative to its largest competitor in a market (Scherer, 1980). This variable implies the advantages associated with a large relative market share. The relative size variable potentially captures some revenue and some cost effects. We hypothesize a positive relation between a business's relative size advantage and its profitability.

The average total operating cost of a business relative to that of its largest competitor is the eighth control variable (Scherer, 1980). In contrast to the relative size variable, the relative cost variable captures only cost advantage effects. The variable measures the difference in the average of all operating costs. We hypothesize a positive relation between a cost advantage for a business and the business's profitability.

In the following section, we discuss the empirical analysis of the relationship between market orientation and business profitability.

Empirical Model

Each of the variables was measured with a seven- or eight-point Likert-type scale, and each is defined as follows:

> *Dependent variable:* ROA; an SBU's ROA in its principal served market segment during the past year relative to all other competitors
>
> *Independent variables:*
>
> - MKTOR: The simple average of an SBU's scores on customer orientation, competitor orientation, and interfunctional coordination; expected sign, +

- Relative size (RSIZE): The size of an SBU's sales revenues in its principal served market segment relative to those of its largest competitor; expected sign, +

- Ease of entry (ENTRY): The likelihood of a new competitor being able to earn satisfactory profits in an SBU's principal served market segment within 3 years after entry; expected sign, −

- Relative costs (RCOST): An SBU's average total operating costs (administrative, production, marketing/sales, etc.) relative to its largest competitor in its principal served market segment; expected sign, −

- Seller concentration (CONC): In an SBU's principal served market segment the percentage of total sales accounted for by the four competitors with the largest sales (including the SBU if appropriate); expected sign, +

- Market growth (MGRO): During the past 3 years the average annual growth rate of total sales in an SBU's principal served market segment; expected sign, +

- Supplier power (SPOW): The extent to which an SBU is able to negotiate lower prices from its suppliers; expected sign, +

- Buyer power (BPOW): The extent to which the customers of an SBU are able to negotiate lower prices from it; expected sign, −

- Technological change (TCHG): The extent to which production or service technology in an SBU's principal served market segment has changed during the past 3 years; expected sign, −

Empirical Results

Ordinary least squares regression analysis was used to test the hypothesis that market orientation and performance are positively associated.[1] To analyze the correlates of market orientation among commodity businesses, we used the t test of differences in means due to the small number of commodity businesses.

The sample of 110 SBUs used in the regression analysis consists of 36 commodity businesses, 23 specialty products businesses, and 51 distribution businesses. The specialty products and distribution businesses are combined into one category, "noncommodity businesses." Dummy variables are used to control for differences between the commodity and noncommodity businesses. Table 3.6 presents the regression results.

In Table 3.6, where there is a statistically significant difference between the regression coefficients for the two types of businesses, both regression coefficients are shown. As hypothesized, the square of MKTOR (SQMKTOR)

Table 3.6 ROA Regression Equations (Standard Errors in Parentheses)

						Variable							
	MKTOR	SQMKTOR	RSIZE	ENTRY	RCOST	CONC	MGRO	SPOW	BPOW	TCHG	Constant	N	$\overline{R}^2$
Expected sign	+	+	+	–	–	+	–	+	–	–			
Commodity business	–7.63* (3.390)	.856* (.393)							1.254** (.273)		19.266** (7.251)		
Combined sample			.192* (.082)	–.035 (.132)	–.583** (.114)	.030 (.119)	–.305** (.086)	.110 (.149)		–.280* (.127)		110	.410
Noncommodity business	.501* (.223)								–.104 (.206)		6.056** (1.808)		

NOTE: BPOW, buyer power; CONC, seller concentration; ENTRY, ease of entry; MGRO, market growth; MKTOR, market orientation; RCOST, relative cost; RSIZE, relative size; SPOW, supplier power; SQMKTOR, square of MKTOR; TCHG, technological change.

$*p \leq .05; **p \leq .01.$

67

is significant for the commodity businesses $(p \le .05)$, and MKTOR is significant for the noncommodity businesses $(p \le .05)$. The nonlinear relationship between market orientation and ROA among the commodity businesses supports the expectation of commodity businesses with a medium level of market orientation earning lower ROA than the commodity businesses that have either the least or the most market orientation. The businesses with the medium level of market orientation are the stuck-in-the-middle businesses, which we discuss later.

Five of the eight control variables are significant at $p \le .05$. (We calculated the variance inflation factor, which indicated no multicollinearity problem among the nine independent variables.) The signs on the coefficients of MGRO and BPOW are opposite the hypothesized signs. The negative sign on MGRO suggests that the SBUs in the sample, for one or more of the four reasons advanced previously, earned lower profits than their competitors with respect to the 3-year market growth rate in their principal served market.

For commodity businesses BPOW has a large and significant $(p \le .01)$ positive coefficient. This result is inconsistent with the conventional assumption of the industrial organization literature (but not that of the marketing literature) that buyers and sellers are opponents. It is not difficult to explain how buyer power could add to the ROA of commodity SBUs: Many commodity businesses, even those that are internally oriented, are attentive to buyers' needs when powerful buyers command their attention. The result is a profitable partnership between efficient commodity businesses and powerful buyers. This explanation is consistent with that of Barrett (1986), who finds that buyer concentration is an important determinant of a seller attending closely to the needs of buyers. A coerced responsiveness to buyers' wants, however, is certainly not the substance of market orientation.

To provide more insight into the nonlinear relation between market orientation and ROA among the commodity businesses, we divided the commodity businesses into three groups based on their market orientation scores: low $(N = 15)$, medium $(N = 14)$, and high $(N = 16)$. The sample size in each group is too small for a multiple regression analysis. We attempted an oblique rotation factor analysis of the independent variables to reduce the set, but we did not achieve convergence.

We therefore ranked the means of the independent and dependent variables for the three groups and tested for significant differences. The statistically significant differences are shown in Table 3.7.

Table 3.7 Low, Medium, and High Market Orientation for Commodity Businesses

	MKTOR		
Variable	Low (N = 15)	Medium (N = 14)	High (N = 16)
ROA	2**** (vs. medium)	3**** (vs. high)	1
MKTOR	3*****	2*****	1***** (vs. low)
Custo	3*****	2*****	1*****
Compo	3*****	2*****	1*****
Coord	3*****	2*****	1*****
Absolute size	1***	3	2****
Ease of entry	1****	2	3***
Four-firm concentration	3	2**	1***
Power over supplier	1****	3	2
HRM	3	2****	1****
SD MKTOR (TMT consensus)	2	3*	1
Customer retention rate	3	2****	1*****
TMT average years in SBU	1	2	3****

NOTE: Values shown are rankings of means (1 = top ranking) and *t* test of differences in means.
*p = .15; **p = .12; ***p ≤ .10; ****p ≤ .05; *****p ≤ .01.

Among the three groups of commodity businesses, the differences in both the mean overall scores for market orientation and the scores of the three components are significant. As expected, the high market orientation group has the highest ROA, and it is significantly different from that of the medium group. The difference in ROA for the low and medium groups is also significant. We also examined the relationship of market orientation to another dependent variable, customer retention rate. This variable measures the success of an SBU in retaining its customers relative to the customer retention success of its principal competitors. Not surprisingly, the businesses with the highest market orientation have the highest customer retention rate—a rate significantly higher than that of both the medium and low market orientation businesses. The businesses with the lowest market orientation have the lowest customer retention rate.

The data in Table 3.7 imply that the high market orientation group has, through its superior market performance, created barriers to entry. The data also suggest that this group of businesses is excellently managed. They score a 1 on human resource management and a 1 on top management team consensus (the variance of the TMT members' scores on market orientation).

Moreover, the top management teams of the high market orientation business have the shortest longevity. Because these managers have the shortest history with their particular SBUs, one may infer that they therefore are perhaps the most able and willing to adapt, especially to undertake the pervasive changes required in adopting a market orientation.

The stuck in the middle medium group occupies the middle ranking in almost all cases. One notable exception is their bottom ranking on TMT consensus on market orientation. The difference between the medium group's score on this variable and that of the high group, although significant at only the .15 level, offers an important possible explanation for the medium group's low market orientation and thus performance. Also, the medium group appears to contain the smallest businesses and to have the least power over suppliers.

We previously mentioned that large businesses may be the most reluctant, or the least able, to adopt a market orientation. Consistent with this expectation, among the three commodity business groups, the businesses in the low group are the largest in absolute size. Their lack of market orientation may also be due in part to a greater management longevity in these businesses. The TMTs in the low group have the largest average number of years in their SBUs. In addition, the low group ranks lowest on human relations management, with a score significantly different from that of the high group. The low HRM score, coupled with the low score on interfunctional coordination (and on the other two dimensions of market orientation), suggests that the human resource management skills in the low group may be inferior to those of the high group. The low group faces the easiest entry of new competitors, a condition that may be due in large part to the low market orientation of the businesses in the low group.

These findings complement the findings of the regression analysis—namely, that among commodity and noncommodity businesses, market orientation is strongly related to profitability. The data imply that the commodity businesses with the greatest market orientation have thereby substantial control over their markets—for example, success in retaining customers and raising entry barriers. The findings also suggest that commodity businesses of varying degrees of market orientation team with strong buyers to form noncoercive, mutually profitable partnerships. The general implication is that commodity businesses with the highest degree of market orientation successfully pursue both differentiation (benefit-addition) strategies and low cost (price-reduction) strategies. Their market orientation greatly increases their strategic options. This implication applies equally for noncommodity businesses.

Discussion

The findings support our hypothesis that for all three types of businesses in a forest products company, market orientation is an important determinant of a business's profitability. Among the noncommodity businesses, the positive relationship between market orientation and profitability appears to be monotonic, whereas among the commodity businesses a positive market orientation-profitability relationship occurs only among businesses that are above the median in their level of market orientation.

For both commodity and noncommodity businesses, relative costs also appear to be an important determinant of profitability. Thus, on average, all three types of businesses can pursue either or both differentiation and low cost strategies.

The results also suggest that market growth is an important determinant of profitability for all three types of businesses, but it affects them differently. For noncommodity businesses, short-term market growth presents a profitable opportunity, whereas for commodity businesses, which in general are less adaptable than noncommodity businesses, short-term market growth appears to reduce profitability.

Also, one may infer that the commodity businesses that are substantially market oriented are able to initiate value-increasing programs with powerful buyers to effect a mutually profitable outcome. Indeed, the commodity businesses that are best able to create superior customer value may even create an economic dependency on the part of otherwise strong buyers.

The following is the more basic issue: How common among all types of businesses is the nonlinear relationship between market orientation and profitability that we observe among the commodity businesses? We suspect that it may be rather common. The forest products industry is by no means unique in comprising a product- or technology-oriented business culture. Business units within organizations that reflect such a culture will move to a market orientation only haltingly and unevenly. We may expect, therefore, that numerous industries, especially basic industries and long-established technology-driven industries, will experience some form of the U-shaped market orientation profitability relationship. The key question is how willing and able are companies to move effectively and efficiently through the stages of culture change to the high profitability of a fully implemented market orientation.

Limitations of the Study

Restricting the study to one large corporation confers both advantages and limitations. The advantages in using one large corporation are that with the uniformly strong support that we received from the corporation's management, we attained easy access to multiple, knowledgeable raters in the SBUs. We also attained a very high response rate. By contrast, if we had examined the same number of stand-alone businesses, it would have been more difficult to identify the TMTs and much more difficult to attain a response rate close to that attained in this study.

The most important potential limitation in using SBUs from one corporation is that a pervasive corporate orientation could overwhelm differences in individual SBU orientations. This problem appears not to exist in the current study, however, because there is considerable variation in responses. On the 7-point scale, responses ranged from 2.8 to 6.1 for customer orientation, from 2.8 to 6.6 for competitor orientation, and from 2.6 to 5.8 for interfunctional coordination (see Table 3.5). The variation in responses indicates that, with respect to the three hypothesized components of market orientation, there is no pervasive corporate culture constraining perceptions.

Implications for Future Research

As an exploratory study, and one in which internal validity considerations often took precedence over external validity, the results, although strong, are necessarily limited in their generalizability. Future studies could expand the potential generalizability by adopting some or all of the following:

Multiple Corporations as the Sampling Frame. Although access to the TMTs of the respondent SBUs and the high response rate were very desirable from a reliability perspective, future studies might focus on a larger sample of organizations to assess the robustness of the market orientation performance relationships found in the current study.

Expanded Sample of Industries. A wide variety of market structures comprised the operating environments of the SBUs in this study, but the SBUs all compete in the same broadly defined industry. Future studies might examine whether the relationships found in this study exist in high-technology industries, in service industries, and in the international environment.

Objective Correlates. The use of multiple respondents in each SBU and the assurance of anonymity for respondents reduces respondent bias. The development and use of objective correlates of market orientation would further increase confidence in the measures. It would also reduce the concern about method variance that accompanies most survey research.

Longitudinal Research Design. The cross-sectional nature of the data in this study restricts conclusions to those of association, not causation. The development of a time series database and testing the market orientation performance relationship in a longitudinal framework would provide more insight into probable causation.

* * *

In addition to testing the robustness of the market orientation performance relationship through the preceding suggestions for modifying the research design, future research might address the following comprehensive issues pertaining to market orientation:

Measurement of Profit Orientation and Long-Range Focus. Our attempt to develop a valid measure of profit orientation and long-range focus as part of a one-dimension construct of market orientation was unsuccessful. Future studies might address this issue by including additional items that represent these constructs and testing their relationship with the three-component model of market orientation and with a business's performance.

Balance Among the Components of a Market Orientation. In addition to further examination of the effect of the magnitude of market orientation on business performance, future studies should examine the effect of the proportions of the components within a given magnitude of market orientation. Some authors (Peters & Austin, 1985; Peters & Waterman, 1982) suggest that customer orientation is the most important component of a market orientation. Their implication is that a given magnitude of market orientation highly skewed to a customer orientation would outperform one in which the three components are more equal. An important research question is whether for a given magnitude of market orientation an approximate equality of the components produces, on average, superior profitability over a substantial inequality of the components, other things being equal. Day and Wensley (1988) suggest that the relative emphasis on customer orientation versus competitor orientation is dependent on features of the competitive environment. This is also an important issue for study.

Creation of a Market Orientation. With the development of a valid measure of market orientation and the demonstration of its significant effect on performance, the most important question to practitioners becomes the following: How does one create and sustain a market orientation? Future studies should examine the relative effectiveness of alternative strategies for implementing and sustaining a market orientation.

Conclusion

This study is an important first step in validating the market orientation performance relationship. For scholars, the implications of this study are clear. This research must be replicated in diverse environments and over time to increase confidence in the nature and power of the theory. For managers, the implications of this study are less clear. Due to the exploratory nature of the research, the generalizability of the findings is limited. The findings do suggest that after controlling for important market-level and business-level influences, market orientation and performance are strongly related. These findings are entirely consistent with the intuition and expectations of both scholars and practitioners during the past three decades regarding the nature and effects of a market orientation. As the first empirical study of the content and effect of a market orientation, this study's findings provide marketing scholars and practitioners a basis beyond mere intuition for recommending a market orientation.

If replications of this research produce findings similar to the current findings, the message to managers is clear. The three components of market orientation—customer orientation, competitor orientation, and interfunctional coordination—must comprise the foundation for a business's efforts to obtain a competitive advantage.

Note

1. The distribution of the regression residuals is similar to the distribution of the individual variables—that is, it has no "tails" and is more centered than a normal distribution. Also, the error terms are more likely to be skewed to the left than to the right. The deviation from the shape of the normal distribution, however, does not suggest any clear form of transformation that would be an improvement. Many of the variables of interest are continuous data. The respondents reported the data in ordinal scales (7-point) or in truncated interval scales, however, instead of in their actual values. This has the effect of narrowing the distribution of the data. As is well-known, with truncated data ordinary least square (OLS) regression analysis may approximate the relationship more precisely over the middle range of values than at the extremities of the data. The other usual caveats regarding OLS are herein offered.

References

Aaker, D. A. (1988). *Strategic market management* (2nd ed.). New York: John Wiley.

Aaker, D. A. (1989). Managing assets and skills: The key to sustainable competitive advantage. *California Management Review, 31*(2), 91-106.

Alderson, W. (1957). *Marketing behavior and executive action.* Homewood, IL: Irwin.

Anderson, P. F. (1982). Marketing, strategic planning and the theory of the firm. *Journal of Marketing, 46*(2), 15-26.

Bain, J. S. (1959). *Industrial organization.* New York: John Wiley.

Barrett, J. (1986, February). Why major account selling works. *Industrial Marketing Management, 15,* 63-73.

Boal, K. B., & Bryson, J. M. (1987). Representation, testing, and policy implications of planning processes. *Strategic Management Journal, 8,* 211-231.

Chamberlin, E. H. (1962). *The theory of monopolistic competition.* Cambridge, MA: Harvard University Press. (Original work published 1933)

Churchill, G. A., Jr. (1979, February). A paradigm for developing better measures of marketing constructs. *Journal of Marketing Research, 16,* 64-73.

Cohen, J., & Cohen, P. (1975). *Applied multiple regression/correlation analysis for the behavioral sciences.* Hillsdale, NJ: Lawrence Erlbaum.

Cronbach, L. (1970). *Essentials of psychological testing.* New York: Harper & Row.

Day, G. S. (1984). *Strategic marketing planning.* New York: West.

Day, G. S., & Wensley, R. (1988). Assessing advantage: A framework for diagnosing competitive superiority. *Journal of Marketing, 52*(2), 1-20.

Demsetz, H. (1974). Two systems of belief about monopoly. In H. J. Goldschmid, H. M. Mann, & J. F. Weston (Eds.), *Industrial concentration: The new learning.* Boston: Little, Brown.

Deshpandé, R., & Webster, F. E., Jr. (1989). Organizational culture and marketing: Defining the research agenda. *Journal of Marketing, 53*(1), 3-15.

Dess, G. G., & Davis, P. S. (1984). Porter's (1980) generic strategies as determinants of strategic group membership and organizational performance. *Academy of Management Journal, 27*(3), 467-488.

Dess, G. G., & Robinson, R. B., Jr. (1984). Measuring organizational performance in the absence of objective measures: The case of the privately held firm and conglomerate business unit. *Strategic Management Journal, 5,* 265-273.

Forbis, J. L., & Mehta, N. T. (1981). Value-based strategies for industrial products. *Business Horizons, 24*(3), 32-42.

Galbraith, C., & Schendel, D. (1983). An empirical analysis of strategy type. *Strategic Management Journal, 4,* 153-173.

Hall, W. K. (1980). Survival strategies in a hostile environment. *Harvard Business Review, 58*(5), 75-85.

Hanan, M. (1985). *Consultative selling.* New York: American Management Association.

Heneman, H. G., III. (1974). Comparisons of self and superior ratings. *Journal of Applied Psychology, 59,* 638-642.

Hise, R. T. (1965). Have manufacturing firms adopted the marketing concept? *Journal of Marketing, 29*(3), 9-12.

Hitt, M. A., & Ireland, R. D. (1986). Relationships among corporate-level distinctive competencies, diversification strategy, corporate structure, and performance. *Journal of Management Studies, 23*(4), 265-298.

Hrebeniak, L. G., & Joyce, W. F. (1985, September). Organizational adaptation: Strategic choice and environmental determinism. *Administrative Science Quarterly, 30,* 336-349.

Jackson, B. B. (1985). *Winning and keeping industrial customers.* Lexington, MA: Lexington Books.

Kerlinger, F. N. (1973). *Foundations of behavioral research.* New York: Holt, Rinehart & Winston.

Kotler, P. (1977). From sales obsession to marketing effectiveness. *Harvard Business Review, 55*(6), 67-75.

Kotler, P. (1984). *Marketing management: Analysis, planning, and control.* Englewood Cliffs, NJ: Prentice Hall.

Kotler, P., & Andreasen, A. R. (1987). *Strategic marketing for nonprofit organizations.* Englewood Cliffs, NJ: Prentice Hall.

Lawton, L., & Parasuraman, A. (1980). The impact of the marketing concept on new product planning. *Journal of Marketing, 44*(1), 19-25.

Levitt, T. (1960). Marketing myopia. *Harvard Business Review, 48*(4), 45-56.

Levitt, T. (1980). Marketing success through differentiation of anything. *Harvard Business Review, 58,* 89-91.

Lusch, R., Udell, J. G., & Laczniak, G. R. (1976). The future of marketing strategy. *Business Horizons, 19*(6), 65-74.

McKee, D. O., Varadarajan, P. R., & Pride, W. M. (1989). Strategic adaptability and firm performance: A market-contingent perspective. *Journal of Marketing, 53*(3), 21-35.

McNamara, C. P. (1972). The present status of the marketing concept. *Journal of Marketing, 36*(1), 50-57.

Miles, R. E., & Snow, C. C. (1978). *Organizational strategy, structure, and process.* New York: McGraw-Hill.

Morris, M. L., & Paul, G. W. (1987). The relationship between entrepreneurship and marketing in established firms. *Journal of Business Venturing, 2,* 247-256.

Nunnally, J. (1978). *Psychometric theory* (2nd ed.). New York: McGraw-Hill.

Ohmae, K. (1982). *The mind of the strategist.* New York: McGraw-Hill.

Pearce, J. A., Robbins, D. K., & Robinson, R. B. (1987). The impact of grand strategy and planning formality on financial performance. *Strategic Management Journal, 8,* 125-134.

Peters, T. J., & Austin, N. (1985). *A passion for excellence.* New York: Random House.

Peters, T. J., & Waterman, R. H. (1982). *In search of excellence.* New York: Random House.

Porter, M. (1980). *Competitive strategy.* New York: Free Press.

Porter, M. (1985). *Competitive advantage.* New York: Free Press.

Scherer, F. M. (1980). *Industrial market structure and economic performance.* Chicago: Rand McNally.

Shapiro, B. P. (1988, November/December). What the hell is "market oriented"? *Harvard Business Review, 66,* 119-125.

Webster, F. E., Jr. (1988, May/June). Rediscovering the marketing concept. *Business Horizons, 31,* 29-39.

Zeithaml, V. A. (1988). Consumer perceptions of price, quality, and value: A means-end model and synthesis of evidence. *Journal of Marketing, 52*(3), 2-22.

Corporate Culture, Customer Orientation, and Innovativeness in Japanese Firms

A Quadrad Analysis

Rohit Deshpandé
John U. Farley
Frederick E. Webster, Jr.

Accepted wisdom holds that customer orientation is a key to long-term profitability. A less accepted corollary is that customer orientation requires continuous innovation. Research also suggests that customer orientation and innovativeness must be an integral part of corporate culture if they are to have a significant influence on managers' decision making and, ultimately, on business performance. There has been, however, little research to test these fundamental assertions.

This study reports on interviews with senior marketing executives in 60 large Japanese firms (all quoted on the Nikkei stock exchange) and their key customers. Results are based on "quadrads" of respondents—a pair of respondents in both the supplier and the customer organizations. Business performance is measured in terms of relative profit, growth, size, and share. The authors found that innovativeness is important—the best market performers are technological leaders in their industries and market pioneers.

Although customers of the best performing firms rated those firms as being highly customer oriented, company self-assessments of customer orientation are uncorrelated with customer assessments. Thus, data from customers are necessary to assess whether a firm is truly customer oriented; such data might be viewed as a "reality check" on company self-assessments.

The authors also found that corporate culture is related to business performance as follows:

- Best performers: market cultures (goal achievement orientation stressing competitive advantage)
- Good performers: adhocracy cultures (creative, entrepreneurial, innovative, and growth oriented)
- Bad performers: clan cultures (cohesive, traditional, family-like, and emphasizing teamwork)
- Worst performers: hierarchy cultures (rule, procedure, and policy oriented)

(Most companies represent a mixture of these culture types; heavier weighting of the market culture, however, is associated with best performance.)

Overall, this study suggests that improving business performance is in fact associated with customer orientation, innovativeness, and a supportive corporate culture. Customer orientation is more than verbal commitment, however. For it to have an impact on performance, customers must perceive it as real. Management is well advised to devote specific attention to creating a culture of basic values and beliefs that are conducive to customer orientation and innovativeness.

There is a clear need to integrate several interconnected lines of recent conceptual thinking and empirical analysis that relate marketing management to overall business strategy. Three related developments intersect to create this need.

First, there has been a return to the dictum of the so-called "marketing concept" with its call for customer orientation and innovation as the focus for all business planning and strategy. Several recent studies and articles document renewed management concern for creating a customer-focused, market-driven enterprise (Houston, 1986; Shapiro, 1988; Webster, 1988).

Second, management literature has been peppered with studies of organizational culture, often involving cross-national comparisons of American, European, and Japanese firms (Davis, 1984; Deal & Kennedy, 1982; Hofstede, 1980). As the study of organizational behavior developed, researchers began to apply rigorous theoretical analysis to understanding organizational cultures (Ouchi, 1980; Smircich, 1983). Toward the end of the 1980s, there was a new awareness within marketing as we began to focus on organizational culture as a field of study and to develop a related research agenda (Deshpandé & Webster, 1989).

Third, there is heightened interest in measuring and understanding business performance, especially as it relates to market share, product quality, sources of competitive advantage, and industry structure (Buzzell & Gale, 1987; Porter, 1980, 1985). Marketing scholars have recently begun to explore the intersection of the marketing concept and business performance (Kohli & Jaworski, 1990; Narver & Slater, 1990, 1991).

The Marketing Science Institute has called for the integration of these three research streams by designating the understanding of customer-oriented organizations (including the cultural and structural factors that relate to being customer oriented) as one of four capital or highest priority research topics (Marketing Science Institute, 1990).

The fundamental question is whether customer orientation, as it relates to corporate culture and in concert with organizational innovativeness, has a measurable impact on business performance. The canons of the marketing concept assert that profit is a reward for a customer orientation (which creates a satisfied customer), but we have only the beginnings of systematic empirical documentation of the presumed relationship (Narver & Slater, 1990). The marketing concept describes a basic set of values and beliefs that puts the customer's interest first, ahead of those of all other stakeholders such as owners, managers, and employees. Responding to customer needs, however, also requires innovation, creating new solutions to customer problems. Thus, to understand the functioning and impact of customer orientation, we should relate it to organizational innovativeness, with the analysis embedded within a framework of organizational culture.

This study reports on a representative national sample of major Japanese firms and their key customers, and using a sampling methodology called a quadrad design, it examines the impact of culture, customer orientation, and innovativeness on business performance. This study makes three contributions: (a) It is the first empirical study to simultaneously relate the concepts of organizational culture, customer orientation, and innovativeness to business performance; (b) it reports on a unique sampling and analytical methodology that involves carefully matched dyad pairs (quadrads) of manufacturers and their key customers; and (c) it extends our emerging knowledge of customer orientation to non-American firms, specifically to large Japanese businesses that have been the focus of much recent scholarly and practitioner interest (Kotabe, Duhan, Smith, & Wilson, 1991; Ohmae, 1985).

Conceptual Background and Hypotheses

Culture, Customer Orientation, and Innovativeness

The field of organizational behavior offers a considerable and very rich theoretical literature on corporate culture. We describe a conceptual framework, grounded in this literature, that lends itself to the definition and measurement of specific cultural variables. We also summarize the less developed literatures on customer orientation and on organizational innovativeness. In addition, we hypothesize relationships between each of these three variables (culture, customer orientation, and innovativeness) and business performance.

Organizational Culture. Deshpandé and Webster (1989) reviewed more than 100 studies in organizational behavior, sociology, and anthropology and defined organizational culture as "the pattern of shared values and beliefs that help individuals understand organizational functioning and thus provide them with the norms for behavior in the organization" (p. 4). One insightful definition described culture as "*why* [italics added] things happen the way they do" versus a description of organizational climate or "*what* [italics added] happens around here" (Schneider & Rentsch, 1988).

Using a framework proposed by Smircich (1983), Deshpandé and Webster (1989) reviewed five alternative theoretical paradigms for studying culture, each with unique marketing research implications (p. 9). One such paradigm, organizational cognition, has been developed more than the others in terms of a formal conceptual framework, specification of variables, and operationalization of measures, and it is therefore the one used in this study. This approach is based in cognitive organization theory (Weick, 1985) and is analogous to the cognitive paradigm in much of consumer behavior research.

This perspective on organizational culture focuses on managerial information processing and views organizations as knowledge systems. Such an information-processing view of organizational functioning is very useful for understanding not only the culture of a firm but also its customer orientation because discussion of the latter has taken an implicit, if not explicit, organizational information-processing approach (Kohli & Jaworski, 1990).

The applicability of such an organizational information-processing perspective to understanding culture and its relationship to marketing strategy is discussed by Webster and Deshpandé (1990). They describe the seminal work of Quinn and colleagues (Quinn, 1988; Quinn & McGrath, 1985; Quinn & Rohrbaugh, 1983), who proposed a "competing values" model of organizational effectiveness. This model suggests that the values and beliefs that are shared by members of an organization (and that represent its culture) can be interpreted in terms of classical Jungian psychological archetypes (Jung, 1923). According to this view, cultural information within organizations is interpreted by individuals in the context of their underlying archetypes. The ways in which culture is experienced and transmitted have been determined to be consistent with these Jungian dimensions (Cameron & Freeman, 1988; Mitroff, 1983). Specifically, the competing values model identifies four cultural types based on the Jungian framework as identified in Figure 4.1 in which the shared beliefs concern dominant organizational attributes, leadership styles, organizational bonding mechanisms, and overall strategic emphases.

As shown in Figure 4.1, there are two key dimensions defining culture types. One axis describes the continuum from organic to mechanistic processes—that is, whether the organizational emphasis is more on flexibility, spontaneity, and individuality or on control, stability, and order. The other axis describes the relative organizational emphasis on internal maintenance (i.e., developing human resources and integration) or on external positioning (i.e., competition and environmental differentiation). The four resulting culture types are labeled clan, hierarchy, adhocracy, and market. These labels are consistent with much of the theory on alternative organizational forms and the use of similar terms by scholars such as Williamson (1975), Ouchi (1980), and Mintzberg (1979).

The bottom right quadrant in Figure 4.1, labeled a market culture, emphasizes competitiveness and goal achievement (Cameron & Freeman, 1988). Transactions are governed by market mechanisms (Ouchi, 1980). The key measure of organizational effectiveness is productivity achieved through these market mechanisms. This culture type is in direct contrast to the set of values expressed in a clan culture (hence the terminology of a competing

ORGANIC PROCESSES (flexibility, spontaneity)

Type: Clan

DOMINANT ATTRIBUTES:
Cohesiveness, participation,
teamwork, sense of family

LEADER STYLE:
Mentor, facilitator, parent figure

BONDING:
Loyalty, tradition, interpersonal
cohesion

STRATEGIC EMPHASES:
Toward developing human
resources, commitment, morale

Type: Adhocracy

DOMINANT ATTRIBUTES:
Entrepreneurship, creativity, adaptability

LEADER STYLE:
Entrepreneur, innovator, risk taker

BONDING:
Entrepreneurship, flexibility, risk

STRATEGIC EMPHASES:
Toward innovation, growth, new resources

INTERNAL MAINTENANCE
(smoothing activities, integration)

EXTERNAL POSITIONING
(competition, differentiation)

Type: Hierarchy

DOMINANT ATTRIBUTES:
Order, rules and regulations,
uniformity

LEADER STYLE:
Coordinator, administrator

BONDING:
Rules, policies and procedures

STRATEGIC EMPHASES:
Toward stability, predictability,
smooth operations

Type: Market

DOMINANT ATTRIBUTES:
Competitiveness, goal achievement

LEADER STYLE:
Decisive, achievement oriented

BONDING:
Goal orientation, production, competition

STRATEGIC EMPHASES:
Toward competitive advantage and market
superiority

MECHANISTIC PROCESSES (control, order, stability)

Figure 4.1. A Model of Organizational Culture Types (Adapted From Cameron &
Freeman [1988] and Quinn [1988])

values approach). In the latter, the emphasis is on cohesiveness, participation, and teamwork. The commitment of organizational members is ensured through participation, and organizational cohesiveness and personal satisfaction are rated higher than financial and market share objectives.

The top right quadrant in Figure 4.1, labeled an adhocracy culture, emphasizes values of entrepreneurship, creativity, and adaptability. Flexibility and tolerance are important, and effectiveness is defined in terms of finding new markets and new directions for growth. Again, the competing set of values is found in the hierarchy culture that stresses order, rules, and regulations. Transactions are under the control of surveillance, evaluation, and direction. Business effectiveness is defined by consistency and achievement of clearly stated goals.

It is important to note that these are modal or dominant culture types rather than mutually exclusive ones. By implication, most firms can and do have elements of several types of cultures, perhaps even within the same strategic business unit. Over time, however, one type of culture emerges as the dominant one. (The process of culture development and subculture conflict is discussed in detail in Deshpandé and Webster [1989].)

The four classifications of culture discussed previously imply varying degrees of business performance in a competitive marketplace. The market culture, characterized by its emphasis on competitive advantage and market superiority, will likely be associated with the best business performance. At the other extreme, we expect a hierarchical culture, with its emphasis on predictability and smooth operations within a bureaucratic organization, to contribute to relatively unsatisfactory business performance. Also, given the focus in an adhocracy culture on innovation, entrepreneurship, and risk taking, we anticipate better market performance than in a clan culture in which loyalty, tradition, and emphasis on internal maintenance could lead to inattention to changing market needs. In a more general sense, the organizational emphasis on external positioning over internal maintenance is likely to be associated with stronger performance. This leads to our first hypothesis:

H_1: Business performance is ranked from best to worst according to the type of organizational culture as follows:

> Market culture
>
> Adhocracy culture
>
> Clan culture
>
> Hierarchical culture

We should also note that the previous hypothesis and the literature we have cited to support it are grounded in corporate rather than national culture. Clearly, the Japanese firms in our sample share a common national culture. We still expect, however, to find diverse corporate cultures. In fact, several authors have suggested that Japanese managers in different firms possess significantly different values (Lincoln & Kalleberg, 1990). Among the most prevalent culture types identified are those labeled bureaucratic, vitalized, clans, hierarchical, and "Theory Z" (Hatvany & Pucik, 1981; Kono, 1988; Ouchi, 1981; Sullivan, 1983).

Customer Orientation. There has been little empirical study of customer orientation. Kohli and Jaworski (1990) point out that discussion of customer orientation (or market orientation, the term they use) has come within the context of implementing the marketing concept. The latter is a taken-for-granted fundamental principle in marketing practice and, perhaps for this reason, has seldom been examined empirically. Kohli and Jaworski's description of customer orientation focuses on an organizationwide generation and dissemination of, and responsiveness to, market intelligence (p. 3). Narver and Slater (1990) reinforce Kohli and Jaworski's conceptualization by defining a market orientation as "the organization culture that most effectively and efficiently creates the necessary behaviors for the creation of superior value for buyers and, thus, continuous superior performance for the business" (p. 21). They further distinguish the three behavioral components of a market orientation as customer orientation, competitor orientation, and interfunctional coordination and argue that on average all three components are equally important.

We note that the conceptual distinction made by Narver and Slater (1990) between a customer and market orientation is not entirely consistent with Kohli and Jaworski's (1990) definition or with the terminology we develop in this chapter. More explicitly, we view customer and market orientations as being synonymous (with the term *market* defined in the conventional manner as the set of all potential customers of a firm [Kotler, 1991]) and hence distinguishable from a competitor orientation, which Narver and Slater define as meaning the "seller understands the short-term strengths and weaknesses and long-term capabilities and strategies of both the key current and the key potential competitors" (pp. 21-22). We agree with Day and Wensley (1988), who conclude that effective marketing strategy requires a balanced mix of customer and competitor analysis. Indeed, we argue that a competitor orientation can be almost antithetical to a customer orientation when the focus is exclusively on the strengths of a competitor rather than on the unmet needs of the customer. We add that Narver and Slater's third behavioral component of interfunctional coordination (defined as the coordinated use of company resources in creating superior value for target customers) is entirely in keeping with the central essence of a customer orientation (as Kohli and Jaworski also argue) and hence should be part of its meaning and measurement.

From the previous discussion, we develop a more formal definition. We define customer orientation as the set of beliefs that puts the customer's interest first, ahead of those of all other stakeholders such as owners, managers, and employees. We view customer orientation as being a part of an overall, but much more fundamental, corporate culture. Hence, a simple focus on information about the needs of actual and potential customers is inadequate without considering the more deeply rooted set of values and beliefs that are likely to consistently reinforce such a customer focus and pervade the organization.

An organization's evaluation of its level of customer orientation should come from its customers rather than merely from the company itself. This latter point is a critical one. We are all familiar with Henry Ford's statement that customers could have a car in any color they wanted as long as it was black. On the basis of the success of the Model T, the Ford Motor Company, prior to the 1920s, viewed itself as being extremely customer oriented. Although customers might have thought otherwise, they had little choice in the matter. Once Alfred Sloan's General Motors began to offer the Chevrolet with more modern features and a variety of colors, Henry Ford's Model T was doomed and Ford's sales and profits sagged disastrously (Halberstam, 1986, pp. 89-90).

One objective of this research is to compare a company's assessment of its own customer orientation with its customer's assessment of its customer orientation to test whether they are related and whether either is significantly related to business performance. On the basis of the assertions of the marketing concept, customer orientation should have a favorable impact on business unit performance, and presumably this should be true regardless of whether customer orientation is measured in terms of the perceptions of the supplier or seller or the customer. Most authors approach customer orientation as an element of corporate culture from the vantage point of the seller (Kohli & Jaworski, 1990; Narver & Slater, 1990). Hence,

H_{2a}: The marketer's self-reported customer orientation is positively related to business performance.

H_{2b}: The marketer's customer orientation, as reported by customers, is positively related to business performance.

Recognizing that customers' and marketers' perceptions may not agree, even though they should (in the normative sense implied by the marketing concept), we offer an additional set of hypotheses:

H_{3a}: Marketers' and customers' perceptions of the marketers' customer orientation will agree.

H_{3b}: The customers' perception of the marketer's customer orientation will be more important than the marketer's own perception in explaining the marketer's business performance.

The latter hypothesis is based in part on Drucker's (1954) comment that marketing is not a specialized activity but rather "the whole business seen from the point of view of its final result, that is, from the customer's point of view" (p. 39). This implies that a customer's perception of the customer orientation of a firm will be more critical for successful business performance than the seller's perceptions.

Organizational Innovativeness. Peter Drucker was one of the first scholars to state the marketing concept (Webster, 1988). In an often-cited passage, Drucker (1954) wrote,

> There is only one valid definition of business purpose: to create a customer. . . . It is the customer who determines what the business is. . . . Because it is its purpose to create a customer, any business enterprise has two—and only these two—basic functions: marketing and innovation. (p. 37)

Although, as the earlier discussion noted, an increased interest in conceptualizing and measuring the marketing concept has emerged, little attention has been devoted recently to Drucker's (1954) second "basic function"—

innovation. In a separate literature (that of diffusion of innovations), however, scholars noted the importance of organizations being innovative (Rogers, 1983). Much of this literature focuses on innovativeness as a dependent variable, presuming it to be important and worthy of study. Increasingly, however, scholars have linked innovativeness to organizational performance, suggesting that a firm needs to be innovative so as "to gain a competitive edge in order to survive and grow" (Gronhaug & Kaufmann, 1988, p. 3). This is an important issue because, as Capon, Farley, and Hoenig (1990) stated, the relationship between organizational factors such as innovativeness and business performance has not been adequately studied. Hence, our final hypothesis:

H_4: The more innovative the firm, the better its performance.

Method

The Unit of Observation: The Quadrad

The substantial literature on the appropriate units of analyses in organizational buying behavior leads to two major conclusions. First, more than one key informant within an organizational unit is needed to develop reliable measures of organizational constructs (Moriarty & Bateson, 1982). This is particularly important for us because we are dealing with some new constructs and operationalizations. Second, the organizational buying behavior literature also stresses the crucial importance of the dyad—that is, measurements of both buyer and seller—to explore the extent of agreement regarding theoretical constructs (Weitz, 1981). The latter is of course especially salient in our study because of our hypotheses relating to customer orientation.

Interestingly, we were unable to locate many studies in which the two major conclusions discussed previously were combined—that is, in which more than one respondent was interviewed in both the buyer and the seller organizations. We note that the methodology described in this chapter refers to an analysis of a matched set of buyer-seller pairs. Previous work attempted to poll both buyers and sellers but used a separate analysis of buyer and seller samples rather than a matched dyads approach (Anderson & Narus, 1990). Hence, we refer to our sampling methodology as a quadrad—that is, the combination of two buyer-seller dyads. The data used in our analysis are derived from 50 such quadrads, each constructed from a set of four interviews—two with a supplier and two with a customer firm of that supplier. For reasons described previously, we believe that the quadrad perspective, although much more time-consuming and expensive, allows for far more precise measurement.

Sample

The sample of 50 firms selected for personal interviews represents a random nth observation sample of firms publicly traded on the Nikkei stock exchange in Tokyo. Two marketing executives from a single business unit of each firm were interviewed in their offices by professional interviewers from a commercial Japanese market research firm. Both executives were asked to respond to survey questions in the context of the same specific product and market situation (hereafter referred to as a "business"). Hence, divisional, rather than corporate, marketing executives were chosen because of their greater familiarity with their customers and the likely reliability of their self-reports (especially on customer orientation). Each respondent was asked to name up to three important customers. The two lists were combined, and a customer was chosen at random. Two purchasing executives at the selected firm were interviewed. If two such interviews could not be arranged, another firm on the list was selected randomly and the interviewing procedure repeated. (Although 60 firms were originally interviewed, 10 observations did not provide a complete set of explanatory measures and were excluded from analyses.) Hence, our analysis is based on 50 sets of four interviews per set (i.e., 50 quadrads). It is also important to note that although this sampling technique is cumbersome and expensive enough to constrain the total number of collectable observations, it also allows us to report on one of the few nationally representative samples of firms in Japan, in which gaining access to the kind of information described in this study is far from easy.

Questionnaire Development

The original questionnaire was prepared in English and translated into Japanese by a Japanese American language instructor. The Japanese questionnaire was refined and modified by the research staff of a major Japanese university. It was then edited and pretested by the Japanese professional market research organization that conducted the fieldwork.

Operationalizations

The operationalizations of the three explanatory constructs (culture, customer orientation, and innovativeness) and the performance measures involved the development of scales. The actual questions used for each construct are listed in Table 4.1. The culture scale was adapted from Cameron and Freeman (1988) and Quinn (1988). The customer orientation scale was developed for this study based on extensive qualitative personal interviewing, a detailed survey of available literature (including the work of Kohli and Jaworski [1990] and Narver and Slater [1990] mentioned earlier), and pretesting in a small sample of firms. The innovativeness scale, adopted from Capon, Farley, and Hulbert (1988), contains both market and strategy measures as suggested by Capon, Farley, Hulbert, and Lehmann (1992). Interrater correlations on individual items for pairs of respondents from a given firm were consistently positive and significant (at $\alpha = .01$), and this measure of reliability was reinforced by high Cronbach's alpha reliability coefficients for all but one scale (as described in more detail later). Hence, the average of the two relevant responses within the quadrad was used in each case to build the scales (i.e., the accepted approach used in organizational sociology studies viz. Hage & Aiken, 1970).

Table 4.2 displays the validated constructs and their properties. Measure validation was performed in two distinct steps. First, items developed for each construct were examined for internal validity. Items with low item-to-total, zero-order correlations were reviewed for their theoretical importance and deleted if they tapped no additional, distinct domain of interest. Second, scale reliability as measured by Cronbach's alpha was performed, and items were deleted as necessary to purify scales if a distinct theoretical domain was already being adequately measured. As can be seen in Table 4.2, all reliability coefficients except one were above .65, thus adequately meeting the standards for such research (Nunnally, 1967). Although clan culture had a lower reliability coefficient, it was retained in the analysis for theoretical purposes because it is part of the broader conceptual framework described earlier (Cameron & Freeman, 1988; Quinn, 1988).

Performance was measured by combining four self-evaluations, each on a three-point ordinal scale, of profitability, size, market share, and growth rate compared with that of the largest competitor for that particular business (i.e., the specific product and market situation being described by the respondents). The performance scale had a Cronbach's alpha of .90. The firms were divided

Table 4.1 Scales Used to Measure Customer Orientation, Organizational Culture, Innovativeness, and Performance

Customer Orientation

The statements below describe norms that operate in businesses. Please indicate your extent of agreement about how well the statements describe the actual norms in your business.

1	2	3	4	5
Strongly disagree	Disagree	Neither agree nor disagree	Agree	Strongly agree

Instruction: Answer in the context of your specific product/market or service/market business

1. We have routine or regular measures of customer service.
2. Our product and service development is based on good market and customer information.
3. We know our competitors well.
4. We have a good sense of how our customers value our products and services.
5. We are more customer focused than our competitors.
6. We compete primarily based on product or service differentiation.
7. The customer's interest should always come first, ahead of the owners.
8. Our products/services are the best in the business.
9. I believe this business exists primarily to serve customers.

[These same items were used with customers with the first-person pronoun replaced by "the supplier," which was identified at the beginning of the interview.]

Culture

[The four culture scores were computed by adding all four values of the A items for Clan, the B items for Adhocracy, the C items for Hierarchy, and the D items for Market. The results shown in Table 4.2 can therefore equal more or less than 100, which would be the result only if respondents distributed points equally on each question. The scale was adapted from Cameron and Freeman (1988) and Quinn (1988).]

These questions relate to what your operation is like. Each of these items contains four descriptions of organizations. Please distribute 100 points among the four descriptions depending on how similar the description is to your business. None of the descriptions is any better than any other, they are just different. For each question, please use all 100 points. You may divide the points in any way you wish. Most businesses will be some mixture of those described.

1. Kind of organization (Please distribute 100 points)

_____ Points for A	(A) My organization is a very personal place. It is like an extended family. People seem to share a lot of themselves.	_____ Points for B	(B) My organization is a very dynamic and entrepreneurial place. People are willing to stick their necks out and take risks.
_____ Points for C	(C) My organization is a very formalized and structural place. Established procedures generally govern what people do.	_____ Points for D	(D) My organization is very production oriented. A major concern is with getting the job done without much personal involvement.

2. Leadership (Please distribute 100 points)

_____
Points for A

(A) The head of my organization is generally considered to be a mentor, sage, or a father or mother figure.

_____
Points for B

(B) The head of my organization is generally considered to be an entrepreneur, an innovator, or a risk taker.

_____
Points for C

(C) The head of my organization is generally considered to be a coordinator, an organizer, or an administrator.

_____
Points for D

(D) The head of my organization is generally considered to be a producer, a technician, or a hard-driver.

3. What holds the organization together (Please distribute 100 points)

_____
Points for A

(A) The glue that holds my organization together is loyalty and tradition. Commitment to this firm runs high.

_____
Points for B

(B) The glue that holds my organization together is a commitment to innovation and development. There is an emphasis on being first.

_____
Points for C

(C) The glue that holds my organization together is formal rules and policies. Maintaining a smooth-running institution is important here.

_____
Points for D

(D) The glue that holds my organization together is the emphasis on tasks and goal accomplishment. A production orientation is commonly shared.

4. What is important (Please distribute 100 points)

_____
Points for A

(A) My organization emphasizes human resources. High cohesion and morale in the firm are important.

_____
Points for B

(B) My organization emphasizes growth and acquiring new resources. Readiness to meet new challenges is important.

_____
Points for C

(C) My organization emphasizes performance and stability. Efficient, smooth operations are important.

_____
Points for D

(D) My organization emphasizes competitive actions and achievement. Measurable goals are important.

Innovativeness

[The innovativeness scale was constructed from the items used by Capon, Farley, and Hulbert (1988) to describe organizational innovativeness.]

In a new product and service introduction, how often is your company:

	Never				Always
First to market with new products and services	1	2	3	4	5
Later entrant in established but still growing markets*	1	2	3	4	5
Entrant in mature, stable markets*	1	2	3	4	5
Entrant in declining markets*	1	2	3	4	5
At the cutting edge of technological innovation	1	2	3	4	5

*Reverse scored in forming the scale.

(continued)

Table 4.1 (Continued)

Performance
Relative to our businesses' largest competitor, we are:

	(1)	(2)	(3)
(a)	Less profitable	About equally profitable	More profitable
(b)	Larger	About the same size	Smaller*
(c)	Have a larger market share	About the same market share	Have a smaller market share*
(d)	Are growing more slowly	Are growing at about the same rate	Are growing faster

*Reverse scored in construction of the scale

Table 4.2 Summary of Statistical Results

				Mean[a]		
Scale	No. of Items	Cronbach's Alpha	All	Low Performers	High Performers	SD
Culture						
Market	4	.82	106.1[b]	92.3	110.8	37.4
Adhocracy	4	.66	78.9[b]	72.5	85.0	26.4
Clan	4	.42	117.0	124.0	114.4	28.8
Hierarchy	4	.71	100.9[b]	111.9	91.0	31.4
Customer orientation						
As evaluated by supplier	9	.69	32.5	32.3	32.3	3.3
As evaluated by customer	9	.83	32.1[b]	31.0	32.7	3.2
Innovativeness	5	.85	17.8[b]	16.9	18.7	2.9

a. Numbers are summations of the four individual components for each culture type.

b. Significant univariate difference between high- and low-performance firms.

into good and poor performers by a median split, with ties at the median assigned to the high-performance group. This procedure was used for two reasons: Because the items are ordinal, it was difficult to develop a summary measure of performance with metric properties. Hence, examining better and poorer performing firms makes some intuitive sense. Furthermore, we were unable to divide the sample into a larger number of size-balanced groups (e.g., good, medium, and poor performers) because of the limited size of the overall sample.

Results

Means of the culture, customer orientation, and innovativeness scores are also shown in Table 4.2. It is interesting to note that although the predominant self-reported culture type is that of a clan, a fact that is consistent with most popular writing about Japanese organizations (Florida & Kenney, 1991), it is evident that all four types of culture are well represented in this sample. As might be expected, this is based on the previously cited work of Sullivan (1983), Hatvany and Pucik (1981), and others who have noted the considerable diversity in both structural and cultural forms in Japanese organizations that is seldom mentioned in more popular writing. Five of seven measures have significant differences for high and low performers, including three of four culture scales, the customer orientation measure provided by the customer, and the innovativeness scale. The two measures not significantly different for high and low performers are the clan culture scale and the marketers' self-rating on customer orientation. We discuss these results later.

Discriminant Function

Because the nature of the quadrad sampling methodology and the treatment of the dependent variable allowed us to group firms in terms of high and low performance, we used a discriminant function to classify high and low performers on the basis of culture, customer orientation, and innovativeness. This also allowed us to make meaningful managerial conclusions about the nature of our findings. Table 4.3 shows the correlations of each explanatory variable with the discriminant function—essentially the partial correlation of each variable with the performance index. The results are consistent with the analysis of the means reported in Table 4.2. In interpreting the results, an important caveat is that our cross-sectional (as opposed to longitudinal) design means that results should be interpreted as factors associated with, rather than necessarily leading to, better performance.

Culture

The coefficients of the four culture types order as expected, supporting Hypothesis 1. Market cultures were associated with the best performance, and adhocracy cultures followed. Both clan and hierarchical cultures were associated with poor performance, with the latter being the worst as hypothesized.

Table 4.3 Partial Relationships of Performance With Culture, Customer
Orientation, and Innovativeness

Explanatory Variable	Partial Correlations With Performance (All Signs as Hypothesized)[a]	Significant?	p
Culture			
Market	.48	Yes	.046
Adhocracy	.39	No	.102
Clan	−.28	No	.239
Hierarchical	−.56	Yes	.021
Customer orientation			
Measured from customer	.52	Yes	.031
Measured from producer	.00	No	.988
Innovativeness	.52	Yes	.034

a. Pooled within-group correlation of prediction from discriminant function with respective explanatory
variable.

The univariate tests were significant for the market and hierarchical cultures,
and the others were not significant due to the relatively small sample size.

Customer Orientation

The marketers' customer orientation as reported by customers is positively related to business performance (H_{2b}), and the customers' perceptions
are significantly more important than the marketers' own perceptions (H_{3b}).
In fact, there is only weak agreement (correlation of .17, $p < .13$) between
the customers' and the marketers' perceptions of customer orientation, so
Hypothesis 3_a was not supported. The extremely low correlation between the
marketers' perceptions and performance (.00, $p < .988$; Table 4.2) also led to
rejection of Hypothesis 2_a.

Innovativeness

Organizational innovativeness is positively related to performance as
per Hypothesis 4. It is interesting to note that this relationship, along with that
of customer-reported customer orientation and performance, was the second
strongest in magnitude (.52; Table 4.3), reinforcing Drucker's (1954) notion
that a customer focus and innovation should be the raison d'être of any busi-

ness. (The strongest coefficient in magnitude is the negative relationship between hierarchical culture types and performance.)

Classification

Overall, the discriminant function classified 73% of the firms correctly into the two performance groups. This is significantly better than chance, based on the proportional chance criterion (Morrison, 1969), which predicts 52% correct classification. For cross-validation, a random subsample of two fifths of the original sample was used to predict the classification of the remainder of the sample with 63% accuracy, again significantly better than chance.

Given the small sample size of 50 quadrads (although this represents 200 individual respondents), we believe that these results are quite strong, especially the correct ordering of culture types in terms of business performance. The results for customer reports of market orientation and for innovativeness are also strong and consistent with our hypotheses. Contrary to our expectations but important for its implications, however, is the lack of a relationship between customer reports and self-reports of customer orientation.

Discussion

This research was designed to evaluate the relationships between corporate culture, customer orientation, innovativeness, and business performance. We began the empirical phase of our work with an examination of Japanese businesses because the opportunity to gather data in that country, as noted earlier, has historically been quite difficult. Although the focus of our study is on corporate rather than national culture, Japan also provided the opportunity to examine these relationships in a setting in which one would expect a strong national background culture to be operating. Future research of this kind that might be performed based on data from American or European companies will allow marketing scholars to compare and contrast findings from different national cultures.

The results for culture types and their relationships with business performance are very encouraging. Responsive (market) and flexible (adhocracy) corporate cultures outperform more consensual (clan) and internally oriented, bureaucratic (hierarchical) cultures. Although the results were not significant for clan-type cultures (perhaps because of lower scale reliability than for the other measures), they were significant for all the others, and all (including clan cultures) were in the expected direction and order. In fact, the results on the highest performance of market cultures are given some credence by recent suggestions that the oft-heard Japanese injunction of *gambatte* (try harder and persist) might explain the dogged perseverance of some Japanese firms in the face of strong competition (Holberton, 1991). For example, Sony continued to push its 8-mm video format despite competition from VHS manufacturers such as JVC and Matsushita. The competitively oriented corporate slogans of market leaders such as toiletries manufacturer Kao ("kill Procter and Gamble"), earth-moving equipment manufacturer Komatsu ("encircle Caterpillar"), and Canon ("best Xerox") are also examples. Indeed, it suggests that the universality of a competitive corporate culture might transcend a more consensually oriented national culture. Again, this is a promising avenue for future empirical research.

The findings on culture types are also theoretically consistent with the competing values model from which the conceptual framework was derived (Quinn, 1988). Specifically, it is interesting that the competing values of the market culture outperformed those of the clan culture (in the diagonally opposite quadrant in Figure 4.1), and those of the adhocracy culture outperformed those of the diagonally opposing hierarchy culture. In Jungian terms (Jung, 1923), this is an illustration of a dominant and a shadow side to the culture of any organization, with each competing for attention at any given time; this point was also made by Mitroff (1983) in his cognitive view of organizational knowledge systems. There is clearly great opportunity for exploring the conflict between dominant and subcultures—an idea articulated by Gregory (1983) in her discussion of native-view paradigms and multiple-culture confrontations.

As Drucker (1954) suggested, we found that customer orientation and innovativeness are both associated with business performance. Simply stated, customer-oriented and innovative firms were the ones that performed better, a basic assertion of the marketing concept. We also discovered, however, that Japanese managers' self-reports of customer orientation are not related to business performance and have no significant relationship to their customers' appraisals of the company's customer orientation. Indeed, it is the customer's assessments that affect business performance—and in the predicted direction. Two interesting possibilities need to be tested in future research: Perhaps the strong national consensus culture in Japan (Florida & Kenney, 1991) makes it difficult for some managers to be self-critical on a matter as important as customer orientation. If so, we might expect to find a stronger correlation between customer and self-reports of customer orientation in American or European firms.

The other possibility is that national differences may not really be important; rather, managers in general, independent of nationality, may not have a good sense of their firm's own customer orientation. This would call into question whether a corporate culture that espouses basic values and beliefs relating to the importance of customer orientation is by itself a contributor to business performance. Some of our other results support the latter possibility. Because customer orientation as a theoretical construct is distinct from each of the four culture types, it appears that relatively good customer orientation is achievable in a variety of cultures and, conversely, that a particular type of culture does not necessarily facilitate customer orientation. Reasoning based on the assertions of the marketing concept creates an expectation that customer orientation would be stronger in market and adhocracy cultures. We found no such relationships in our data.

On a technical level, the data requirements for this kind of work are very demanding. We have shown that self-reporting on customer orientation is potentially inaccurate, so data from customers are required. Similarly, because customers cannot be expected to profile suppliers' cultures clearly, data from suppliers are also needed. If we couple these requirements with the need for reliable measures on both the supplier and the customer side, we find that we need a complex and expensive research design such as the quadrad design used in this study.

That firms that are "customer oriented" or "market driven" are successful is often taken as a matter of faith. It is, of course, a matter of degree because no firm can ignore customers completely, and a complete customer orientation (from the customer's point of view) is probably neither achievable nor economically desirable (Narver & Slater, 1990). Many marketing managers, however, are uncertain of the customer orientedness of their firms—a fact demonstrated by the inability of our sample of suppliers to accurately assess how their customers feel about the matter. Van de Ven (1990) stressed the importance of accurate market feedback to the general success of the firm, and in this study there is an indication of relatively inaccurate feedback. Many marketing managers are also uncertain about what kinds of change and what types of organizational culture might be needed to move toward a more customer-oriented posture; external goal orientation and creativity (which do not necessarily occur simultaneously) are cultural characteristics that appear to favor customer orientation, and to achieve these the commitment of top management is required. Finally, other manifestations of customer orientation, such as successful product and service innovation, may be more important to success than internal culture or orientation, which may be facilitators rather than causers. These are clearly matters for future research.

References

Anderson, J. C., & Narus, J. A. (1990). A model of distributor firm and manufacturer firm working partnerships. *Journal of Marketing, 54*(1), 42-58.

Buzzell, R. D., & Gale, B. T. (1987). *The PIMS principles: Linking strategy to performance.* New York: Free Press.

Cameron, K. S., & Freeman, S. J. (1988). *Cultural congruence, strength and type: Relationships to effectiveness* [Working paper]. Ann Arbor: University of Michigan, School of Business.

Capon, N., Farley, J. U., & Hoenig, S. (1990, October). Determinants of financial performance: A meta-analysis. *Management Science, 36*(10), 1143-1159.

Capon, N., Farley, J. U., & Hulbert, J. (1988). *Corporate strategic planning.* New York: Columbia University Press.

Capon, N., Farley, J. U., Hulbert, J., & Lehmann, D. R. (1992, February). Profiles of product innovators among large U.S. manufacturers. *Management Science, 38,* 157-169.

Davis, S. M. (1984). *Managing corporate culture.* Cambridge, MA: Ballinger.

Day, G. F., & Wensley, R. (1988). Assessing advantage: A framework for diagnosing competitive superiority. *Journal of Marketing, 52*(2), 1-20.

Deal, T. E., & Kennedy, A. E. (1982). *Corporate culture.* Reading, MA: Addison-Wesley.

Deshpandé, R., & Webster, F. E., Jr. (1989). Organizational culture and marketing: Defining the research agenda. *Journal of Marketing, 53*(1), 3-15.

Drucker, P. F. (1954). *The practice of management.* New York: Harper & Row.

Florida, R., & Kenney, M. (1991, June). Transplanted organizations: The transfer of Japanese industrial organization to the U.S. *American Sociological Review, 56,* 381-398.

Gregory, K. L. (1983, September). Native-view paradigms: Multiple cultures and conflicts in organizations. *Administrative Science Quarterly, 28,* 359-376.

Gronhaug, K., & Kaufmann, G. (1988). *Innovation: A cross-disciplinary perspective.* Oslo: Norwegian University Press.

Hage, J., & Aiken, M. (1970). *Social change in complex organizations.* New York: Random House.

Halberstam, D. (1986). *The reckoning.* New York: Avon.

Hatvany, N., & Pucik, C. V. (1981). Japanese management practices and productivity. *Organizational Dynamics, 9*(4), 5-21.

Hofstede, G. (1980). *Culture's consequences: International differences in work-related values.* Beverly Hills, CA: Sage.

Holberton, S. (1991, June 21). Why sheer persistence is the key to Japanese success. *Financial Times,* 14.

Houston, F. S. (1986). The marketing concept: What it is and what it is not. *Journal of Marketing, 50*(2), 81-87.

Jung, C. G. (1923). *Psychological types.* London: Routledge Kegan Paul.

Kohli, A. K., & Jaworski, B. J. (1990, April). Market orientation: The construct, research propositions, and managerial implications. *Journal of Marketing, 54*(2), 1-18. (See also Chapter 2)

Kono, T. (1988). *Changing corporate culture.* Tokyo: Kodansha.

Kotabe, M., Duhan, D. F., Smith, D. K., Jr., & Wilson, R. D. (1991). The perceived veracity of PIMS strategy principles in Japan: An empirical inquiry. *Journal of Marketing, 55,* 26-41.

Kotler, P. (1991). *Marketing management* (7th ed.). Englewood Cliffs, NJ: Prentice Hall.

Lincoln, J. R., & Kalleberg, A. L. (1990). *Culture, control and commitment: A study of work organization and work attitudes in the U.S. and Japan.* Cambridge, UK: Cambridge University Press.

Marketing Science Institute. (1990). *Research priorities 1990-1992: A guide to MSI research programs and procedures.* Cambridge, MA: Author.

Mintzberg, H. (1979). *The structuring of organizations.* Englewood Cliffs, NJ: Prentice Hall.

Mitroff, I. I. (1983). *Stakeholders of the organizational mind.* San Francisco: Jossey-Bass.

Moriarty, R. T., & Bateson, J. E. G. (1982, May). Exploring complex decision making units: A new approach. *Journal of Marketing Research, 19*(2), 182-191.

Morrison, D. G. (1969, May). On the interpretation of discriminant analysis. *Journal of Marketing Research, 6*(2), 156-163.

Narver, J. C., & Slater, S. F. (1990). The effect of a market orientation on business profitability. *Journal of Marketing, 54*(3), 20-35. (See also Chapter 3)

Narver, J. C., & Slater, S. F. (1991). *Increasing a market orientation: An exploratory study of the programmatic and market-back approaches* [Working paper]. Seattle: University of Washington, Graduate School of Business Administration.

Nunnally, J. (1967). *Psychometric theory.* New York: McGraw-Hill.

Ohmae, K. (1985). *Triad power.* New York: Free Press.

Ouchi, W. G. (1980, March). Markets, bureaucracies, and clans. *Administrative Science Quarterly, 25,* 129-141.

Ouchi, W. G. (1981). *Theory Z.* Reading, MA: Addison-Wesley.

Porter, M. E. (1980). *Competitive strategy.* New York: Free Press.

Porter, M. E. (1985). *Competitive advantage.* New York: Free Press.

Quinn, R. E. (1988). *Beyond rational management.* San Francisco: Jossey-Bass.

Quinn, R. E., & McGrath, M. R. (1985). Transformation of organizational cultures: A competing values perspective. In P. J. Frost, L. F. Moore, M. R. Louis, C. Lundberg, & J. Martin (Eds.), *Organizational culture.* Beverly Hills, CA: Sage.

Quinn, R. E., & Rohrbaugh, J. (1983). A spatial model of effectiveness criteria: Toward a competing values approach to organizational analysis. *Management Science, 29*(3), 363-377.

Rogers, E. M. (1983). *Diffusion of innovations* (3rd ed.). New York: Free Press.

Schneider, B., & Rentsch, J. (1988). Managing climates and cultures: A futures perspective. In J. Hage (Ed.), *Futures of organizations.* Lexington, MA: Lexington Books.

Shapiro, B. P. (1988, November/December). What the hell is "market oriented"? *Harvard Business Review, 66,* 119-125.

Smircich, L. (1983, September). Concepts of culture and organizational analysis. *Administrative Science Quarterly, 28*(3), 339-358.

Sullivan, J. J. (1983). A critique of theory Z. *Academy of Management Review, 8,* 132-142.

Van de Ven, A. H. (1990). Trends in organizations: The need for organizational change. In G. S. Swartz (Ed.), *Organizing to become market-driven* (Report No. 90-123). Cambridge, MA: Marketing Science Institute.

Webster, F. E., Jr. (1988, May/June). The rediscovery of the marketing concept. *Business Horizons, 31*(3), 29-39.

Webster, F. E., Jr., & Deshpandé, R. (1990). *Analyzing corporate cultures in approaching the global marketplace* (Report No. 90-111). Cambridge, MA: Marketing Science Institute.

Weick, K. E. (1985). The significance of corporate culture. In P. J. Frost, L. F. Moore, M. R. Louis, C. Lundberg, & J. Martin (Eds.), *Organizational culture* (pp. 381-389). Beverly Hills, CA: Sage.

Weitz, B. A. (1981). Effectiveness in sales interactions: A contingency framework. *Journal of Marketing, 45,* 85-103.

Williamson, O. E. (1975). *Markets and hierarchies: Analysis and antitrust implications.* New York: Free Press.

Market Orientation

Antecedents and Consequences

Bernard J. Jaworski
Ajay K. Kohli

Market orientation is the implementation of the marketing concept and is defined as comprising three sets of activities: (a) organizationwide generation of market intelligence pertaining to current and future customer needs, (b) internal dissemination of the intelligence within the organization, and (c) organizationwide responsiveness to the intelligence. The purpose of this study was to empirically assess both the influence of organizational factors hypothesized to affect market orientation and the impact of market orientation on business performance.

Jaworski and Kohli conducted two cross-sectional mail surveys to obtain data from two samples of American business units. The first sample included 222 businesses (strategic business units) and employed a multiple-informant design. Informants were requested to respond to questions designed to measure market orientation, its antecedents, and its consequences. Regression analyses were performed to test the hypotheses. The second sample included 230 managerial responses. The results from the two samples were remarkably consistent.

The first set of findings indicated that market orientation is aided by (a) visibility of top management emphasis on market orientation, (b) the presence of reward systems that recognize and reward employees for tracking and responding to market needs, (c) connectedness of departments within the organization, and (d) decentralized decision making. Market orientation appears to be hindered by risk aversion of top management and by interdepartmental conflict.

The second set of findings indicated that market orientation is positively related to business performance. Moreover, the relationship between market orientation and business performance appears to be robust across business environments characterized by different levels of market turbulence, competitive intensity, or technological turbulence. Finally, a market orientation appears to increase employees' commitment to their organizations and their esprit de corps.

Recent years have witnessed a renewed emphasis on delivering superior quality products and services to customers (Bitner, 1990; Day & Wensley, 1988; Parasuraman, Zeithaml, & Berry, 1985). Because customer needs and expectations evolve, delivering consistently high-quality products and services requires continuous tracking and quick response to changing marketplace needs—that is, being market oriented. More formally, market orientation is the organizationwide generation of market intelligence, dissemination of that intelligence among departments, and organizationwide responsiveness to it (Kohli & Jaworski, 1990).

Why are some organizations more market oriented than others? Remarkably, this fundamental issue has not been addressed in any empirical study to date. Several propositions pertaining to the antecedents of market orientation have been advanced by Kohli and Jaworski (1990). As they point out, however, these propositions need empirical validation. Although market orientation is posited to lead to greater customer satisfaction and greater organizational commitment on the part of employees, this has not been subjected to empirical testing.

Narver and Slater (1990) report empirical support for the often assumed or implied relationship between market orientation and business performance. Arguments that market orientation may have a strong or a weak effect on business performance depending on environmental conditions, such as market turbulence and competitive intensity, have been advanced in the literature (Houston, 1986). Such variations in the impact of market orientation on performance have yet to be empirically investigated.

The purpose of this research is to address the previously noted gaps in our knowledge. Specifically, we use two national studies to investigate (a) the role of three sets of factors posited in the literature to affect market orientation, (b) the hypothesized effect of market orientation on business performance and employees, and (c) the role of environmental characteristics in moderating the relationship between market orientation and business performance. This research sheds light on the relative importance of many organizational factors that help or hinder market orientation and the impact of such an orientation on employees and business performance.

In addition to testing theory, the research findings are useful to managers who are building market-oriented organizations (Day, 1990). This research addresses the issue of whether all businesses should be market oriented. This is important because devoting resources to developing market orientation may be wasteful if the orientation does not lead to better performance. Finally, this research sheds light on the impact of market orientation on employees, an aspect that has been underemphasized in previous research.

We first provide a brief review of the literature on market orientation and discuss hypotheses pertaining to its antecedents and consequences. Next, we describe two large-scale field studies undertaken to test these hypotheses and describe the results. We conclude with a discussion of the managerial relevance of our findings and note future research directions.

Background Hypotheses

Introduced in the early 1950s, the marketing concept represents a cornerstone of marketing thought. Given its widely acknowledged importance, however, it is remarkable how little research has focused on the implementation of the marketing concept, referred to as market orientation. There exists only a small set of conceptual articles that offer preliminary suggestions for engendering market orientation (Felton, 1959; Stampfl, 1978; Webster, 1988).

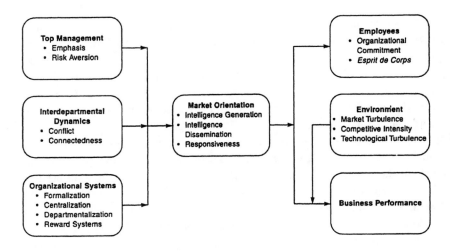

Figure 5.1. Antecedents to and Consequences of a Market Orientation

In addition, very few empirical studies have been conducted, and these primarily concern the extent to which organizations have adopted the marketing concept rather than the antecedents or consequences of market orientation (Barksdale & Darden, 1971; Hise, 1965; Lusch, Udell, & Laczniak, 1976; McNamara, 1972). There is, however, a strong resurgence of academic and practitioner interest in market orientation (Deshpandé & Webster, 1989; Houston, 1986; Linden, 1987; Narver & Slater, 1990; Olson, 1987; Shapiro, 1988).

Using a theories-in-use approach described by Zaltman, LeMasters, and Heffring (1982), Kohli and Jaworski (1990) find that market orientation is composed of three sets of activities: (a) organizationwide generation of market intelligence pertaining to current and future customer needs, (b) dissemination of this intelligence among departments, and (c) organizationwide responsiveness to it. This responsiveness is composed of two sets of activities: response design (i.e., using market intelligence to develop plans) and implementation (i.e., executing such plans). The three-component concept also makes possible a more focused analysis of the role of any given antecedent of market orientation. (As will be discussed later, the same antecedent may have a different effect on the different components of market orientation.) We therefore adopt the three-component concept of market orientation.

Figure 5.1 identifies the key constructs included in this study. We hypothesize three sets of antecedents pertaining to top management, interdepartmental factors, and organizational systems to be related to market orientation. Furthermore, we hypothesize that market orientation is related both to the commitment and esprit de corps of employees and to business performance. Finally, we hypothesize that the link between market orientation and business performance is moderated by market turbulence, competitive intensity, and technological turbulence. Because a fairly detailed discussion of these hypotheses is provided by Kohli and Jaworski (1990), we offer only a brief synopsis.

Antecedents to Market Orientation

The first set of antecedents included in this study pertain to top management. Several authors suggest that top managers play a critical role in shaping an organization's values and orientation (Felton, 1959; Hambrick & Mason, 1984; Webster, 1988). The central theme in their research is that unless employees get clear signals from top managers about the importance of being responsive to customer needs, the organization is not likely to be market oriented (Levitt, 1969, p. 244; Webster, 1988, p. 37). Top management reinforcement of the importance of market orientation is likely to encourage employees to track changing markets, share market intelligence, and be responsive to market needs. We therefore expect the following:

H_1: The greater the top management emphasis on market orientation, the greater the (a) market intelligence generation, (b) intelligence dissemination, and (c) responsiveness of the organization.

A second antecedent to market orientation relates to top managers' risk posture. Responding to changing market needs often calls for the introduction of new products and services. New products, services, and programs often run a high risk of failure and tend to be more visible than established products. Kohli and Jaworski (1990) argue that if top management demonstrates a willingness to take risks and accept occasional failures, junior managers are more likely to propose and introduce new offerings in response to changing customer needs. In contrast, if top management is risk averse and intolerant of failures, subordinates are less likely to focus on generating or disseminating market intelligence or responding to customer needs.
We therefore expect the following:

H_2: The greater the risk aversion of top management, the lower the (a) market intelligence generation, (b) intelligence dissemination, and (c) responsiveness of the organization.

The second set of factors hypothesized to affect market orientation pertains to interdepartmental dynamics. A particularly important factor is interdepartmental conflict (i.e., the tension among departments arising from the incompatibility of actual or desired responses [Gaski, 1984; Raven & Kruglanski, 1970, p. 70]). Several authors point to interdepartmental conflict as an inhibitor of market orientation (Felton, 1959; Levitt, 1969; Lusch et al., 1976). Essentially, interdepartmental conflict is likely to inhibit communication among departments (Ruekert & Walker, 1987), thereby lowering market intelligence dissemination. In addition, tension among departments is likely to inhibit response to market needs, thereby hampering market orientation. We did not expect interdepartmental conflict to affect intelligence generation because it does not affect the information-acquisition process in any given department. Hence,

H$_3$: The greater the interdepartmental conflict, the lower the (a) market intelligence dissemination and (b) responsiveness of the organization.

In addition, we posit that market orientation is affected by interdepartmental connectedness (i.e., the degree of formal and informal contact among employees in various departments). Several related streams of research suggest that connectedness facilitates interaction and exchange of information as well as actual use of market information (Cronbach et al., 1981; Deshpandé & Zaltman, 1982; Patton, 1978). We therefore expect that the more connectedness there is, the more likely employees are to exchange market intelligence and respond to it in a concerted fashion (Kohli & Jaworski, 1990). We did not expect interdepartmental connectedness to affect intelligence generation. Thus,

H$_4$: The greater the interdepartmental connectedness, the greater the (a) market intelligence dissemination and (b) responsiveness of the organization.

The third set of antecedents posited to affect market orientation pertains to organizational structure and systems. We first consider three structural variables: formalization, centralization, and departmentalization. Formalization is the degree to which rules define roles, authority relations, communications, norms and sanctions, and procedures (Hall, Haas, & Johnson, 1967). Centralization is the extent to which decision-making authority resides with top management only (Aiken & Hage, 1968). Departmentalization refers to the number of departments into which organizational activities are divided.

Research to date suggests that both formalization and centralization are inversely related to use of market information (Deshpandé & Zaltman, 1982; Hage & Aiken, 1970; Zaltman, Duncan, & Holbek, 1973). In this chapter, using market information means designing and implementing programs based on market intelligence—that is, organizational responsiveness. Thus, as Stampfl (1978) argues, it appears that formalization and centralization are inversely related to that responsiveness. Similarly, Lundstrom (1976) and Levitt (1969) discuss departmentalization as a barrier to communication (and hence dissemination of market intelligence).

Interestingly, there is reason to believe that organizational structure may not affect all three components of market orientation in the same fashion. As noted earlier, because market orientation involves doing something new or different in response to market conditions, it may be viewed as a form of innovative behavior. Zaltman et al. (1973, p. 62) find innovative behavior to be composed of two stages: the initiation stage (i.e., awareness and decision-making stage) and the implementation stage (i.e., carrying out the decision). In this chapter, we consider the initiation stage equivalent to intelligence generation, dissemination, and response design. The implementation stage is equivalent to actual response.

Zaltman et al. (1973) draw on numerous studies to argue that organizational characteristics, such as formalization, centralization, and departmentalization, may have opposite effects on each stage of the innovative behavior. In particular, they indicate that although these characteristics may hinder the initiation of innovative behavior, they may actually facilitate the implementation of innovative behavior. This suggests that formalization, centralization, and departmentalization may be inversely related to market intelligence generation, dissemination, and design of response but positively related to implementation of response. We therefore hypothesize the following:

H_5: The greater the formalization of an organization, (a) the less it will tend to generate, disseminate, and plan a response to market information but (b) the more effective its response implementation.

H_6: The greater the centralization of an organization, (b) the less it will tend to generate, disseminate, and plan a response to market information but (b) the more effective its response implementation.

H_7: The greater the departmentalization of an organization, (a) the less it will tend to generate, disseminate, and plan a response to market information but (b) the more effective its response implementation.

The last antecedent investigated in this study relates to the measurement and reward system of an organization. Literature on the subject suggests that measurement and reward systems are instrumental in shaping the behavior of employees (Anderson & Chambers, 1985; Hopwood, 1974; Jaworski, 1988; Lawler & Rhode, 1976). In the current context, Webster (1988) argues that "the key to developing a market-driven, customer-oriented business lies in how managers are evaluated and rewarded" (p. 38). He observes that if managers are primarily evaluated on short-term profitability and sales, they are likely to focus on these criteria and neglect factors such as customer satisfaction that ensure the long-term health of an organization. We expect that individuals in organizations that emphasize customer satisfaction and market-oriented behavior as bases for administering rewards will more readily generate, disseminate, and respond to market intelligence. That is,

H_8: The greater the reliance on market-based factors in evaluating and rewarding managers, the greater the (a) generation, (b) dissemination, and (c) response of the organization to market intelligence.

Consequences of Market Orientation

Market orientation is frequently posited to improve business performance. The argument is that market-oriented organizations—that is, those that respond to customer needs and preferences—can better satisfy customers and hence perform better. The study by Narver and Slater (1990) is the first to test empirically and provide support for the link between market orientation and business performance. Because that study uses data from a single corporation and asks each informant to perform the relatively demanding task of rating on a Likert-type scale the return on assets of his or her organization relative to competitors, it is important that this central link receive additional empirical attention. The following is the formal hypothesis to be tested:

H_9: The more market oriented an organization is, the better it will perform.

The next set of consequences examined in the study focuses on employees. The research reported by Kohli and Jaworski (1990) suggests that market orientation affords many psychological and social benefits to employees. Specifically, market orientation is argued to lead to a sense of pride in belonging to an organization in which all departments and individuals work toward the common goal of satisfying customers. Kohli and Jaworski posit that accomplishing this objective results in employees sharing a feeling of contributing to the organization and thus having a commitment to it. The following is the formal testable hypothesis:

H_{10}: The greater the market orientation, the greater the (a) esprit de corps and (b) organizational commitment of employees.

As noted earlier, several scholars suggest that the link between market orientation and performance is likely to depend on environmental context. In this study, we include three environmental characteristics that, according to Kohli and Jaworski (1990), influence the link between market orientation and performance. First, we consider market turbulence—the rate of change in the composition of customers and their preferences. Organizations operating in turbulent markets are more likely to need to modify their products and services continually to satisfy their customers. In contrast, an organization's products and services are likely to need relatively little modification in stable markets in which customers' preferences do not change much. In other words, market orientation is likely to be more strongly related to performance in turbulent markets than in stable markets. Stated formally,

H_{11}: The greater the market turbulence, the stronger the relationship between market orientation and business performance.

A second environmental factor that moderates the link between market orientation and business performance is competitive intensity. As Houston

(1986) and Kohli and Jaworski (1990) observe, in the absence of competition, an organization may perform well even if it is not very market oriented. This is because customers are stuck with the organization's products and services. In contrast, under conditions of intense competition, customers have many options, and organizations that are not very market oriented will probably lose out. Thus, market orientation is expected to be a more important determinant of performance under conditions of intense competition. That is,

$H_{12:}$ The greater the competitive intensity, the stronger the relationship between market orientation and business performance.

The third environmental factor that moderates the relationship between market orientation and business performance is technological turbulence—the rate of technological change. Market orientation is a means of developing a competitive advantage because it enables an organization to understand customer needs and offer products and services that meet those needs. Although market orientation is an important means of obtaining competitive advantage, there are others. One is technology. Organizations working with nascent technologies may be able to obtain a competitive advantage via technological innovation, thereby diminishing, but not eliminating, the importance of market orientation. In contrast, organizations working with stable (mature) technologies are poorly positioned to use technology to obtain competitive advantage and must rely on market orientation to a greater extent. For additional arguments along similar lines, see Bennett and Cooper (1981), Houston (1986), Kaldor (1971), and Tauber (1974). The previous discussion suggests the following:

$H_{13:}$ The greater the technological turbulence in an industry, the weaker the relationship between market orientation and business performance.

Data Collection

Sample 1

The sample for our first study (Sample 1) was drawn from the member companies of the Marketing Science Institute (MSI) and the top 1,000 companies (in sales revenues) listed in the Dun and Bradstreet (D&B) *Million Dollar Directory*. We employed a multiple-informant design in this study.

A letter from the MSI executive director was mailed to a senior executive at all 49 MSI member companies with a request to participate in the study. We requested that each executive provide the names of a senior marketing and a senior nonmarketing executive in one or more of the strategic business units (SBUs) of the company so that researchers could contact them. Thirteen companies agreed to participate in the study and provided names of executives in 27 SBUs. We mailed a copy of the questionnaire, a personalized letter, and return envelope to the two informants in each SBU and sent a reminder postcard approximately 1 week after the initial mailing. Three weeks later, we mailed a replacement copy of the questionnaire and another personalized letter. The response rate was 88.9% for the marketing executives and 77.8% for the nonmarketing executives.

From the D&B sampling frame, we selected 500 companies from among the top 1,000 by selecting every other listing. The initial contact was made with the chief executive officer (CEO) of each company via a personalized letter requesting the company's participation in the study. A total of 21 companies could not be reached because of incorrect addresses, resulting in an effective base of 479 companies. We requested that the CEOs provide the names of two senior executives (one marketing and one nonmarketing) in their SBUs to serve as informants. A total of 102 companies agreed to participate, and we obtained 229 SBU names, including 206 for marketing and 187 for nonmarketing executives. Researchers then contacted informants in these SBUs and requested that they complete and return the study questionnaire per the procedure described for the MSI companies. The response rate was 79.6% for the marketing executives and 70% for the nonmarketing executives.

The previous procedures resulted in responses from a total of 222 business units. For the purpose of analysis, the responses of the two informants were averaged to obtain scores for each business unit. In the relatively few instances in which only one informant provided data, these data were used to represent business unit scores.

Sample 2

To cross-validate the findings from the previous study, data were obtained from a second sample (Sample 2). The sampling frame for the second sample was the American Marketing Association membership roster, from which we selected 500 names at random, after first eliminating those whose titles suggested that they were relatively low in the organizational hierarchy. From this set, 13 individuals could not be reached because of incorrect addresses, resulting in an effective base of 487. We used the three-wave mailing procedure described earlier. A total of 230 responses were obtained for a response rate of 47.2%.

Instrument Development and Refinement

The study used existing scales for measuring the organizational characteristics of formalization, centralization, and departmentalization. Scales for other constructs included in the study were not available in the literature. Hence, the first step in developing our study entailed creating new scales. A four-phase iterative procedure was adopted for the purpose.

First, we independently generated a large pool of items for each of the constructs included in the study. We were careful to capture the domain of each construct as closely as possible. For example, we generated multiple items to correspond to each of the three components of market orientation. From this pool of items, we selected a subset, using the criteria of uniqueness and the ability to convey different shades of meaning to informants (Churchill, 1979). Several items were reverse scored to minimize response set bias.

Next, because of the centrality of the market orientation scale, its items were tested for clarity and appropriateness in personally administered pretests with 27 managers from marketing and nonmarketing departments as well as from top management. In completing a questionnaire, managers were asked to indicate any ambiguity they found in the items or any other difficulty they had in responding and to offer any suggestions. On the basis of their feedback, we eliminated or added some items and modified others.

This was followed by another phase of pretests in which the scales for all constructs were clearly marked and presented to seven academic experts. We asked them to evaluate the items critically for domain representativeness, item specificity, and clarity of construction. On the basis of their detailed critiques, some items were eliminated and others revised to improve their specificity and precision.

The items thus developed and refined were subjected to another phase of pretests involving personal interviews with seven managers. We asked these managers to complete a questionnaire that included the items as they applied to their business unit. At this stage, very few concerns were raised, and we made only very minor refinements. A brief description of the final scale items follows. The complete scales are provided in Appendix 5.A.

Market orientation was measured by a 32-item scale. Of these items, 10 pertain to market intelligence generation, 8 to intelligence dissemination, and 14 to responsiveness at the business unit level. Of the 14 responsiveness items, 7 measure the extent to which an organization develops plans in response to market intelligence (response design), and the remaining 7 assess the actual implementation of these plans (response implementation). Woven into items measuring the three components (generation, dissemination, and responsiveness) are issues related to the needs and preferences of customers and end-users, competitors' moves, and regulatory trends. Sample items for the three components include the following: "In our business unit, intelligence on our competitors is generated independently by several departments," "We have interdepartmental meetings at least once a quarter to discuss market trends and developments," and "Customer complaints fall on deaf ears in this business unit" (reverse scored). Each item was scored on a 5-point scale ranging from "strongly disagree" to "strongly agree."

Top management emphases on market orientation and risk tolerance were measured by two separate scales. The first scale is composed of four items (e.g., "Top managers repeatedly tell employees that this business unit's survival depends on its adapting to market needs"). Items in this scale focus on the verbal reinforcement that top managers provide for market-oriented activities. The risk-aversion scale is composed of six items (e.g., "Top managers in this business unit like to 'play it safe' ") and measures top managers' disposition toward innovative action in the face of risk and uncertainty. Items were scored on a 5-point scale ranging from strongly disagree to strongly agree.

The two constructs pertaining to the interdepartmental dynamics of conflict and connectedness were each measured by seven-item scales. The conflict items pertain to the extent to which the goals of the different departments are incompatible and tension prevails in interdepartmental interactions (e.g., "Protecting one's departmental turf is considered to be a way of life in this business unit"). The connectedness items measure the extent to which individuals in a department are networked to various levels of hierarchy in other departments (e.g., "In this business unit, it is easy to talk with virtually anyone you need to, regardless of rank or position"). Items were scored on a 5-point scale ranging from strongly disagree to strongly agree.

Formalization and centralization were measured by the widely used scales developed by Aiken and Hage (1968). The seven-item formalization scale assesses the extent to which jobs in the organization are codified and an emphasis on observing rules prevails (e.g., "How things are done around here is left up to the person doing the work"; reverse coded). The five-item centralization scale assesses the degree of hierarchical authority in an organization (e.g., "A person who wants to make his own decisions would be quickly discouraged here"). All items were scored on a 5-point scale ranging from strongly disagree to strongly agree.

Departmentalization was measured by a count of the number of departments in the business unit. Reward-system orientation was measured by a six-item scale that assesses the extent to which customer relations, customer satisfaction, and market-oriented behavior are used to evaluate and reward individuals in the organization (e.g., "Customer satisfaction assessments influence senior managers' pay in this business unit"). We used a 5-point scoring format (1 = strongly disagree; 5 = strongly agree) for these items.

Market turbulence, competitive intensity, and technological turbulence were measured by three scales comprising six, six, and five items, respectively. The items for the market turbulence scale assess the extent to which an organization's customers tend to change over time (e.g., "We are witnessing demand for our products and services from customers who never bought them before"). Competitive intensity scale items assess the behavior, resources, and ability of competitors to differentiate (e.g., "Anything that one competitor can offer, others can match readily"). Technological turbulence items measure the extent to which technology in an industry is in a state of flux (e.g., "The technology in our industry is changing rapidly"). We used a 5-point scoring format (1 = strongly disagree; 5 = strongly agree) for all items.

Business performance was measured using two distinct approaches reflected in the literature—judgmental and objective. The judgmental measure asked informants for their assessment of the overall performance of the business and overall performance relative to major competitors, rated on a 5-point scale ranging from "poor" to "excellent." The objective measures related to the dollar share of the served market and the return on shareholders' equity.

Organizational commitment and esprit de corps were measured by two 7-item scales. The organizational commitment items measure the extent to which a business unit's employees are fond of the organization, view their future tied to that of the organization, and are willing to make personal sacrifices for the business unit (e.g., "Employees often go above and beyond the call of duty to ensure this business unit's well-being"). The esprit de corps scale assesses the team spirit of the organization (e.g., "People in this business unit are genuinely concerned about the needs and problems of each other"). All items were scored on a 5-point scale ranging from strongly disagree to strongly agree.

The reliability of each scale was estimated by computing its coefficient alpha. Items that exhibited low inter-item correlations were eliminated to improve the internal consistency of the scales. The reliability coefficient of each of the refined scales is reported in Appendix 5.A (except for the overall responsiveness construct, which has a reliability coefficient of .89). As may be seen from the appendix, the refined scales generally have good to excellent reliability coefficients, and these are above the levels recommended by Nunnally (1978).

Analyses and Results

Hypotheses H_1 through H_8 relate to the antecedents of market orientation. These were tested by estimating the following regression equations:

$$Y_1 = \beta_1 X_1 + \beta_2 X_2 + \ldots + \beta_8 X_8 + e_1$$
$$Y_2 = \beta_1 X_1 + \beta_2 X_2 + \ldots + \beta_8 X_8 + e_2$$
$$Y_3 = \beta_1 X_1 + \beta_2 X_2 + \ldots + \beta_8 X_8 + e_3$$
$$Y_4 = \beta_1 X_1 + \beta_2 X_2 + \ldots + \beta_8 X_8 + e_4$$

where Y_1 denotes overall market orientation; Y_2 through Y_4 denote market intelligence generation, market intelligence dissemination, and responsiveness, respectively; X_1 through X_8 correspond to (1) top management emphasis on market orientation, (2) top management risk aversion, (3) interdepartmental conflict, (4) interdepartmental connectedness, (5) formalization, (6) centralization, (7) departmentalization, and (8) reward system orientation; and e is the error term. Because we hypothesized that interdepartmental conflict and connectedness would affect intelligence dissemination and responsiveness but not intelligence generation (H_3 and H_4), conflict and connectedness were not included as predictors of intelligence generation in the second equation listed previously. The results obtained from estimating the four equations with Sample 1 and Sample 2 are provided in Tables 5.1 and 5.2.

Table 5.1 Antecedents of Market Orientation: Standardized Regression Coefficients Estimated With Sample 1

Independent Variable	Dependent Variable			
	Market Orientation	Intelligence Generation	Intelligence Dissemination	Responsiveness
Top management emphasis	.24***	.27***	.25***	.20**
Top management risk aversion	ns	ns	ns	−.24***
Interdepartmental conflict	−.17*	—	−.27***	−.23**
Interdepartmental connectedness	.20**	—	ns	ns
Formalization	ns	ns	ns	ns
Centralization	−.22**	ns	−.14*	−.22**
Departmentalization	ns	ns	ns	ns
Reward system orientation	.30***	.39***	.24***	.16*
R^2	.63	.34	.49	.54
N	134	144	154	150

*$p < .05$; **$p < .01$; ***$p < .001$. ns, not significant.

Table 5.2 Antecedents of Market Orientation: Standardized Regression Coefficients Estimated With Sample 2

Independent Variable	Dependent Variable			
	Market Orientation	Intelligence Generation	Intelligence Dissemination	Responsiveness
Top management emphasis	.24***	.20*	.28***	.24***
Top management risk aversion	ns	ns	ns	−.12*
Interdepartmental conflict	−.28***	—	−.20*	−.32***
Interdepartmental connectedness	.22**	—	.27**	ns
Formalization	ns	ns	ns	ns
Centralization	ns	−.34**	ns	ns
Departmentalization	ns	ns	ns	ns
Reward system orientation	.31***	.38***	.20**	.19**
R^2	.58	.33	.38	.55
N	123	130	138	138

*$p < .05$; **$p < .01$; ***$p < .001$. ns, not significant.

In addition, recall that H_5 through H_7 hypothesized that formalization, centralization, and departmentalization would have opposite effects on the two components of responsiveness—design and implementation. Accordingly, two additional regression equations were estimated by incorporating response design and implementation as the dependent variables and the eight independent variables noted previously. The results obtained for the effects of formalization, centralization, and departmentalization on the two components of responsiveness in both samples were identical to those obtained for overall responsiveness reported in Tables 5.1 and 5.2.

H_9 and H_{10} pertain to the effect of market orientation on business performance and employees' organizational commitment and esprit de corps. These were tested by regressing performance (using in turn the judgmental measure and the objective measures of market share and return on equity) on market orientation.[1] To control for the effects of additional determinants of performance, six control variables were incorporated as independent variables in the regression equations. The control variables relate to competitive intensity, buyer power, supplier power, entry barriers, pressure from competitors' products, and product quality. The literature suggests that these variables are important determinants of performance (Boulding & Staelin, 1990; Jacobson & Aaker, 1987; Porter, 1980). We developed measures of these variables specifically for this study. Similarly, employees' organizational commitment and esprit de corps were separately regressed on market orientation and the control variables to test H_9 and H_{10}. The results obtained are reported in Tables 5.3 and 5.4.

Finally, H_{11} through H_{13} hypothesize that the impact of market orientation is contingent on the level of market turbulence, competitive intensity, and technological turbulence in a given industry. To test for the moderating effect of these three variables, a split-group analysis was performed as follows with both Sample 1 and Sample 2 separately (Arnold, 1982). First, the sample was sorted in ascending order of a moderator variable (e.g., market turbulence) and then split at the median to form two groups—one with relatively low market turbulence and the other with relatively high market turbulence. Performance was regressed on market orientation and the six control variables discussed previously in the full sample while allowing all regression coefficients to take on different values in the two subgroups. To test for the moderating effects of market turbulence, the regression equation was re-estimated, this time constraining the coefficient associated with market orientation to take on the same value in the two subgroups. The Chow (1960) test

Table 5.3 Consequences of Market Orientation: Standardized Regression
Coefficients Estimated With Sample 1

	Dependent Variable				
Independent Variable	Overall Performance	Market Share	ROE	Organizational Commitment	Esprit de Corps
Market orientation	.23**	ns	ns	.44***	.51***
Product quality	.24**	ns	ns	.18*	.18*
Competitive intensity	ns	−.39***	ns	ns	ns
Buyer power	ns	ns	−.40*	ns	ns
Supplier power	ns	.22*	ns	ns	ns
Entry barriers	ns	ns	ns	ns	ns
Substitutes	ns	ns	ns	ns	ns
R^2	.18	.06	.22	.31	.40
N	145	112	53	153	153

*$p < .05$; **$p < .01$; ***$p < .001$. *ns*, not significant.

Table 5.4 Consequences of Market Orientation: Standardized Regression
Coefficients Estimated With Sample 2

	Dependent Variable				
Independent Variable	Overall Performance	Market Share	ROE[a]	Organizational Commitment	Esprit de Corps
Market orientation	.36***	ns	—	.66***	.58***
Product quality	ns	ns	—	ns	ns
Competitive intensity	ns	−.21*	—	ns	ns
Buyer power	ns	ns	—	ns	ns
Supplier power	ns	ns	—	ns	ns
Entry barriers	ns	ns	—	ns	ns
Substitutes	ns	ns	—	ns	ns
R^2	.25	.11	—	.50	.39
N	136	89	—	139	135

a. This regression model was not estimated owing to the limited number of cases available for the analysis.
*$p < .05$; ***$p < .001$. *ns*, not significant.

was performed to assess the statistical significance of the difference in the regression coefficients of the market orientation variable across the low and high market turbulence subgroups. The hypothesized moderating effects of competitive intensity and technological turbulence were tested in a similar fashion by re-sorting the samples using these variables in turn and proceeding as discussed previously.

Findings and Discussion

Focusing on the antecedents to market orientation, there is strong convergence in the findings from the two samples. The only exceptions relate to the role of interdepartmental connectedness and organizational centralization (see Tables 5.1 and 5.2). Overall, the results suggest that several factors drive the market orientation of a business. The amount of emphasis that top managers place on market orientation seems to affect the generation of market intelligence (Sample 1: $\beta = .27, p < .001$; Sample 2: $\beta = .20, p < .05$), its dissemination within the organization (Sample 1: $\beta = .25, p < .001$; Sample 2: $\beta = .28, p < .001$), and the responsiveness of the organization (Sample 1: $\beta = .20, p < .01$; Sample 2: $\beta = .24, p < .001$). It thus seems important that top managers continually emphasize the need for tracking and responding to market developments. The risk aversion of top management does not appear to affect intelligence generation or dissemination but seems to have a negative effect on the responsiveness of the organization (Sample 1: $\beta = -.24, p < .001$; Sample 2: $\beta = -.12, p < .05$). These findings support our expectation that responding to market developments entails tolerating some risk, and that if top managers are unwilling to assume any risk the organization is less likely to be responsive to customers.

Interdepartmental conflict, as expected, appears to inhibit intelligence dissemination (Sample 1: $\beta = -.27, p < .001$; Sample 2: $\beta = -.20, p < .05$) and the responsiveness of an organization (Sample 1: $\beta = -.23, p < .01$; Sample 2: $\beta = -.32, p < .001$). This supports our expectation that employees of organizations in which tension prevails are less likely to share market information and to work together to satisfy customer needs. Results from both samples suggest that a feeling of connectedness among employees promotes market orientation. The results from Sample 2 suggest that connectedness facilitates the dissemination of intelligence within an organization ($\beta = .27, p < .01$), thereby improving its market orientation. Curiously, in Sample 1, connectedness does not appear to be related to intelligence dissemination, although it is related to overall market orientation ($\beta = .20, p < .01$). These results call for additional research to examine the link between connectedness and market orientation.

Market orientation appears to be very strongly related to the reward systems of the organization (Sample 1: $\beta = .30, p < .001$; Sample 2: $\beta = .31$, $p < .001$). Organizations that reward employees based on customer satisfaction, good customer relations, and so on tend to be more market oriented. Comparisons of the standardized regression coefficients in both Sample 1 and Sample 2 suggest that the design of reward systems has the strongest impact on market orientation from among the set included in the study. The right reward systems appear to facilitate all three components of market orientation intelligence generation (Sample 1: $\beta = .39, p < .001$; Sample 2: $\beta = .38$, $p < .001$), intelligence dissemination (Sample 1: $\beta = .24, p < .001$; Sample 2: $\beta = .20, p < .01$), and responsiveness (Sample 1: $\beta = .16, p < .05$; Sample 2: $\beta = .19, p < .01$).

The results from both samples suggest that centralization of decision making serves as a barrier to market orientation. The patterns of results for this variable in the two samples, however, are different. In Sample 1, centralization is inversely related to intelligence dissemination ($\beta = -.14, p < .05$) and responsiveness ($\beta = -.22, p < .01$), and in Sample 2 centralization is inversely related to intelligence generation ($\beta = -.34, p < .01$).

Contrary to our hypotheses, formalization does not appear to be related to market orientation. This result parallels in part the results reported by Narver and Slater (1991), who suggest that programmatic approaches (e.g., changing structure or staffing) to improving market orientation may not be effective. It is often argued that emphasis on rules makes an organization less adaptable to external change. Although the results suggest that formalization is unrelated to market orientation, an alternative interpretation is that mere emphasis on rules is less relevant than the precise nature of the rules in an organization. In other words, it is possible that rules, if properly designed, may facilitate rather than hinder market orientation. For example, an organization may mandate that various departments get together every month for a market assessment meeting. Such a rule is likely to enhance intelligence dissemination. Similarly, other rules may mandate fast response to customer complaints or other developments, thereby improving market orientation. The lack of a relationship between departmentalization and market orientation similarly suggests that the sheer number of departments is less important than the connectedness or level of conflict among them.

We now discuss the hypothesized effects of market orientation on business performance and employees. As shown in Tables 5.3 and 5.4, market orientation appears to be significantly related to business performance when overall performance is assessed using judgmental measures (Sample 1: β = .23, $p < .01$; Sample 2: β = .36, $p < .001$). In contrast, market orientation does not appear to be related to performance using the more objective measures of market share and return on equity. These results appear to provide somewhat mixed support for the importance of market orientation. Several issues warrant mention in this context, however.

First, it is unclear whether market share is a particularly appropriate indicator of performance. For example, it is possible that certain high-performing companies may deliberately pursue a "focus" strategy and not be concerned about market share (Porter, 1980). The literature is replete with examples of low-share companies outperforming high-share companies (e.g., Inland Steel vs. USX). In such instances, market share may be a less accurate indicator of performance than judgmental assessments that take into account the particular strategy of a company.

Furthermore, the zero-order correlation of market orientation with return on equity (ROE) is .26 and statistically significant ($p < .05$). Although the results of the regression analysis suggest that market orientation is unrelated to ROE, one must be cautious in drawing conclusions from this result for three reasons. First, it is possible that there is a lag in the effect of market orientation on ROE—that is, that market orientation leads to higher ROE over a relatively long period of time. If so, such effects may not be captured in the cross-sectional design employed in the study. Second, information on ROE was provided by only a small fraction of our informants. Specifically, the number of cases available for estimation of the relationship between market orientation and ROE in Sample 1 was 53. Because of the relatively small sample size, it is premature to place much confidence in the results obtained from the regression analyses. Finally, although the study employed senior managers as informants, the possibility of errors in financial information, particularly from managers in departments other than finance, cannot be completely ruled out. On the basis of these considerations, we place more confidence in the results obtained using judgmental measures of performance.

The results reported in Tables 5.3 and 5.4 provide strong support for the hypothesized effects of market orientation on employees' organizational commitment (Sample 1: β = .44, $p < .001$; Sample 2: β = .66, $p < .001$) and esprit de corps (Sample 1: β = .51, $p < .001$; Sample 2: β = .58, $p < .001$). It appears that market orientation nurtures a bonding among employees and promotes a feeling of belonging to a team that is dedicated to meeting customer needs.

Finally, we discuss the effect of market turbulence, competitive intensity, and technological turbulence on the link between market orientation and performance (H_{11}-H_{13}). The differences in regression coefficients associated with market orientation are not statistically significant ($p < .05$) in environments characterized by high and low levels of the three moderator variables in both samples. These results do not support the hypothesized moderating effects for any of the three variables. In other words, the link between market orientation and performance appears to be robust among contexts characterized by varying levels of market turbulence, competitive intensity, and technological turbulence.

Conclusion

Managerial Implications

The purpose of the study was to empirically test several hypotheses regarding the antecedents to and consequences of market orientation. The findings suggest that the market orientation of a business is an important determinant of its performance, regardless of the market turbulence, competitive intensity, or technological turbulence of the environment in which it operates. Thus, it appears that managers should strive to improve the market orientation of their businesses. It should be noted that although a relationship between market orientation and ROE was not found in this study, the limited data on ROE and several other considerations discussed earlier make it difficult to place a great deal of confidence in this particular result.

This study suggests that several factors are important determinants of market orientation. Specifically, market orientation appears to be facilitated by the emphasis that top managers place on market orientation by continually reminding employees that it is critical for them to be sensitive and responsive to market developments. In addition, market orientation appears to require a certain level of risk tolerance on the part of senior managers and a willingness to accept an occasional failure as a normal part of doing business. In the absence of such willingness, employees at the lower levels of an organization are unlikely to want to respond to market developments with new products, services, or programs.

Although the role of top managers in engendering market orientation is important, it appears that the nature of interdepartmental dynamics also plays a very important role. Interdepartmental conflict appears to reduce market orientation, whereas interdepartmental connectedness appears to facilitate it. Therefore, it may be useful to promote interdepartmental connectedness through physical proximity and telematics (e.g., computer hookups and voice mail). Although some level of interdepartmental conflict is unavoidable, it appears to be useful to reduce the level of conflict by offering various means, such as interdepartmental training and sports programs, and by focusing departmental performance objectives on customer satisfaction.

The role of market-based reward systems and decentralized decision making in engendering market orientation appears to be strong, suggesting that reward systems should take into account an individual's ability to sense and respond to market needs. In addition, the negative relationship between centralization and market orientation suggests that it may be useful to allow lower-level employees to make decisions rather than concentrate decision making in the upper echelons of an organization. Although formalization and departmentalization do not appear to affect market orientation, it appears that the content of formal rules rather than their mere presence is important. Similarly, the manner in which the various departments interact with each other appears to be a more important determinant of market orientation than the sheer number of departments in a business.

Research Directions

There appear to be several areas in need of further research. Perhaps the most important relates to an assessment of the impact of market orientation on financial measures of performance. Because one possible reason for the lack of a relationship between market orientation and ROE found in this study may be the lag in the effect of market orientation on financial performance, it would be useful to assess the relationship between market orientation and financial performance using longitudinal designs.

Also, it would be useful to assess the role of additional factors in influencing the market orientation of an organization. For example, do certain characteristics of employees (e.g., personality and attitudes) help or hinder market orientation? Similarly, some of the variables included in this study deserve further study. For example, we hypothesized that formalization would affect market orientation, but we found no relation between the two. Future research is needed to assess the characteristics of rules that facilitate or hinder market orientation.

Finally, this study employs a cross-sectional analysis of many businesses. Although providing important insights into the determinants of market orientation, the study does not shed much light on the process involved in improving market orientation. In this regard, it would be useful to conduct in-depth studies of a few organizations engaged in this process to determine what factors influence improving the market orientation of a business.

Appendix 5.A: Scales

Scale	Scale Item	Coefficient Alpha
Market orientation (intelligence generation)	1. In this business unit, we meet with customers at least once a year to find out what products or services they will need in the future.	.71
	2. Individuals from our manufacturing department interact directly with customers to learn how to serve them better.	
	3. In this business unit, we do a lot of in-house market research.	
	4. We are slow to detect changes in our customers' product preferences.	
	5. We poll end-users at least once a year to assess the quality of our products and services.	
	6. We often talk with or survey those who can influence our end-users' purchases (e.g., retailers, distributors).	
	7. We collect industry information through informal means (e.g., lunch with industry friends, talks with trade partners).	
	8. In our business unit, intelligence on our competitors is generated independently by several departments.	
	9. We are slow to detect fundamental shifts in our industry (e.g., competition, technology, regulation).	
	10. We periodically review the likely effect of changes in our business environment (e.g., regulation) on customers.	

Scale	Scale Item	Coefficient Alpha
Market orientation (intelligence dissemination)	1. A lot of informal "hall talk" in this business unit concerns our competitors' tactics or strategies.[a]	.82
	2. We have interdepartmental meetings at least once a quarter to discuss market trends and developments.	
	3. Marketing personnel in our business unit spend time discussing customers' future needs with other functional departments.	
	4. Our business unit periodically circulates documents (e.g., reports, newsletters) that provide information on our customers.	
	5. When something important happens to a major customer or market, the whole business unit knows about it in a short period.	
	6. Data on customer satisfaction are disseminated at all levels in this business unit on a regular basis.	
	7. There is minimal communication between marketing and manufacturing departments concerning market developments.	
	8. When one department finds out something important about competitors, it is slow to alert other departments.	
Market orientation (response design)	1. It takes us forever to decide how to respond to our competitors' price changes.	.78
	2. Principles of market segmentation drive new product development efforts in this business unit.	
	3. For one reason or another we tend to ignore changes in our customers' product or service needs.	
	4. We periodically review our product development efforts to ensure that they are in line with what customers want.	
	5. Our business plans are driven more by technological advances than by market research.	
	6. Several departments get together periodically to plan a response to changes taking place in our business environment.	
	7. The product lines we sell depend more on internal politics than real market needs.	
Market orientation (response implementation)	1. If a major competitor were to launch an intensive campaign targeted at our customers, we would implement a response immediately.	.82
	2. The activities of the different departments in this business unit are well coordinated.	
	3. Customer complaints fall on deaf ears in this business unit.	

Scale	Scale Item	Coefficient Alpha
	4. Even if we came up with a great marketing plan, we probably would not be able to implement it in a timely fashion. 5. We are quick to respond to significant changes in our competitors' pricing structures. 6. When we find out that customers are unhappy with the quality of our service, we take corrective action immediately. 7. When we find that customers would like us to modify a product or service, the departments involved make concerted efforts to do so.	
Top management emphasis	1. Top managers repeatedly tell employees that this business unit's survival depends on its adapting to market trends. 2. Top managers often tell employees to be sensitive to the activities of our competitors. 3. Top managers keep telling people around here that they must gear up now to meet customers' future needs. 4. According to top managers here, serving customers is the most important thing our business unit does.	.66
Top management risk aversion	1. Top managers in this business unit believe that higher financial risks are worth taking for higher rewards. 2. Top managers here accept occasional new product failures as being normal.[a] 3. Top managers in this business unit like to take big financial risks. 4. Top managers here encourage the development of innovative marketing strategies, knowing well that some will fail. 5. Top managers in this business unit like to "play it safe." 6. Top managers around here like to implement plans only if they are very certain that they will work.	.85
Interdepart-mental conflict	1. Most departments in this business get along well with each other. 2. When members of several departments get together, tensions frequently run high. 3. People in one department generally dislike interacting with those from other departments. 4. Employees from different departments feel that the goals of their respective departments are in harmony with each other.	.87

Scale	Scale Item	Coefficient Alpha
	5. Protecting one's departmental turf is considered to be a way of life in this business unit.	
	6. The objectives pursued by the marketing department are incompatible with those of the manufacturing department.	
	7. There is little or no interdepartmental conflict in this business unit.	
Interdepartmental connectedness	1. In this business unit, it is easy to talk with virtually anyone you need to, regardless of rank or position.	.80
	2. There is ample opportunity for informal "hall talk" among individuals from different departments in this business unit.	
	3. In this business unit, employees from different departments feel comfortable calling each other when the need arises.	
	4. Managers here discourage employees from discussing work-related matters with those who are not their immediate superiors or subordinates.	
	5. People around here are quite accessible to those in other departments.	
	6. Communications from one department to another are expected to be routed through "proper channels."[a]	
	7. Junior managers in my department can easily schedule meetings with junior managers in other departments.	
Formalization	1. I feel that I am my own boss in most matters.	.76
	2. A person can make his own decisions without checking with anybody else.	
	3. How things are done around here is left up to the person doing the work.	
	4. People here are allowed to do almost as they please.	
	5. Most people here make their own rules on the job.	
	6. The employees are constantly being checked on for rule violations.	
	7. People here feel as though they are constantly being watched to see that they obey all the rules.	
Centralization	1. There can be little action taken here until a supervisor approves a decision.	.88
	2. A person who wants to make his own decision would be quickly discouraged here.	
	3. Even small matters have to be referred to someone higher up for a final answer.	
	4. I have to ask my boss before I do almost anything.	
	5. Any decision I make has to have my boss's approval.	

Scale	Scale Item	Coefficient Alpha
Reward system orientation	1. No matter which department they are in, people in this business unit get recognized for being sensitive to competitive moves.	.73
	2. Customer satisfaction assessments influence senior managers' pay in this business unit.	
	3. Formal rewards (i.e., pay raise, promotion) are forthcoming to anyone who consistently provides good market intelligence.	
	4. Salespeople's performance in this business unit is measured by the strength of relationships they build with customers.	
	5. Salespeople's monetary compensation is almost entirely based on their sales volume.[a]	
	6. We use customer polls for evaluating our salespeople.	
Organizational commitment	1. Employees feel as though their future is intimately linked to that of this organization.	.89
	2. Employees would be happy to make personal sacrifices if it were important for the business unit's well-being.	
	3. The bonds between this organization and its employees are weak.	
	4. In general, employees are proud to work for this business unit.	
	5. Employees often go above and beyond the call of duty to ensure this business unit's well-being.	
	6. Our people have little or no commitment to this business unit.	
	7. It is clear that employees are fond of this business unit.	
Esprit de corps	1. People in this business unit are genuinely concerned about the needs and problems of each other.	.90
	2. A team spirit pervades all ranks in this business unit.	
	3. Working for this business unit is like being a part of a big family.	
	4. People in this business unit feel emotionally attached to each other.	
	5. People in this organization feel like they are "in it together."	
	6. This business unit lacks an esprit de corps.	
	7. People in this business unit view themselves as independent individuals who have to tolerate others around them.	

Scale	Scale Item	Coefficient Alpha
Overall performance	1. Overall performance of the business unit last year. 2. Overall performance relative to major competitors last year.	.83
Market turbulence	1. In our kind of business, customers' product preferences change quite a bit over time. 2. Our customers tend to look for new product all the time. 3. Sometimes our customers are very price sensitive, but on other occasions, price is relatively unimportant.[a] 4. We are witnessing demand for our products and services from customers who never bought them before. 5. New customers tend to have product-related needs that are different from those of our existing customers. 6. We cater to much the same customers that we used to in the past.	.68
Competitive intensity	1. Competition in our industry is cutthroat. 2. There are many promotion wars in our industry. 3. Anything that one competitor can offer, others can match readily. 4. Price competition is a hallmark of our industry. 5. One hears of a new competitive move almost every day. 6. Our competitors are relatively weak.	.81
Technological turbulence	1. The technology in our industry is changing rapidly. 2. Technological changes provide big opportunities in our industry. 3. It is very difficult to forecast where the technology in our industry will be in the next 2 to 3 years.[a] 4. A large number of new product ideas have been made possible through technological breakthroughs in our industry. 5. Technological developments in our industry are rather minor.	.88

a. These items were eliminated based on the scale refinement procedure described in the text.

Note

1. Information about ROE in Sample 2 was provided by only 20 informants; this precluded an estimation of the effect of market orientation on ROE in this sample. In Sample 1, two cases with extreme values on ROE were eliminated to improve the accuracy of the parameter estimates.

References

Aiken, M., & Hage, J. (1968). Organizational independence and intraorganizational structure. *American Sociological Review, 33,* 912-930.

Anderson, P., & Chambers, T. (1985). A reward/measurement model of organizational buying behavior. *Journal of Marketing, 49*(2), 7-23.

Arnold, H. J. (1982, April). Moderator variables: A clarification of conceptual, analytic, and psychometric issues. *Organizational Behavior and Human Performance, 29,* 143-174.

Barksdale, H. C., & Darden, B. (1971). Marketers' attitude toward the marketing concept. *Journal of Marketing, 35*(4), 29-36.

Bennett, R., & Cooper, R. (1981, June). Beyond the marketing concept. *Business Horizons, 22,* 76-83.

Bitner, M. J. (1990). Evaluating service encounters: The effects of physical surroundings and employee responses. *Journal of Marketing, 54*(2), 69-82.

Boulding, W., & Staelin, R. (1990, October). Environment, market share, and market power. *Management Science, 36,* 1160-1177.

Chow, G. C. (1960, July). Test of equality between sets of coefficients in two linear regressions. *Econometrika, 28,* 591-605.

Churchill, G. A., Jr. (1979, February). A paradigm for developing better measures of marketing constructs. *Journal of Marketing Research, 16,* 64-73.

Cronbach, L. J., et al. (1981). *Toward reform in program evaluation.* San Francisco: Jossey-Bass.

Day, G. S. (1990). *Market driven strategy: Processes for creating value.* New York: Free Press.

Day, G. S., & Wensley, R. (1988). Assessing advantage: A framework for diagnosing competitive superiority. *Journal of Marketing, 52*(2), 1-20.

Deshpandé, R., & Webster, F. E., Jr. (1989). Organizational culture and marketing: Defining the research agenda. *Journal of Marketing, 53*(1), 3-15.

Deshpandé, R., & Zaltman, G. (1982, February). Factors affecting the use of market research information: A path analysis. *Journal of Marketing Research, 19,* 14-31.

Felton, A. P. (1959, July/August). Making the marketing concept work. *Harvard Business Review, 37,* 55-65.

Gaski, J. F. (1984). The theory of power and conflict in channels of distribution. *Journal of Marketing, 48*(3), 9-29.

Hage, J., & Aiken, M. (1970). *Social change in complex organizations.* New York: Random House.

Hall, R. H., Haas, J. E., & Johnson, N. J. (1967, December). Organizational size, complexity, and formalization. *American Sociological Review, 32,* 903-991.

Hambrick, D. C., & Mason, P. A. (1984). Upper echelons: The organization as a reflection of its top managers. *Academy of Management Review, 9*(2), 193-206.

Hise, R. T. (1965). Have manufacturing firms adopted the marketing concept? *Journal of Marketing, 29*(3), 9-12.

Hopwood, A. (1974). *Accounting and human behavior.* London: Haymarket.

Houston, F. S. (1986). The marketing concept: What it is, what it is not. *Journal of Marketing, 50*(2), 81-87.

Jacobson, R., & Aaker, D. A. (1987). The strategic role of product quality. *Journal of Marketing, 51*(4), 31-44.

Jaworski, B. J. (1988). Toward a theory of marketing control: Environmental context, control types, and consequences. *Journal of Marketing, 52*(3), 23-39.

Kaldor, A. G. (1971). Imbricative marketing. *Journal of Marketing, 35*(2), 19-25.

Kohli, A. K., & Jaworski, B. J. (1990). Market orientation: The construct, research propositions, and managerial implications. *Journal of Marketing, 54*(2), 1-18. (See also Chapter 2)

Lawler, E. E., & Rhode, J. G. (1976). *Information and control in organizations.* Pacific Palisades, CA: Goodyear.

Levitt, T. (1969). *The marketing mode.* New York: McGraw-Hill.

Linden, W. B. (1987, April). *Marketing marketing: The Ryder system story.* Paper presented at the Marketing Science Institute conference "Developing a Marketing Orientation," Cambridge, MA.

Lundstrom, W. J. (1976, Fall). The marketing concept: The ultimate in bait and switch. *Marquette Business Review, 20,* 214-230.

Lusch, R. F., Udell, J. G., & Laczniak, G. R. (1976, December). The practice of business. *Business Horizons, 19,* 65-74.

McNamara, C. P. (1972). The present status of the marketing concept. *Journal of Marketing, 36*(1), 50-57.

Narver, J. C., & Slater, S. F. (1990). The effect of a market orientation on business profitability. *Journal of Marketing, 54*(4), 20-35. (See also Chapter 3)

Narver, J. C., & Slater, S. F. (1991). *Becoming more market oriented: An exploratory study of the programmatic and market-back approaches* [Working paper]. Seattle: University of Washington.

Nunnally, J. C. (1978). *Psychometric theory* (2nd ed.). New York: McGraw-Hill.

Olson, D. (1987, April). *When consumer firms develop a marketing orientation.* Paper presented at the MSI conference "Developing a Marketing Orientation," Cambridge, MA.

Parasuraman, A., Zeithaml, V. A., & Berry, L. L. (1985). A conceptual model of service quality and its implications for future research. *Journal of Marketing, 49*(4), 41-50.

Patton, M. Q. (1978). *Utilization focused evaluation.* Beverly Hills, CA: Sage.

Porter, M. E. (1980). *Competitive strategy.* New York: Free Press.

Raven, B. H., & Kruglanski, A. W. (1970). Conflict and power. In P. Swingle (Ed.), *The Structure of Conflict* (pp. 69-109). New York: Academic Press.

Ruekert, R., & Walker, O. (1987). Marketing's interaction with other functional units: A conceptual framework and empirical evidence. *Journal of Marketing, 51,* 1-19.

Shapiro, B. P. (1988, November/December). What the hell is "market oriented"? *Harvard Business Review, 66,* 119-125.

Stampfl, R. W. (1978, Spring). Structural constraints, consumerism, and the marketing concept. *MSU Business Topics, 26,* 5-16.

Tauber, E. M. (1974, June). How marketing discourages major innovation. *Business Horizons, 17,* 22-26.

Webster, F. E., Jr. (1988, May/June). Rediscovering the marketing concept. *Business Horizons, 31,* 29-39.

Zaltman, G., Duncan, R., & Holbek, J. (1973). *Innovations and organizations.* New York: John Wiley.

Zaltman, G., LeMasters, K., & Heffring, M. (1982). *Theory construction in marketing.* New York: John Wiley.

Market Orientation, Performance, and the Moderating Influence of Competitive Environment

Stanley F. Slater
John C. Narver

Market orientation is a business culture that is outwardly focused; its primary objective is to profitably create superior value for customers. Market-oriented businesses are customer driven, competitor knowledgeable, and interfunctionally committed to understanding and capitalizing on opportunities for value creation throughout the value chain. Research has shown that market orientation is positively related to business performance, after controlling for theoretically important market- and business-level factors.

Two award-winning articles in the *Journal of Marketing* suggest that a business's market environment might influence the relationship between market orientation and performance. Day and Wensley (1988) suggest that environment might affect the necessary focus, either customer or competitor, in a market orientation. For example, they suggest that in markets with a low concentration of competitors, the emphasis should be on customers. A competitor emphasis would be called for in high-concentration markets. Kohli and Jaworski (1990) suggest that certain characteristics of market environment might affect the strength (or the importance) of the relationship between market orientation and performance. For example, the relationship would be stronger in low-growth than in high-growth environments.

135

Slater and Narver tested for these moderator effects in a sample of 107 business units from two *Fortune* 500 corporations operating in industrial markets. They recruited knowledgeable respondents from the top management teams of each business unit. As recommended by Sharma, Durand, and Gur-Arie (1981), they first tested for moderator effects using multiple regression analysis with a multiplicative interaction term and eight theoretically important control variables. If the interaction term was not significant, they divided the sample at the median of the hypothesized environmental moderator and tested whether the partial correlation coefficients between the predictor and criterion variables were significantly different between the two subsamples. They found evidence to suggest that environment may have a moderating effect on the relationship between market orientation and performance.

Slater and Narver conclude by cautioning managers about the wisdom of trying to fine-tune their business's market-oriented behaviors. First, as a form of business culture, market orientation is expensive and time-consuming to develop. Also, in the long run, all markets will experience slowing growth and increased competition, the conditions that require market-driven behaviors. They suggest that the wise course is for a business to become market oriented while the environment is forgiving rather than to wait until market orientation is a competitive necessity. By that time, it may be too late.

For the past three decades, the subject of market orientation in one form or another (Kotler, 1977; Levitt, 1960; Shapiro, 1988; Webster, 1988) has had the center stage in the theory and practice of marketing. Curiously, however, only recently have researchers constructed a theory of the antecedents and consequences of market orientation, developed a valid measure of the construct, and tested its effect on business performance.

Kohli and Jaworski (1990) describe and offer a theory of market orientation. They write, "A market orientation appears to provide a unifying focus for the efforts and projects of individuals and departments within the organization, thereby leading to superior performance" (p. 13).

Narver and Slater (1990) develop a measure of market orientation and test its effect on business performance. Narver and Slater's measure of market orientation consists of three behavioral components—customer orientation, competitor orientation, and interfunctional coordination—all of which are critical and related to creating sustainable superior value for customers. Although their cross-sectional study does not prove causality, they find a substantial positive relationship between the magnitude of a business's market orientation and its profitability, after controlling for important firm- and market-level influences on profitability.

Although we accept the proposition that market orientation has a general and positive effect on business performance, two award-winning articles (Day & Wensley, 1988; Kohli & Jaworski, 1990) suggested that competitive environment might affect the market orientation-performance relationship. There is a long tradition of support for the theory that environment moderates the effectiveness of organizational characteristics. The practical beginning of this stream is Lawrence and Lorsch's (1967) study of the influence of a business's technological, market, and economic setting on its pattern of organization and administration. During the past decade, many strategy and marketing scholars interested in the moderating influence of competitive environment have focused on the Miles and Snow (1978) typology of strategic adaptation. Numerous studies (Hambrick, 1983; McKee, Varadarajan, & Pride, 1989; Snow & Hrebeniak, 1980) have found that the effectiveness of "a particular strategic orientation is contingent on the dynamics of the market" (McKee et al., 1989, p. 21). The purpose of this study is to test whether competitive environment influences the form and effectiveness of a business's external orientation.[1]

On the basis of the articles by Day and Wensley (1988) and Kohli and Jaworski (1990), there are two principal possible moderator effects of competitive environment on market orientation (Figure 6.1). First, the competitive environment (e.g., the rate of market growth) could affect the strength of the market orientation-performance relationship (Kohli & Jaworski, 1990). Second, the competitive environment (e.g., the number and power of competitors) could affect the focus of the external emphasis within a market orientation—that is, a greater emphasis on customer analysis relative to competitor analysis, or vice versa, within a given magnitude of market orientation (Day & Wensley, 1988).

Whether these moderating effects exist is of substantial interest to both scholars and managers. If they do, a business could benefit from adjusting its magnitude and emphasis on market orientation through the selective allocation of human or financial resources. For example, if Day and Wensley (1988) and Kohli and Jaworski (1990) are correct, a business in the early stages of a

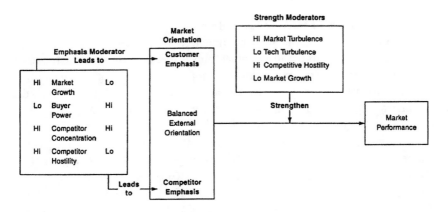

Figure 6.1. The Moderating Influence of Competitive Environment on the Market Orientation-Performance Relationship

NOTE: Strength moderators are suggested by Kohli and Jaworski (1990), and emphasis moderators are suggested by Day and Wensley (1988).

market's development, when there are few competitors and growth is rapid, might benefit from a competitor emphasis during the early stages of developing a market orientation.

This study tests for both the strength and the emphasis of moderator effects on the relationship between market orientation and business performance. The study uses a cross-sectional design and therefore cannot prove causality. The inclusion of numerous, theoretically important control variables should increase confidence in our findings, however. We first discuss potential moderators of the strength of the market orientation-performance relationship; we then discuss moderators of the emphasis of market orientation (i.e., customers and competitors).

Moderators of the Strength of the Market Orientation-Performance Relationship

Kohli and Jaworski (1990) write,

> Our study suggests that though a market orientation is likely to be related to business performance in general, under certain conditions it may not be

critical. . . . Managers of businesses operating under these conditions
should pay close attention to the cost-benefit ratio of a market orientation.
(p. 15)

Kohli and Jaworski (1990) argue that, considering the necessary commitment of resources, a business will carefully assess the expected benefits
and expected costs in increasing its market orientation. They identify four
contexts in which, due to an "environmental moderator," the expected costs
of increasing or maintaining a market orientation may exceed expected benefits and, therefore, a market orientation may not be strongly related to business performance. The four environmental characteristics that Kohli and Jaworski propose as moderators of the market orientation-performance linkage
are market turbulence, technological turbulence, competitive intensity, and
economic strength.

In a recent working paper, Jaworski and Kohli (1992) report results of
a study of the antecedents and consequences of a market orientation. In that
study, they test for the moderating effects of market turbulence, competitive
intensity, and technological turbulence on the market orientation-performance
relationship and find no evidence of a moderating role for environment.

Their measures of business performance lead us to question this finding, however. They used three measures: a subjective measure of "overall performance" of the business unit, return on equity (ROE), and market share. As
they acknowledge, market share leadership is not an objective for all businesses and may not be an appropriate performance measure. ROE is a function of return on assets (ROA) and capital structure. Although market orientation should affect ROA, it should have little influence on capital structure,
thus diluting its influence on ROE. Their measure of overall performance is
so general that it allows interpretation in almost any manner. Consequently,
some respondents may be referring to growth, others to profitability, and others to quality improvement. There is also the possibility of a functional bias
among respondents, and although there were two respondents for many of their
subject business units, responses were averaged without reporting interrater
reliability. Thus, we believe that the question of whether there are moderators
of the market orientation-performance relationship remains unanswered.

The original Kohli and Jaworski propositions suggest the specific hypotheses to be tested. The theory underlying each proposition is described in
Kohli and Jaworski (1990) and is not repeated in its entirety here.

Propositions and Hypotheses

Market Turbulence Proposition. The greater the market turbulence, the stronger the relationship between a market orientation and business performance.

Kohli and Jaworski's (1990) theory underlying the proposition is that

> when there is a fixed set of customers with stable preferences, a market orientation is likely to have little effect on performance because little adjustment to a marketing mix is necessary to cater effectively to stable preferences of a given set of customers. (p. 14)

Therefore, we hypothesize the following:

H_1: The greater the extent of market turbulence, the greater the positive impact of market orientation on performance.

Technological Turbulence Proposition. The greater the technological turbulence, the weaker the relationship between a market orientation and business performance.

As Kohli and Jaworski (1990) define it, *technology* refers to the entire process of transforming inputs to outputs and delivering those outputs to the customer. They hold that in industries characterized by rapidly changing technology, a market orientation may not be as important as it is in technologically stable industries because many of the major innovations will be developed by R&D efforts outside the industry. Thus, we hypothesize the following:

H_2: The lesser the extent of technological turbulence, the greater the positive impact of market orientation on performance.

Intensity of Competition Proposition. The greater the competition, the stronger the relationship between a market orientation and business performance.

Kohli and Jaworski's (1990) argument is that the greater the competition, the more aggressive a business must be in discovering customer desires and creating superior customer value in satisfying them. Thus, the greater the competition, the more a business must be market oriented to attain superior performance. Therefore,

H_3: The greater the extent of competitive hostility, the greater the positive impact of market orientation on performance.

Strength of the Economy Proposition. The weaker the general economy, the stronger the relationship between a market orientation and business performance.

According to Kohli and Jaworski (1990), the stronger the demand faced by a business, the more the business may be able to "get away with" not being very market oriented. This implies that in a market characterized by strong demand growth, demand may exceed supply and customers will more readily accept what is offered. Conversely, in markets in which there is little demand growth, businesses must exert more effort to understand how they can provide superior value by more effectively satisfying buyer needs. This leads to the following hypothesis:

H_4: The lower the rate of market growth, the greater the positive impact of market orientation on performance.

Moderators of the Relative Emphasis in a Market Orientation: Customers or Competitors

Businesses that have an ability to learn about their markets and act quickly on that information are best positioned to achieve and maintain competitive advantage (Day, 1991; DeGeus, 1988; Senge, 1990). This ability to learn quickly has become more important as markets change in character and complexity and the availability of market information and the need for common managerial interpretations of the information (Day, 1991) increases. Managers cope with the vast amounts of this rapidly changing and often conflicting market information through the processes of selective attention and simplification (Pfeffer & Salancik, 1978). The most common outcomes are the adoption of either a customer-focused or a competitor-centered market perspective. By adopting one or the other perspective, a manager attempts to reduce the complexity of the market-monitoring task and determines the information to be gathered and how it should be screened and interpreted (Day

& Wensley, 1988, p. 2). Customer focus is a relative emphasis on collecting and processing customer-oriented information, and competitor centering is a relative emphasis on competitor-oriented information.

It is of course possible that focusing primarily on either customers or competitors could lead to "a partial and biased picture of reality" (Day & Wensley, 1988, p. 2), and that balance between the two perspectives is more desirable. The purpose of this phase of the study is to determine whether there are conditions that favor either a customer or a competitor emphasis over balance. We now consider the suggested moderating effects (Day & Wensley, 1988) of a business's competitive environment on a business's choice of external emphasis.

Theory and Hypotheses

Daft, Sormunen, and Parks (1988) find that, in general, uncertainty in the competitive environment influences the extent and type of environmental scanning. Day and Wensley (1988) provide a foundation for how the competitive environment might influence a manager's selection of a particular relative emphasis within a market orientation: "When market demand is predictable, the competitive structure is concentrated and stable, and there are a few powerful customers, the emphasis is necessarily on competitors" (p. 17). They suggest the following: "In dynamic markets with shifting mobility barriers, many competitors, and highly segmented end-user markets, a tilt toward a customer focus is mandatory" (p. 17). They provide little rationale, however, for the necessity of the respective emphases. In the following sections, we offer our rationale for how four dimensions of competitive environment (market growth, buyer power, competitor concentration, and competitor hostility) suggested by Day and Wensley (1988) might influence a manager's selection of either a customer or a competitor emphasis in a market orientation.

Although all our hypotheses are stated in terms of the conditions that would favor a customer emphasis (e.g., high rate of market growth), the implication is that the opposite (i.e., low rate of market growth) would favor a competitor emphasis. In justifying each hypothesis, we discuss both the conditions that favor a customer emphasis and those that favor a competitor emphasis.

Market Growth. Some authors argue that in slower growth markets, customer needs are relatively predictable and the strategic emphasis is on price (Hax & Majluf, 1984; Porter, 1980), including heavy trade allowances and consumer promotions (Peter & Donnelly, 1988). To avoid uneconomical pricing decisions, businesses must pay very close attention to their production, marketing, and development costs relative to those of the competition (Day, 1990). The implication is that this heavy emphasis on cost during the slower growth periods requires a competitor emphasis (Day & Wensley, 1988).

Successful new product introductions are typically followed by a period of rapid growth. Recent evidence (von Hippel, 1986) points to the importance of the user (particularly the lead user or early adopter) in the development and evaluation of new products. Maidique and Zirger (1984) conclude that new product success is more likely when the developing organization has an "in-depth understanding of the customers" (p. 201). Consequently, a customer emphasis seems to be desirable during the high-growth period following new product introductions.

The importance of a customer emphasis also extends to the later growth stage of a product. During this period, emphasis must be on meaningful differentiation from the numerous emulators that will enter the market and on discovering and exploiting opportunities for market segmentation. An important objective is to establish a strong brand franchise through substantial service to dealers and customers. Although competitor intelligence is important during this stage, customer analysis is even more critical.

In summary, the implication is a positive relationship between market growth and the importance of a customer emphasis. Accordingly, we hypothesize the following:

H_5: The higher the rate of market growth, the greater the positive impact of customer emphasis on performance.

Buyer Power. Powerful buyers exert pressure on prices or force sellers to provide higher quality or more services. Buyers are especially powerful when they account for a large proportion of sales, the products they purchase are undifferentiated or unimportant to the quality of the final product, or they face few switching costs (Porter, 1980, p. 24).

Powerful buyers can demand concessions from sellers. Of course, sellers must necessarily be sensitive to these demands if they wish to attract and retain these buyers. Powerful customers are usually very clear about what they expect and require from suppliers, so competitive advantage is most likely to stem from an in-depth understanding of competitors' strengths and weaknesses. For example, cost information on competitors' products is very important because it may reveal a competitor's threshold for pain in aggressive pricing situations.

In contrast, buyers with little power are often smaller, and their needs are less well-known. In markets with many small buyers, it may be more difficult to understand all their needs. The truly customer-driven business attempts to develop a deeper understanding of these needs, which generates additional ways to create value for buyers. Such customer emphasis will also allow the seller to capture price premiums through value-based pricing (Forbis & Mehta, 1981). Thus, the marginal benefit of a customer emphasis is expected to be higher when buyer power is low. Therefore, we hypothesize the following:

H_6: The lower the power of the buyer, the greater the positive impact of customer emphasis on performance.

Competitor Concentration. In highly concentrated markets, there is a small number of relatively powerful competitors. In a concentrated market, because of the interdependence among the leading competitors, any of the leading competitors can significantly alter competitive intensity in the market. Increased intensity is reflected in aggressive pricing and advertising, numerous product introductions, and increasing services (Porter, 1980). Because of the substantial impact that any one leading competitor can have on competitive intensity, a competitor emphasis is essential. This is demonstrated in the airline industry, in which competitive moves are quickly matched.

In markets with numerous competitors, competitor monitoring is both more difficult and potentially less important because no one competitor has the capacity or resources to substantially alter the balance of power among the sellers. In this environment, focusing on the buyers' value equations, while staying abreast of competitive developments, is the approach most likely to work. We therefore hypothesize the following:

H_7: The lower the degree of competitor concentration, the greater the positive impact of customer emphasis on performance.

Competitor Hostility. The degree of competitor hostility is determined by the breadth and aggressiveness of competitive actions. A hostile environment is characterized by competitors who attack each other aggressively on numerous strategic dimensions (e.g., pricing, promotion, product development, and distribution). In a market in which the "rules" of competition are stable, a business that pays close attention to competitors' costs and strategies may uncover competitive weaknesses that represent opportunities to develop a competitive advantage.

If the rules are not stable, however (e.g., competitors move back and forth between strategic groups; Porter, 1980, p. 134), monitoring competitors closely is difficult. Day and Wensley (1988) suggest, "In dynamic markets with shifting mobility barriers, many competitors, and highly segmented end-user markets, a customer focus is mandatory" (p. 17). The necessity of this emphasis results from the constantly changing rules of competition, which greatly complicate competitor monitoring and could lead to misperceptions of competitive structure. Thus, we hypothesize the following:

H_8: The higher the degree of competitive hostility, the greater the positive impact of customer emphasis on performance.

Research Design

The Sample

The sample consists of 81 strategic business units (SBUs) in a forest products company and 36 SBUs in a diversified manufacturing corporation, both of which are listed among the *Fortune* 500 largest industrial firms. The 81 forest products company SBUs are a subset of the sample from the study described in Narver and Slater (1990).[2]

An SBU is an organizational unit with a defined business strategy and a manager with sales and profit responsibility (Aaker, 1988). In both these corporations, SBUs are substantial, autonomous organizational entities. Within each SBU, the top management team was identified by the responsible group executive, and each member was sent a questionnaire titled "Business Practices Survey" that contained questions concerning the SBU's competitive practices and strategies, competitive environment, and performance in its principal served market segment. We used multiple, knowledgeable members of the top management team to offset biases of individual respondents and to reduce measurement error (Huber & Power, 1985). We report interrater reliability in Table 6.1.

In the forest products corporation, the response rate was 84%, which yielded an average of 3.3 respondents per SBU. The diversified manufacturing corporation had a 74% response rate, for an average of 7.4 respondents per SBU. Within each SBU, top management team responses were aggregated,

Table 6.1 Descriptive Statistics and Reliabilities

Variable	Mean	SD	Reliability
ROA	4.56	1.36	.70
Sales growth	4.59	1.27	.64
New product success	4.47	1.23	.67
Market orientation	4.68	0.60	.80
Relative emphasis (customer/competitor)	1.04	0.68	NA
Relative size	3.85	1.80	.90
Relative cost	4.02	1.13	.90
Market growth	5.58	3.98	.74
Ease of entry	3.15	0.97	.71
Buyer power	3.99	0.78	.88
Market turbulence	4.90	0.81	.79
Technological turbulence	4.38	0.67	.54
Competitive hostility	4.69	0.68	.62
Four-firm concentration	5.53	1.02	.80

NOTE: Interrater reliability for single-item scales was calculated with the formula for within-group interrater reliability for a single-item estimator (James, Demaree, & Wolf, 1984) and is the median score for all of the SBUs. Reliability for multi-item scales is Cronbach's alpha.

and an average score on the constructs of interest was calculated for the SBU. Due to missing values for some variables, the final sample includes 107 of the 117 SBUs (91.5%) sampled.

Tests for Moderator Effects

A moderator effect implies that the moderator variable (environment) modifies the form of the relationship (i.e., the slope of the regression line as represented by the regression coefficient) between the predictor variable (market orientation or relative emphasis) and the criterion variable (performance). The appropriate technique for identifying moderator effects is moderated regression analysis (Sharma, Durand, & Gur-Arie, 1981).

To test for moderators, we multiply the value for market orientation and relative emphasis, respectively, by the values for the hypothesized environmental moderators, creating eight multiplicative interaction terms. We regress performance on market orientation, relative emphasis, the environmental dimensions, the interaction terms, and nine control variables that may affect a business's performance and, thus, need to be controlled in analyzing the effect of market orientation. The nine variables are relative size, relative cost, market growth, ease of entry, buyer power, market turbulence, technological turbulence, competitor concentration, and competitive hostility. The effect of control variables on business performance is described in Narver and Slater (1990). The test for determining whether an interaction exists is the *t* test of the regression coefficient for the multiplicative interaction term.

In some cases, a variable will influence the strength of the relationship between the predictor and the criterion variables (i.e., the proportion of variance explained by the predictor as represented by the coefficient of determination or the correlation coefficient) but will not interact with the predictor. This type of moderator is termed a homologizer variable (Sharma et al., 1981). The appropriate approach for testing homologizers is regression analysis within subgroups. Because our concern is with the strength of the relationship, the regression coefficient must be converted to a partial correlation coefficient. A significant difference between the partial correlation coefficients for the predictor and criterion variables in the subgroups indicates the presence of a homologizer.

Following Sharma et al. (1981), the moderator hypotheses are tested first with moderated regression analysis in the entire sample. If the interaction term is statistically significant, a moderator effect is present. If the interaction is not significant, we then determine whether the hypothesized moderator is related to either the predictor or criterion variables. If there is a significant relationship, then the environmental dimension is not a moderator but an exogenous, predictor, intervening, antecedent, or suppressor variable. If there is no relationship, we test for homologizer effects by splitting the sample at the median of the hypothesized moderator and performing regression analysis within the subgroups.

Definition of Variables

The measures for all variables are provided in Appendix 6.A. The following sections provide a description of the variables used in the analyses.

Market Orientation. We use the Narver and Slater (1990) measure of market orientation. Both the Kohli and Jaworski (1990) and the Narver and Slater constructs explicitly consider customer orientation and interfunctional coordination. Narver and Slater also give explicit consideration to the role of competitor orientation, whereas Kohli and Jaworski consider it in the context of the relationship between market orientation and competitive advantage.

The similarity of the Narver and Slater and Kohli and Jaworski constructs is considerable and is not at issue.

Narver and Slater (1990) developed subscales to measure the customer orientation (α in this study = .878), competitor orientation (α = .726), and interfunctional coordination (α = .774) components of market orientation in accordance with the recommendations of Cronbach (1970), Kerlinger (1973), and Churchill (1979). They report significant evidence of reliability, convergent validity, discriminant validity, concurrent validity, and thus construct validity of the components based on the relationships among the components and with other theoretically related variables. A business's magnitude of market orientation is the average of its scores on the three components of market orientation.

Relative Emphasis (Customer vs. Competitor). Relative emphasis is measured as the ratio of a business's score on the customer orientation subscale to its score on the competitor orientation subscale. This results in a single value for each SBU, with high values signifying customer emphasis and low values signifying competitor emphasis. The numerous information acquisition and dissemination items in the customer and competitor orientation scales capture the market monitoring concept of which Day and Wensley (1988) are concerned.

The relative emphasis measure describes the importance of customer orientation relative to competitor orientation without regard to the overall magnitude of market orientation. Although this measure uses the customer orientation and competitor orientation scales from the market orientation measure, this poses no multicollinearity problem because the correlation of market orientation with the emphasis measure is less than .1, indicating that they are measuring fundamentally different constructs.

Control Variables

Relative Size. Relative size measures the size of a business relative to that of its largest competitor and is included to control for size-related performance benefits (Buzzell & Gale, 1987). We expect a positive relationship between a business's relative size and its performance.

Relative Cost. Relative cost is included in the analysis as a control variable because of its theoretical influence on business profitability (Scherer,

1980). Relative cost measures the average total operating costs of a business relative to those of its largest competitor in its principal served market segment. A low relative cost implies a cost advantage; thus, we expect a negative relationship between relative cost and business performance.

Ease of Entry. Ease of entry is the likelihood of a new entrant being able to earn satisfactory profits in its principal served market segment within 3 years after entry. Easy entry implies a disadvantage to current competitors; therefore, we expect a negative relationship between ease of entry and business performance.

Market Growth. Market growth is the approximate average annual growth rate of total sales in a business's principal served market segment during the past 3 years. Because high market growth denotes a more favorable environment, we expect a positive relationship between rate of market growth and business performance.

Buyer Power. Buyer power is the extent to which buyers are able to negotiate lower prices from sellers (Porter, 1980). Strong buyer power implies low profit margins for sellers; thus, we expect a negative relationship between buyer power and business performance.

Market Turbulence. As Kohli and Jaworski (1990) note, market turbulence—changes in the composition of customers and their preferences—is a subset of the environmental turbulence construct. Miller (1987) developed measures of the dynamism, heterogeneity, and hostility components of environmental turbulence. Kohli and Jaworski's market turbulence is very similar to "heterogeneity," which Miller describes as the change in diversity of production methods and marketing tactics required to cater to customers' needs. It seems likely that the greater the change in customer preferences, the greater the required diversity of value creation efforts to satisfy those needs. Therefore, we believe the Miller construct of heterogeneity adequately captures the meaning of "market turbulence." Because market turbulence implies changing market strategies in the face of changing customer needs, we expect a negative relationship with business performance.

Technological Turbulence. Dess and Beard (1984) describe both environmental turbulence and dynamism as changes that are unpredictable and difficult to plan for in advance. Miller's (1987) "dynamism" construct is composed of "the amount and unpredictability of change in customer tastes, *production or service technologies* [italics added], and modes of competition" (p. 74). The two items of Miller's four-item scale that best reflect Kohli and Jaworski's (1990) concept of technological turbulence are the magnitude of changes in production and service technology and the magnitude of changes in R&D activity. Therefore, these two items comprise our scale of technological turbulence. Again, because a high rate of technological change requires increased investment in research and development and in state-of-the-art production capabilities, we expect a negative relationship between technological turbulence and business performance.

Competitor Hostility. Kohli and Jaworski (1990) found that numerous executives noted that the "degree of competition" in an industry had a substantial influence on the importance of a market orientation (p. 14). They cited examples of how the breadth, predictability, and rate of change of competitors' market activities affected their relationships with customers. To measure the degree of competition, we use Miller's (1987) hostility scale. The scale consists of three items: the predictability of a business's key competitors' market activities, the hostility of a business's key competitors, and the breadth of a business's key competitors' market activities (e.g., pricing and service). Intense competition is expected to be negatively related to business performance.

Competitor Concentration. Competitor concentration is the proportion of sales revenue in the SBU's principal served market segment accounted for by the four largest firms, including the subject SBU if appropriate. According to neoclassical economic theory, high concentration should result in higher performance for the major competitors because they recognize the advantages of avoiding price competition.

Market Performance. Market performance is measured as the top management team's assessment of the SBU's ROA, sales growth, and new product success relative to those of all other competitors in the SBU's principal served market during the past year. Relative performance is used to control for performance differences due to differences among the SBU's different industries and served markets. Subjective measures of performance are commonly used in research on private companies or on business units of large corporations. Previous studies have found a strong correlation between subjective assessments and their objective counterparts (Dess & Robinson, 1984; Pearce, Robbins, & Robinson, 1987).

Results of Tests for Moderators

Table 6.1 reports means, standard deviations, and reliabilities, and Table 6.2 reports correlations among the predictor, control, moderator, and criterion variables.

Table 6.3 contains results of the tests for main effects of market orientation, relative emphasis (customer or competitor), and the control variables on ROA, sales growth, and new product success. It is important to note that market orientation is the only predictor variable that is significant for all three dependent variables. As expected, there is no main effect for relative emphasis. Relative size and relative cost are significant predictors for both ROA and new product success. Coefficients for dimensions of competitive environment are significant for only 3 of 18 possible occurrences.

Relevant results of the moderated regression analyses and the subgroup analyses are reported in Tables 6.4 and 6.5. Subgroup analysis is performed only when there is no pure moderator effect and when there is no significant correlation between the hypothesized moderator and either the predictor or criterion variables. Table 6.4 reports results of the tests of the influence of competitive environment on the relationship between market orientation and ROA, sales growth, and new product success, respectively. Table 6.5 reports results of the tests of the influence of competitive environment on the relationship between relative emphasis in a market orientation and ROA, sales growth, and new product success, respectively.

The only difference between the moderated regression models and the main effects models reported in Table 6.3 is the inclusion of the interaction terms. Therefore, for the moderated regression analysis, only the coefficients and standard errors for the multiplicative interaction terms are shown. For the subgroup analysis, the partial correlation coefficient for market orientation and performance in each subgroup is reported in Table 6.4, and the partial correlation coefficient for relative emphasis and performance is reported in Table 6.5.

As shown in Table 6.4, none of the coefficients for the multiplicative interaction terms is statistically significant. The differences in the magnitude of the partial correlation coefficients of market orientation between the high and low environmental dimension subgroups are significant ($p < .05$),

Table 6.2 Correlation Analysis

Variable					Correlation Coefficient							
	1	2	3	4	5	6	7	8	9	10	11	12
ROA												
Sales growth	.293**											
New product success	.124	.545**										
Market orientation	.415**	.476**	.301**									
Relative size	.199*	.148	.297**	.066								
Relative cost	-.428**	-.121	.112	-.314**	.193*							
Market growth	-.146	-.004	-.143	-.113	.226*	.156						
Ease of entry	-.059	-.180	-.045	-.100	.056	-.026	.156					
Buyer power	-.298**	-.120	-.113	-.139	-.221*	.154	-.167	-.137				
Market turbulence	.157	.254**	.254	.342	-.147	-.240*	-.453**	.008	-.050			
Technological turbulence	-.018	.127	.143	.036	-.005	-.027	.026	.087	-.146	.056		
Competitive hostility	-.154	-.370**	-.255**	-.236*	-.119	.216*	.130	.024	.078	-.292**	-.112	
Firm concentration	.116	-.188*	.016	.074	.151	-.184	.167	-.069	-.003	-.174	-.062	.089

$*p \leq .05; **p \leq .01.$

152

Table 6.3 Tests for Main Effects

Results of Regression Analyses
Regression Coefficients (Standard Errors)
N = 107

Variable	ROA	Sales Growth	New Product Success
Market orientation	.63** (.20)	.91*** (.19)	.52** (.20)
Relative emphasis	−.67 (1.10)	.04 (1.06)	−.14 (1.11)
Relative size		.17** (.07)	.08 (.06)
Relative cost	−.38*** (.11)	.03 (.10)	.26* (.10)
Market growth	−.06 (.03)	.04 (.03)	−.04 (.03)
Ease of entry	−.08 (.12)	−.35** (.11)	−.06 (.12)
Buyer power	−.37** (.15)	−.01 (.14)	−.08 (.15)
Market turbulence	−.06 (.16)	.23 (.16)	.26 (.16)
Technological turbulence	−.09 (.16)	.11 (.15)	−.20 (.17)
Competitive hostility	.06 (.23)	−.41* (.22)	−.19 (.23)
F	6.47***	6.35***	3.91***
Adjusted R^2	.34	.34	.22

$*p \leq .05; **p \leq .01; ***p \leq .001.$

however, for market turbulence with ROA as the dependent variable, for technological turbulence with new product success as the dependent variable, and for market growth with sales growth as the dependent variable.

Thus, there is partial support for Hypotheses 1, 2, and 4 because the results indicate that market turbulence, technological turbulence, and market growth influence the strength of the relationship between market orientation and business performance through a homologizer moderator effect (Sharma et al., 1981). Next, we discuss the results of the tests for the presence of environmental moderators on the relationship between relative emphasis in a market orientation and performance.

The multiplicative interaction terms for relative emphasis and competitive environment are significant ($p < .10$) for market growth with sales growth as the dependent variable and for competitor concentration and competitor hostility with ROA as the dependent variable. Furthermore, the difference

Table 6.4 Tests for Moderator Effects: The Influence of Competitive Environment on Market Orientation and Performance

Results of Regression Analyses
Regression Coefficients (Standard Errors)

Hypothesis No.	Variable	DV = ROA			DV = Sales Growth			DV = New Product Success		
		Multiplicative Action	Market Orientation Subgroups Analysis		Multiplicative Interaction	Market Orientation Subgroups Analysis		Multiplicative Interaction	Market Orientation Subgroups Analysis	
			Low	High		Low	High		Low	High
H_1	Market turbulence	-.358 (.256)	1.0401[a,b] (.283)	.295 (.367)	-.53[a] (.24)	M		-.35 (.25)	C	
H_2	Technological turbulence	-.377 (.266)	.699[a] (.292)	.293 (.288)	-.53[a] (.25)	1.12[a] (.28)	.63[a] (.29)	-.31 (.27)	.96[a,b] (.30)	.17 (.30)
H_3	Competitive hostility	.240 (.383)	.484 (.278)	.763[a] (.336)	.691 (.36)	M		.57 (.38)	C	
H_4	Market growth	-.010 (.057)	.681[a] (.252)	.660[a] (.325)	-.05 (.05)	1.10[a,b] (.22)	.65 (.34)	-.04 (.06)	.561 (.28)	.32 (.31)

NOTE: *C*, no moderator effect, correlated with predictor or criterion variables; *M*, moderator variable.
a. Coefficient is significant at $p \le .05$.
b. Coefficients are different at $p \le .05$ (one-tailed) when converted to partial correlation coefficients and employing Fisher's z test (Hambrick & Lei, 1985).

Table 6.5 Tests for Moderator Effects: The Influence of Competitive Environment on Relative Emphasis and Performance

Results of Regression Analyses
Regression Coefficients (Standard Errors)

Hypothesis No.	Variable	DV = ROA			DV = Sales Growth			DV = New Product Success		
		Multiplicative Interaction	Market Orientation Subgroups Analysis		Multiplicative Interaction	Market Orientation Subgroups Analysis		Multiplicative Interaction	Market Orientation Subgroups Analysis	
			Low	High		Low	High		Low	High
H_5	Market growth	-.217 (.188)	.63 (1.53)	-.24 (1.79)	-.038 (.182)	7.080 (1.34)	-.41 (1.89)	-.119 (.190)	1.24 (1.71)	-2.20 (1.66)
H_6	Buyer power	-.136 (.273)	C		.304 (.261)	-1.11 (1.72)	3.23[a,b] (1.58)	.069 (.275)	-2.46[b] (1.75)	2.06 (2.00)
H_7	Four-firm concentration	-.022 (0.95)	2.02 (1.75)	-3.48[a,b] (1.49)	-.136 (.090)	.11 (1.55)	1.98 (1.62)	.072 (.095)	-.31 (1.58)	.90 (1.81)
H_8	Competitive hostility	-.106[b] (.245)	-2.00[b] (1.86)	-1.08 (1.71)	.219 (2.34)	C		-.031 (.246)	C	

NOTE: C, no moderator effect, correlated with predictor or criterion variables.

a. Coefficient is significant at $p \le .05$.

b. Coefficients are different at $p \le .05$ (one-tailed) when converted to partial correlation coefficients and employing Fisher's z test (Hambrick & Lei, 1985).

155

between the partial correlation coefficients for relative emphasis and performance in the low and high buyer power subgroups is different ($p < .05$) for both sales growth and new product success. Thus, there is also evidence of a moderator role for competitive environment on the relative emphasis in a market orientation.

Statistically significant evidence of either a moderator or a homologizer effect is found in 8 of 24 (eight moderator dimensions $\times$ three performance variables) analyses conducted. Either a moderator or a homologizer effect is found for six of the eight hypotheses on at least one of the performance variables. Because this is a somewhat larger proportion than would be expected by chance, we conclude that there is limited support for an environmental moderator effect on both the strength of the market orientation-performance relationship and the appropriateness of particular relative emphases on customers or competitors in a market orientation.

Limitations and Suggested Future Research

A significant limitation of this study is its cross-sectional design. Although the inclusion of an extensive set of control variables rules out some alternative explanations for our findings, others are not readily dismissed. For example, managers may infer their market orientation from their market performance—that is, the better their market performance, the more they believe they are market oriented. Also, better managers may be more market oriented. They may also be more innovative, be better motivators, or do a better job of managing costs, however. In these cases, market orientation does not necessarily cause better performance; instead, it is related to better performance because it is also related to a third variable that affects market orientation and performance.[3] An important step for future research to rule out these alternative explanations is the collection and analysis of longitudinal data.

The use of different sources of data for some of these variables also deserves attention. For example, all our performance measures are subjective and relative. It would be interesting to understand the effect of market orientation on objective measures of performance. Also, Deshpandé, Farley, and Webster (1992) indicate that managers and customers may have quite different perspectives on the market orientedness of a business. Reconciling these differences would contribute to understanding how managers derive their perceptions of their involvement in market-oriented behaviors and could improve our measures of market orientation.

Some of our scale reliabilities are lower than the .70 level recommended by Nunnally (1978); they exceed the .50 level, however, which is considered adequate for exploratory research by Van de Ven and Ferry (1979; see also Miller, 1987). It is not uncommon for studies in marketing to use scales with reliabilities in this range (Frazier & Rody, 1991; Katabe, 1990; Kohli, 1989; Noordewier, John, & Nevin, 1990). Moreover, we are not surprised by the low levels of internal consistency in the technological turbulence and competitive hostility scales because they respectively measure different sources of technological turbulence and hostility in the environment. Cronbach's alpha is a measure of internal consistency that would be maximized by measuring similar sources of technological turbulence and hostility.

Discussion

The results of this study extend Narver and Slater's (1990) finding of a strong relationship between market orientation and ROA by demonstrating that this relationship also applies to sales growth and new product success. In general, businesses that apply significant resources to understanding their customers and competitors and coordinate the activities of all functions of the business for an integrated value-creation effort achieve higher relative profitability, sales growth, and new product success. Market orientation is a guide to product development, promotional strategy, pricing decisions, and manufacturing management as well as other customer value-creating functions. When these functions are not guided by market forces and when they are not coordinated to produce consistent superior value for customers, competitive advantage will be fleeting at best and most likely unattainable.

This study is also the first to provide evidence of the influence of competitive environment on the strength and nature of the market orientation-performance relationship. Kohli and Jaworski (1990) propose that market turbulence, technological turbulence, the strength of competition, and the strength of the economy are moderators of the market orientation-performance linkage. Examining the four market orientation-performance linkages with moderated regression analysis and regression analysis within subgroups, we find evidence of environment modifying the strength of the market orientation-performance relationship. It is important to note that because this study uses cross-sectional data, it does not demonstrate causality.

Contrary to Kohli and Jaworski's (1990) proposition, however, we find market orientation to be more important in the low market turbulence subgroup than in the high-turbulence group. Why is market orientation apparently as important during times of low market turbulence as it is during high turbulence? When Kohli and Jaworski say "cater effectively" to customers, do they mean that a business provides merely the benefits that the customers desire—that is, the "expected product" (Levitt, 1980)—or do they mean that a business discovers additional relevant benefits for the buyers and thereby creates consistently greater value for them than they perceive as being available from any other source? Clearly, "catering to customers" can have two meanings. In a stable market, all competitors will find it easy to understand and satisfy the customer's minimum expectations. This, however, leaves all sellers equal in the eyes of the buyer, and thus will force a seller to reduce his or her price to create the largest value for the buyer. Of course, the seller's competitors will respond in kind, inducing the first seller to retaliate and so on, thereby creating and reinforcing a price-driven and low-profit market. A market orientation enables a business to escape this outcome. Therefore, it follows that in both unstable and stable markets, to create superior value for customers other than by price, a market orientation is required.

The empirical support for the existence of environmental moderators of the market orientation-performance relationship invites careful consideration of how best to manage a business. A market orientation is a particular form of business culture. As previously noted, increasing and maintaining a magnitude of market orientation is a complex process requiring considerable expenditure of money and time. This fact raises important questions about the wisdom of a business's attempting to fine-tune its market orientation to match environmental conditions.

One must ask whether the influential environmental conditions are sufficiently permanent for it to be reasonable for a business to attempt to "adjust" its market orientation to them, given the complexity of changing a market orientation (i.e., culture). Hence, how rapidly can a business increase or decrease its market orientation to "adapt" to an increase in demand or in competitive hostility? In short, if it is even possible, is it cost-effective for a business to continuously attempt to adjust the magnitude of its market orientation in relation to various "moderators"?

The following is an even more fundamental question: Why should a market-oriented business necessarily be influenced by "environmental moderators"? With its external focus and commitment to innovation, a market-oriented business should be prepared to achieve and sustain competitive advantage in any environmental condition. Indeed, a substantially market-oriented business should find more opportunities in any environment than should its less market-oriented competitors (Kirzner, 1979). This is supported by our finding in this study that the coefficient for market orientation is positive in all environments studied.

As Day (1990) notes, "Sooner or later all market arenas lose their luster, as sales growth stagnates, profit margins are squeezed, and competition intensifies. Management cannot wait until this has happened to take action" (p. 13). Action means continuously striving to create superior value for customers. Becoming and remaining market oriented are essential to continuously creating superior value. In summary, the rebuttable presumption is that businesses that are more market oriented are best positioned for success under any environmental conditions.

This study also finds support for the proposition that an appropriate match between competitive environment and type of external emphasis in a market orientation is associated with higher levels of performance. Contrary to our hypothesis, however, although the coefficients for relative emphasis are different in the high and low buyer power subsets for both sales growth and new product success, a customer emphasis is beneficial in the high buyer power subset. It is likely that by uncovering latent needs or through more effective value differentiation, a customer emphasis reduces buyer power, leading to superior performance.

In any case, we agree with Day and Wensley's (1988) suggestion that there is a probable danger from overemphasis on either customers or competitors because either preoccupation may obscure or preclude opportunities to create value for buyers that stem from the lesser emphasis. Furthermore, competitive environments are unstable. Mobility barriers rise and fall, and market growth and buyer power may increase or decrease. Thus, although short-term adjustments will always be necessary, theory suggests that a long-term approximate balance among the components is expected to be the most profitable.

Conclusion

This study supports the proposition that environment moderates both the strength of the market orientation-performance relationship and the effectiveness of different relative emphases within a market orientation. We believe, however, that it would be risky for a manager to attempt to adjust the business's market orientation to match current market conditions. First, "adjusting" a business's magnitude of market orientation is complex, time-consuming, and expensive. Second, market conditions are transient. As Day (1990) notes, in the long run, all markets will encounter slow growth, hostility, and changing buyer preferences, all of which are conditions that require a high magnitude of market orientation (Kohli & Jaworski, 1990). It is better to invest in becoming market oriented while the environment is somewhat munificent rather than to wait until it has become hostile.

We suggest, however, that managers seek to increase the business's overall magnitude of market orientation but remain flexible enough to shift resources in the short run between a customer and competitor orientation as market conditions change. We believe that businesses should avoid becoming locked into a particular external emphasis because market opportunities and threats are fluid.

Most important, however, is the development of a market orientation. Being market oriented is the basis for creating superior value for buyers, the underpinning of competitive advantage. Accordingly, being market oriented can never be a negative.

Appendix 6.A: Questionnaire

Market Orientation Questionnaire Items [On the actual instrument, some items are worded negatively to avoid a response bias and the labels "Custo" (customer), "Compo" (competitor), and "Coord" (coordination) do not appear.]*

Business Practices: In answering, use the following response scale and place the most appropriate number in the blank space to the left of each statement. Please respond to each statement.

Not at all	To a very slight extent	To a small extent	To a moderate extent	To a considerable extent	To a great extent	To an extreme extent
1	2	3	4	5	6	7

In our business—

Compo	_____	Our salespeople regularly share information within our business concerning competitors' strategies.
Custo	_____	Our business objectives are driven primarily by customer satisfaction.
Compo	_____	We rapidly respond to competitive actions that threaten us.
Custo	_____	We constantly monitor our level of commitment and orientation to serving customers' needs.
Coord	_____	Our top managers from every function regularly visit our current and prospective customers.
Coord	_____	We freely communicate information about our successful and unsuccessful customer experiences across all business functions.
Custo	_____	Our strategy for competitive advantage is based on our understanding of customers' needs.
Coord	_____	All of our business functions (e.g., marketing/sales, manufacturing, R&D, finance/accounting, etc.) are integrated in serving the needs of our target markets.
Custo	_____	Our business strategies are driven by our beliefs about how we can create greater value for customers.
Custo	_____	We measure customer satisfaction systematically and frequently.
Custo	_____	We give close attention to after-sales service.
Compo	_____	Top management regularly discusses competitors' strengths and strategies.
Coord	_____	All of our managers understand how everyone in our business can contribute to creating customer value.
Compo	_____	We target customers where we have an opportunity for competitive advantage.

*Custo	Item from customer orientation subscale
Compo	Item from competitor orientation subscale
Coord	Item from interfunctional coordination subscale

Business's Competitive Environment

Circle the number representing your best estimate of your business's competitive environment. Leave questions blank for which you cannot make at least a rough estimate.

Relative Size: In your principal served market segment (PSMS), what is the approximate size of your sales revenue compared to that of your largest competitor?

1	2	3	4	5	6	7	8
<.25	.50	.75	1.0	1.25	1.50	1.75	>2.0
Less than			(Equal to)				More than twice

Relative Cost: In your PSMS, how do your *per-unit* operating costs (including all of administrative, production, rent or equivalent, marketing/sales, etc.) compare to those of your largest competitor?

1	2	3	4	5	6	7	8
<.25	.50	.75	1.0	1.25	1.50	1.75	>2.0
Less than			(Equal to)				Greater than

Market Growth: Over the last 3 years, what has been the average annual growth rate of total sales in your PSMS?

_____%

Ease of Entry: What is the likelihood of a new competitor in your PSMS being able to earn satisfactory profits within 3 years after entry?

1	2	3	4	5	6	7	8
Extremely low							Extremely high

Buyer Power: How successful are your customers in negotiating lower prices from you?

Not at all	To a very slight extent	To a small extent	To a moderate extent	To a considerable extent	To a great extent	To an extreme extent
1	2	3	4	5	6	7

Competitor Concentration: Currently in your PSMS, approximately what percentage of total sales is accounted for by the four largest competitors? (Include yourself if appropriate as one of the four largest competitors.)

1	2	3	4	5	6	7
<10%	11–25%	26–40%	41–55%	56–70%	71–85%	86–100%

Changes in Business's Competitive Environment
Over the Past 3 Years

Circle the number representing your best estimate of how the competitive environment in your PSMS has changed over the past 3 years. Leave questions blank for which you cannot make at least a rough estimate.

Heterogeneity: The diversity in our marketing practices needed to serve our different customers has substantially:

1	2	3	4	5	6	7
Increased			No change			Decreased

Technological Turbulence: Production/service technology has changed:

1	2	3	4	5	6	7
Very much			Somewhat			Very little

Research and development activity has substantially:

1	2	3	4	5	6	7
Increased			No change			Decreased

Competitor Hostility: The market activities of our key competitors have become substantially:

1	2	3	4	5	6	7
Less predictable			No change			More predictable

Our key competitors have become substantially:

1	2	3	4	5	6	7
More hostile			No change			Less hostile

The market activities of our key competitors now affect our business in:

1	2	3	4	5	6	7
Many more areas (e.g., pricing, production, marketing, delivery, service, etc.)			No change			Far fewer areas

Business Performance

Use the 7-point scale shown below to rate the three dimensions of your business's performance. Rate how well your business has performed relative to all other competitors in your PSMS over the past year. Leave blank any dimension for which you cannot make at least a rough estimate.

1	2	3	4	5	6	7
<10%	11–25%	26–40%	41–55%	56–70%	71–85%	86–100%

Example: If you believe that your return on investment is greater than that of approximately 60% of all competitors in your PSMS, rate yourself a 5 for return on investment.

	Rating
Return on investment*	____
New product success rate	____
Sales growth	____

*For this study, we consider CROI, ROI, ROA, and RONA to be equivalent.

Notes

1. See Dess, Ireland, and Hitt (1990) for an excellent review and discussion of the importance of industry effects from both a theoretical and a methodological perspective.

2. The forest products company SBUs from the Narver and Slater (1990) study that are excluded from this study primarily use telemarketing. By its nature, telemarketing restricts the extent and depth of customer contact, which is of prime interest in this study. Thus, these SBUs are not included.

3. We are indebted to Richard Staelin for his thoughts on this subject.

References

Aaker, D. (1988). *Strategic market management* (2nd ed.). New York: John Wiley.

Buzzell, R. D., & Gale, B. T. (1987). *The PIMS principles*. New York: Free Press.

Churchill, G. A., Jr. (1979, February). A paradigm for developing better measures of marketing constructs. *Journal of Marketing Research, 16,* 64-73.

Cronbach, L. (1970). *Essentials of psychological testing* (3rd ed.). New York: Harper & Row.

Daft, R. L., Sormunen, J., & Parks, D. (1988). Chief executive scanning, environmental characteristics, and company performance: An empirical study. *Strategic Management Journal, 9*(2), 123-139.

Day, G. S. (1990). *Market driven strategy*. New York: Free Press.

Day, G. S. (1991). *Learning about markets* (Report No. 91-117). Cambridge, MA: Marketing Science Institute.

Day, G. S., & Wensley, R. (1988). Assessing advantage: A framework for diagnosing competitive superiority. *Journal of Marketing, 52*(2), 1-20.

DeGeus, A. P. (1988, March/April). Planning as learning. *Harvard Business Review, 66,* 70-74.

Deshpandé, R., Farley, J. U., & Webster, F. E., Jr. (1992). *Corporate culture, customer orientation, and innovativeness in Japanese firms: A quadrad analysis* (Report No. 92-100). Cambridge, MA: Marketing Science Institute. (See also Chapter 4)

Dess, G. G., & Beard, D. W. (1984, March). Dimensions of organizational task environments. *Administrative Science Quarterly, 29,* 52-73.

Dess, G. G., Ireland, R. D., & Hitt, M. A. (1990). Industry effects and strategic management research. *Journal of Management, 16,* 7-27.

Dess, G. G., & Robinson, R. B., Jr. (1984). Measuring organizational performance in the absence of objective measures: The case of the privately-held firm and conglomerate business unit. *Strategic Management Journal, 5,* 265-273.

Forbis, J. L., & Mehta, N. T. (1981). Value-based strategies for industrial products. *Business Horizons, 24*(3), 32-42.

Frazier, G., & Rody, R. (1991). The use of influence strategies in interfirm relationships in industrial product channels. *Journal of Marketing, 55*(1), 52-69.

Hambrick, D., & Lei, D. (1985). Toward an empirical prioritization of contingency variables for business strategy. *Academy of Management Journal, 28*(4), 763-788.

Hambrick, D. C. (1983). Some tests of the effectiveness and functional attributes of Miles and Snow's strategic types. *Academy of Management Journal, 26,* 5-26.

Hax, A. C., & Majluf, N. S. (1984). *Strategic management: An integrative perspective*. Englewood Cliffs, NJ: Prentice Hall.

Huber, G. P., & Power, D. J. (1985). Retrospective reports of strategic-level managers: Guidelines for increasing their accuracy. *Strategic Management Journal, 6,* 171-180.

James, L., Demaree, R., & Wolf, G. (1984). Estimating within-group interrater reliability with and without response bias. *Journal of Applied Psychology, 69,* 85-98.

Jaworski, B. J., & Kohli, A. K. (1992). *Market orientation: Antecedents and consequences* (Report No. 92-104). Cambridge, MA: Marketing Science Institute. (See also Chapter 5)

Katabe, M. (1990). Corporate product policy and innovative behavior of European and Japanese multinationals. *Journal of Marketing, 54*(2), 19-33.

Kerlinger, F. (1973). *Foundations of behavioral research*. New York: Holt, Rinehart & Winston.

Kirzner, I. M. (1979). *Perception, opportunity, and profit*. Chicago: University of Chicago Press.

Kohli, A. K. (1989). Effects of supervisory behavior: The role of individual differences among salespeople. *Journal of Marketing, 53*(4), 40-50.

Kohli, A. K., & Jaworski, B. J. (1990). Market orientation: The construct, research propositions, and managerial implications. *Journal of Marketing, 54*(2), 1-18. (See also Chapter 2)

Kotler, P. (1977). From sales obsession to marketing effectiveness. *Harvard Business Review, 55*(6), 67-75.

Lawrence, P. R., & Lorsch, J. W. (1967). *Organization and environment.* Boston: Harvard Business School Press.

Levitt, T. (1960). Marketing myopia. *Harvard Business Review, 38*(4), 45-56.

Levitt, T. (1980). Marketing success through differentiation of anything. *Harvard Business Review, 58,* 83-91.

Maidique, M. A., & Zirger, B. J. (1984). A study of success and failure in product innovation: The case of the U.S. electronics industry. *IEEE Transactions on Engineering Management, EM-31*(4), 192-203.

McKee, D. O., Varadarajan, P. R., & Pride, W. M. (1989). Strategic adaptability and firm performance: A market-contingent perspective. *Journal of Marketing, 53*(3), 21-35.

Miles, R. E., & Snow, C. C. (1978). *Organizational strategy, structure, and process.* New York: McGraw-Hill.

Miller, D. (1987). The structural and environmental correlates of business strategy. *Strategic Management Journal, 8,* 55-76.

Narver, J., & Slater, S. (1990). The effect of a market orientation on business profitability. *Journal of Marketing, 54*(4), 20-35. (See also Chapter 3)

Noordewier, T., John, G., & Nevin, J. (1990). Performance outcomes of purchasing arrangements in industrial buyer-vendor relationships. *Journal of Marketing, 54*(4), 80-93.

Nunnally, J. (1978). *Psychometric theory* (2nd ed.). New York: McGraw-Hill.

Pearce, J., Robbins, D., & Robinson, R. (1987). The impact of grand strategy and planning formality on financial performance. *Strategic Management Journal, 8,* 125-134.

Peter, J. P., & Donnelly, J. H., Jr. (1988). *A preface to marketing management.* Plano, TX: Business Publications.

Pfeffer, J., & Salancik, G. R. (1978). *The external control of organizations: A resource dependence perspective.* New York: Harper & Row.

Porter, M. (1980). *Competitive strategy.* New York: Free Press.

Scherer, F. M. (1980). *Industrial market structure and economic performance.* Chicago: Rand McNally.

Senge, P. M. (1990, Fall). The leader's new work: Building learning organizations. *Sloan Management Review,* 7-23.

Shapiro, B. P. (1988, November/December). What the hell is "market oriented"? *Harvard Business Review, 66,* 119-125.

Sharma, S., Durand, R. M., & Gur-Arie, O. (1981, August). Identification and analysis of moderator variables. *Journal of Marketing Research, 18,* 291-320.

Snow, C. C., & Hrebeniak, L. G. (1980, June). Strategy, distinctive competence, and organizational performance. *Administrative Science Quarterly, 25,* 317-336.

Van de Ven, A. H., & Ferry, D. L. (1979). *Measuring and assessing organizations.* New York: John Wiley.

von Hippel, E. (1986, July). Lead users: A source of novel product concepts. *Management Science, 32,* 791-805.

Webster, F. E., Jr. (1988, May/June). Rediscovering the marketing concept. *Business Horizons, (31),* 29-39.

Does Market Orientation Matter for Small Firms?

Alfred M. Pelham
David T. Wilson

Although the philosophy of market orientation or "being close to the customer" has regained currency, its implementation in business seldom goes beyond lip service. Because of the abstract nature of market orientation and the difficulty of influencing employee behavior, only a minority of top managers devote sufficient time and effort to build a market-oriented corporate culture. Instead, many managers continue to focus on concrete, controllable factors, such as financial management and cost reduction.

Empirical studies of large firms have determined that market orientation—defined here as firmwide activities designed to understand customers and competitors and to constantly increase customer satisfaction—is linked to profitability. For small firms, however, it could be argued that market orientation is a less critical ingredient of success because these companies have fewer customers and simpler organizational structures and are more adaptable to marketplace changes.

To examine this issue, Pelham and Wilson developed a model of small firm performance that incorporated market orientation along with a variety of other firm and industry variables suggested by the management literature, including market environment, business strategy, and organizational structure. They then tested the relationships among these variables over time using longitudinal data from The Center for Entrepreneurship at Eastern Michigan University. Survey respondents were the presidents or chief executive officers of small Michigan firms in a variety of industries.

Contrary to traditional management theory, changes in market environment, business strategy, and organizational structure had only modest impacts on small firm performance. For the sample studied, regression results instead indicated that a high level of market orientation and an increase in sales growth or market share were the only significant, direct determinants of improved profitability. Market orientation was also one of the few important determinants of more effective new product development and higher product quality.

Although the authors found only a weak association between low cost strategy and performance, increased use of this approach can boost sales or market share in the short run. For small firms with limited funds, however, emphasizing a low cost strategy reduces the resources available for new product or market development. Shifting to an innovation/niche/differentiation strategy, in contrast, had no short-term influence on performance, but it did strongly and positively affect new product or market development—and ultimately profitability.

An organizational structure accommodating differences in product lines had a significant but negative impact on revenue growth or market share. Although it may appear that expanding organizational structure to accommodate more product lines is a positive move, for small firms it can mean having too few resources devoted to existing markets and product lines. The result may therefore be disappointing market shares and sales in all segments.

Although changes in organizational structure variables, such as formalization, coordination, and control systems, did not directly affect small firm profitability, these variables had a strong influence on market orientation. Similarly, although changes in firm strategy do not directly affect profitability, a strategy of innovation or premium pricing was also strongly associated with market orientation.

In conclusion, small firms cannot compete successfully by blindly duplicating the strategies and practices of large firms. Rather than attempt to combat the cost advantages that large firms enjoy, small firm managers can achieve a sustainable competitive advantage by instilling market-oriented behaviors in employees. This orientation, in turn, enables small companies to focus on their areas of strength—innovation, flexibility, and greater value added for carefully targeted customer groups.

Of course, developing market-oriented norms and practices is difficult, and few managers understand the causal relationships between market orientation practices and performance. A customer focus, however, makes a firm more responsive to the changing demands of the marketplace than its competitors, large or small. With a strong market orientation, small firms should be able to improve marketing effectiveness and profitability.

Although every student in Marketing 101 learns that market orientation—"being close to customers"—should drive business, they apparently forget this concept as soon as they become managers. In fact, academics were the only ones discussing the marketing concept until U.S. businesses began to emulate the Japanese management approach in the 1980s. Today, however, urged on by popular writers such as Tom Peters and Robert Waterman (1982), market orientation is making a comeback in American business.

This revival likely motivated the efforts of Kohli and Jaworski (1990) and Narver and Slater (1990) to define the role that the marketing concept plays in business performance. These studies suggest that market orientation does indeed improve the profitability of strategic business units in large firms.

Our study expands on this and other business performance research by integrating market orientation into models that incorporate several other potentially important variables, including market environment, business strategy, and organizational structure. We also examine the impact of business position variables such as revenue growth or firm share performance, new product or market development performance, and relative product quality performance.

The focus here is on small firms. It could be argued that market orientation is less important for these businesses because they have a more cohesive culture, less complex organization, and fewer customers. At the same time, however, market orientation may in fact be an even more important determinant of success for small firms because it may provide a companywide framework for objectives, decisions, and actions. This framework may be crucial to performance because small firms often lack systematic decision making and strategic thinking (for a review of the impact of planning on small business performance, see Robinson & Pearce, 1984).

Another unique aspect of small firms is that the president or owner has a much greater opportunity to influence the actions of employees than the manager of a strategic business unit or president of a large firm. The president of a small firm can thus be more influential in fostering a companywide market orientation.

Model and Propositions

Our model draws on the management literature—specifically, industrial organization theory, organization theory, and business policy theory—to define expected relationships between small firm performance and market structure, organizational structure, and firm strategy. Figure 7.1 illustrates the relationships predicted by the management literature. As Table 7.1 shows, however, management theory does not agree on the direction of influence of these variables. Moreover, Park and Mason (1990) have demonstrated the poor fit of existing models of performance, which all ignore at least some of the influences.

Our model takes a comprehensive view by incorporating market orientation along with all the potential determinants of performance. Market orientation has been found to have a significant impact on business performance (Jaworski & Kohli, 1993; Narver & Slater, 1990). We employ Narver and Slater's definition of market orientation: Market orientation is the "organization culture . . . that most effectively and efficiently creates the necessary behaviors for the creation of superior value for buyers and, thus, superior performance for the business" (p. 21). Necessary behaviors include those that promote the following (Narver & Slater, 1990, pp. 21-22):

- An understanding of one's target buyers to be able to create superior value for them continuously
- An understanding of competitive short-term strengths and weaknesses and long-term capabilities and strategies
- A coordinated utilization of company resources in creating superior value for target customers

Our model also incorporates firm structure variables, including formalization, coordination, and control systems, because research indicates that formal planning has a strong positive impact on performance (Robinson & Pearce, 1984). Small firms, however, are known to lack formal planning.

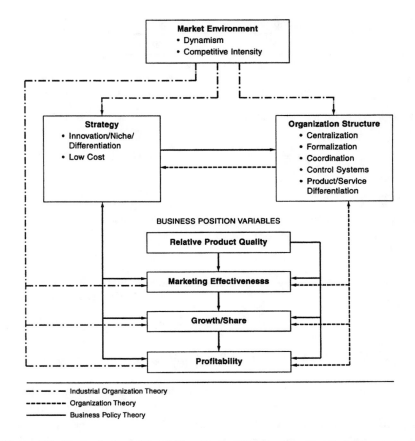

Figure 7.1. Determinants of Small Firm Profitability Predicted by the Management Literature

Market environment variables such as competitive intensity and market dynamism are also included because their influence on performance is a much-debated topic. Some studies indicate that industry characteristics, or their interaction with strategy, have only a minor impact on performance (Hansen & Wernerfelt, 1989; Prescott, 1986). Venkatraman and Prescott (1990), however, found that in mature, stable, or declining industries, strategy choice is crucial to profitability. Small firms with limited financial resources may thus be particularly vulnerable to market environment characteristics, or they may be particularly resilient because of their greater flexibility.

Table 7.1 Predicted Relationships of Key Constructs

Source	Relationship	Reference
Industrial organization theory	Market environment → firm strategy	Porter (1979), Park and Mason (1990)
	Market environment → performance	Venkatraman and Prescott (1990)
Organization theory	Market environment → firm structure	Lawrence and Lorsch (1967), Miles and Snow (1978)
	Firm structure → performance	Hill and Pickering (1986), Park and Mason (1990)
Business policy theory	Firm strategy → firm structure	Grinyer, Yasai-Ardekanii, and Al-Bazzaz (1980)
	Firm strategy → performance	Hambrick (1983), Park and Mason (1990)
	Share → profitability	Buzzell (1981, 1987)
	Product quality → profitability	Jacobson (1988), Venkatraman and Prescott (1990)

Market Orientation Should Affect Profits Indirectly

A small firm emphasizing activities that seek to understand customer needs and to satisfy those needs should have high relative product quality and therefore premium pricing, which in turn should lead to greater profitability. With its greater understanding of the environment, the market-oriented firm should also have greater marketing effectiveness (defined by new product and market development success) and greater revenue growth or market share. This should also lead to increased profitability. Stated formally,

$P_{1:}$ A high level of market orientation in small firms positively influences the level of relative product quality.

$P_{2:}$ A high level of market orientation in small firms positively influences marketing effectiveness.

$P_{3:}$ A high level of market orientation in small firms positively influences increases in revenue growth or market share.

Market Orientation Should Affect Profits Directly

Our supposition that a strong market orientation leads to greater profitability is based in part on the logic of the strong culture hypothesis (Dennison, 1984; Weick, 1985) and in part on the logic of sustainable competitive advantage (Day & Wensley, 1983, 1988; Reed & DeFillippi, 1990). The strong culture hypothesis suggests that strongly held beliefs and norms that are pervasive throughout the organization can provide cohesiveness and focus in strategies and tactics. If most employees in the firm hold beliefs about the importance of satisfying customers, these beliefs translate into norms that provide consistency in employees' behavior and the firm's strategies and tactics. The results should be fewer defects, lower costs, greater customer satisfaction, greater potential to charge premium prices, and higher profitability.

Critics of this hypothesis charge that common cultural traits across many organizations oversimplify the complex mix of firm characteristics that can affect performance (Barney, 1986; Saffold, 1988). There is empirical evidence, however, that certain types of strong corporate cultures do have a positive influence on performance (Dennison, 1984; Gordon & Tomaso, 1992). For example, Deshpandé, Farley, and Webster (1993) found that market cultures emphasizing competitiveness, goal achievement, and strategic focus on competitive advantage are associated with higher performance levels than clan, adhocracy, and hierarchy cultures.

A market-oriented small firm may in fact possess a sustainable competitive advantage. This advantage may develop because of the difficulty of establishing such a culture and because few managers may understand the relationship between market-oriented behaviors and performance. Thus, market orientation may provide those attributes Reed and DeFillippi (1990) define as critical for sustaining a competitive advantage—that is, attributes that are difficult to achieve and copy and that are causally ambiguous. We therefore expect the following:

P_4: A high level of market orientation in small firms positively influences increases in profitability.

Influence of Internal and External Environments

Jaworski and Kohli (1993) studied internal antecedents to market orientation, including organizational structure. Citing Deshpandé and Zaltman's

(1982) study, they suggest that interdepartmental connectedness is important to the dissemination of and responsiveness to market information. They argue (per Zaltman, Duncan, & Holbek, 1973) that formalization can have a negative impact on market orientation if the emphasis on rules makes the organization less adaptive to the environment; it can, however, have a positive impact on market orientation if the rules enhance customer satisfaction.

Jaworski and Kohli (1993) also suggest that formalization, centralization, and departmentalization may inhibit innovative behavior but enhance the implementation stage of innovative behavior. Their results indicate, however, that interdepartmental connectedness significantly and positively influences market orientation, but that formalization, centralization, and departmentalization have no effect.

Our focus, however, is on small firms, which tend to have high levels of centralization and low levels of formalization, departmentalization, and control systems. These organizational structure variables may therefore play a role in the extent of market orientation in small firms. As managers increase the levels of formalization, differentiation in structure, decentralization, and control systems in their companies, they should increasingly value market information gathering and dissemination. We therefore hypothesize the following:

P_5: Increases in formalization, product differentiation structure, decentralization, and control systems positively influence the level of market orientation in small firms.

Narver and Slater (1990) also note a significant correlation between market orientation and growth or differentiation strategy. In a firm that pursues such a strategy, there should be a tendency to emphasize cultural norms that favor a customer orientation. Firms that pursue a maintenance-, defense-, or retrenchment-type strategy, in contrast, should have a low market orientation. Although our measures of strategy are slightly different, we expect the same relationships to exist in small firms. Hence,

P_6: Increases in the use of innovation/niche/differentiation strategy in small firms positively influence the level of market orientation.

Consistent with industrial organization theory's claim that the market environment constrains firm strategy, we expect that industry dynamism and competitive intensity influence the level of a firm's market orientation. Changing perceptions of a more hostile or more dynamic market environment could

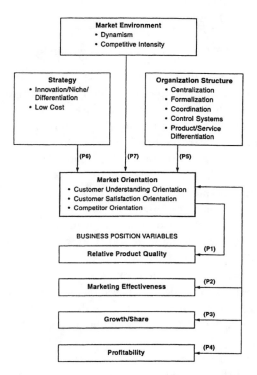

Figure 7.2. Expanded Model of Small Firm Profitability

directly encourage small firm managers to emphasize external activities designed to understand and satisfy customers and to monitor competition. Hence,

> P_7: Increases in perceived levels of market dynamism or competitive intensity (market structure) positively influence the level of market orientation in small firms.

Figure 7.2 depicts our expanded model that integrates the antecedents and consequences of market orientation. Note that, because we are primarily interested in the significance of the antecedents and consequences of market orientation, we did not formally present propositions based on the other relationships presented in the management literature. We did, however, test for these relationships and will discuss the results as they apply to expectations based on industrial organization theory, organization theory, and business policy theory.

Testing the Model

We tested our propositions by examining parameter significance in a model using year-to-year differences in the dependent and independent variables. Because of the small sample size and the complexity of some models, we supplemented multiple regression with stepwise regression as a check on parameter insignificance. Also, because of potentially small year-to-year differences, we examined correlations of variables.

The database was developed by The Center for Entrepreneurship at Eastern Michigan University in 1992 and 1993 and measures a broad spectrum of internal firm and external industry variables. The center's panel comprises 370 Michigan firms (30% manufacturing, 28% wholesaling, 24% business services, and 18% construction), with an average of 21.5 employees and $2.9 million in sales. Because we added marketing orientation and relative product quality questions in the midst of their telephone interview schedule in 1993, and because we needed complete responses to all measures for both years, our regression models are based on only 68 firms.

The market orientation and relative product quality variables thus reflect a one-time measurement. The lack of longitudinal data may reduce confidence in the causal effects of market orientation, although we believe that a firm's culture forms over a long time and a measure taken once within a 3- or 4-year period is likely to be representative. Even in small firms, which have considerably more flexibility than large firms, modifying employee behavior is a slow and difficult process.

Measurement Sources

The survey questions for each construct appear in Appendix 7.A. All measures use 7-point semantic differential or agree/disagree scales, with the exception of formalization, which uses a yes or no series of questions. Each construct has at least three measures. All construct measures represent the average score for each firm on the items addressing that construct.

Market Orientation. The nine market orientation questions are based on Pelham's (1993) analysis of measures of market orientation as used by Narver and Slater (1990) and Jaworski and Kohli (1993). Pelham's study of 160 small manufacturing firm presidents and sales managers found that Narver and Slater's measures achieved the best reliability and validity scores.

Organizational Structure. The items measuring the organizational structure variable of product line differentiation (i.e., differences across product lines in method of production, customer buying habits, and nature of competition) are drawn from Miller (1988). The items that address centralization, control systems, and formalization are based on Miller and Droge's (1986) study. An example of a centralization measure is the organization level at which decisions about worker dismissals are made. A control systems measure is the extent of use of cost centers. A formalization measure is the use or nonuse of written job descriptions. A coordination measure is the frequency of decisions made by departments working together.

Market Environment. Competitive intensity measures are taken from Khandwalla (1977). An example of this type of measure is the extent of threat from price competition. Dynamism measures are from Miller and Droge's (1986) study. An example is the frequency of change in customer needs.

Performance. Performance measures are based on the firm presidents' responses to questions assessing whether results were above or below expectations. Profitability is a composite of five measures: operating profits, profit-to-sales ratio, cash flow, return on investment, and return on assets.

Business Strategy. An example of a low cost strategy measure is the degree to which the firm emphasizes continuing, overriding concern for the lowest unit cost. In contrast, a measure of an innovation/niche/differentiation strategy is the degree to which the firm emphasizes developing and refining products.

Measure and Construct Reliability

The Center for Entrepreneurship found coefficient alpha scores for the previously discussed variables ranging from .63 to .88. The average of .75 represents an acceptable level of reliability for research of this type (Van de Ven & Ferry, 1979).

We also used LISREL measurement model analysis, which provides a more rigorous assessment of convergent and discriminant validity. The scores for each variable indicate good measurement reliability and good convergent and discriminant validity (see Appendix 7.A). To determine if parameter insignificance was due to independent variable multicollinearity, we ran forward stepwise regression models. Variance inflation factor analysis indicated no significant parameter distortion due to multicollinearity.

Table 7.2 Impacts of Independent Variables (Beta Coefficients; $N = 68$)

	Dependent Variable[a]				
Independent Variable[a]	Market Orientation	Relative Product Quality	Marketing Effectiveness	Growth/ Share	Profitability
Innovation/niche/ differentiation strategy	.01	−.11	.12	−.03	.00
Low cost strategy	−.15	−.03	−.27*	.24*	.12
Centralization	.13	−.11	−.02	.12	.10
Formalization	.24*	.07	−.01	−.03	.02
Coordination	.03	.01	.01	−.12	.04
Product differentiation	−.01	−.02	.11	−.27**	.08
Control systems	.12	.12	.19	−.17	−.07
Market dynamism	.06	.05	.13	−.07	.17
Competitive intensity	−.18	−.11	.24*	−.20	−.02
Market orientation[b]		.31*	.24*	−.01	.29*
Marketing effectiveness				.44*	−.09
Relative product quality[b]			.19	.12	.09
Growth/share					.57*
Model R^2	.25	.22	.43	.33	.55
Adjusted R^2	.13	.12	.30	.18	.44
Model F	2.3*	1.7	4.8**	2.2*	5.0**
Reduced model R^2	.12	.07	.32	.19	.47

a. Changes in response from 1992 to 1993.

b. Data available for only 1 year.

*$p < .05$; **$p < .01$.

Appendix 7.B provides a correlation matrix of variables for both 1992 and 1993. Despite the subjective nature of many of the respondents' judgments, most of the correlations between 1992 and 1993 responses are reasonably high (formalization, .67; centralization, .35; coordination, .59; and control systems, .59). Appendix 7.C provides the means and standard deviations for the variables in both years.

We calculated beta weights for parameter estimation from standardized data. Indirect influences were computed using a path analysis method suggested by Duncan (1971) that was based on multiplication of beta weights.

Results

Table 7.2 provides the regression results of model testing using year-to-year differences in variables. This table omits the results of tests for paths

Table 7.3 Comparison of Regression Parameters and Year-to-Year Correlations

Dependent Variable	Independent Variable	Regression Beta Parameter	Correlation of Independent Variable in Year 1 to Dependent Variable in Year 2
Coordination	Innovation/niche/ differentiation strategy	.17 (ns)	.33 (.01)
Innovation/niche/ differentiation strategy	Formalization	.01 (ns)	.22 (.05)
	Control systems	−.21 (ns)	.27 (.05)
Control systems	Competitive intensity	−.04 (ns)	.26 (.01)
Formalization	Competitive intensity	.15 (ns)	.23 (.05)
Marketing effectiveness	Market dynamism	.13 (ns)	.34 (.01)
	Formalization	−.01 (ns)	.24 (.05)
	Coordination	.01 (ns)	.23 (.05)
	Control systems	.19 (ns)	.27 (.01)
	Low cost strategy	−.27 (.05)	.11 (ns)
	Innovation/niche/ differentiation strategy	.12 (ns)	.54 (.01)
Growth/share	Low cost strategy	.24 (.04)	−.01 (ns)
	Product differentiation structure	−.27 (.03)	.14 (ns)
	Relative product quality (current year only)	.12 (ns)	.27 (.01)
Profitability	Relative product quality (current year only)	.09 (ns)	.42 (.01)
Market orientation	Formalization	.24 (.05)	.16 (ns)
	Coordination	.03 (ns)	.25 (.05)
	Control systems	.12 (ns)	.28 (.05)
	Innovation/niche/ differentiation strategy	.01 (ns)	.26 (.05)
	Competitive intensity	−.18 (ns)	.37 (.01)

NOTE: Beta parameters are for year-to-year differences in variables. Numbers in parentheses refer to significance levels. *ns,* not significant.

among market environment, organizational structure, and firm strategy because of the lack of parameter significance and low model R^2 levels. The weakness of these relationships, although contrary to the management literature, is understandable given the relatively low levels of formalization, coordination, and control systems in small firms. Table 7.3 presents significant correlation results between variables in 1992 and 1993, indicating how previous levels of one variable may influence current levels of another.

The correlations indicate that, as the management literature suggests, perceptions of the market environment are related to organizational structure. For instance, perceptions of competitive intensity are positively associated with formalization and control systems, whereas perceptions of dynamism are positively associated with coordination. Increased structure is a natural organizational adaptation to greater environmental uncertainty.

This also explains the significant correlation between perceptions of competitive intensity and greater use of a low cost strategy. When small firms believe they are threatened, they tend to emphasize cost cutting, including adding systems to monitor costs better. At the same time, however, the correlation between perceptions of market dynamism and innovation or premium-pricing strategy suggests that when small firm managers perceive a change toward a more opportunistic environment, they tend to emphasize an innovation strategy.

The only significant ($p < .05$) influence on firm strategy from performance feedback loops revealed by regression analysis was the negative ($-.31$) impact of increased marketing effectiveness on the low cost strategy. This implies that positive feedback from new product and market development activities tends to encourage a shift from cost cutting to innovation.

Market Environment and Performance

Our results indicate that changes in the market environment have minimal effects on respondents' assessments of their firms' performance. Changes in market dynamism also have no significant impact on any of the performance variables. Increased competitive intensity only influences the assessment of marketing effectiveness ($.24, p < .05$). These results were duplicated in stepwise regression, indicating that multicollinearity or parameter instability does not account for the lack of significance.

The finding that change in competitive intensity has no significant impact on change in growth or share differs from Jaworski and Kohli's (1993) results for large firms. This difference may reflect the use of different performance measures or the greater ability of small firms to adapt to changes in the environment. The minimal impact of perceptions of competitive intensity is also suggested by the lack of significant correlations between previous-year competitive intensity and any performance variable.

Organizational Structure and Performance

The only change in an organizational structure variable having a significant ($p < .05$) impact on performance is the negative effect ($-.27$) of greater product line differentiation on growth or share. This result implies that, in the short term, spreading limited resources across too many product lines may have a detrimental impact on growth or share in current and new markets, relative to expectations.

Although the minor importance of changes in organizational structure conflicts with the expectations of organization theory, it must be remembered that the small firms in this study have little structure. Our results, however, do support expectations in the small business management literature that high levels of formalization, coordination, and control systems in the previous year have a positive impact on marketing effectiveness in the current year.

Firm Strategy and Performance

Although greater reliance on a low cost strategy significantly ($p = .05$) and negatively ($-.27$) influences marketing effectiveness, it significantly and positively ($.24$) influences growth or share. The lack of significant correlations between the previous extent of low cost strategy and any performance variable, however, suggests that these effects may be only short term.

Changes in innovation/niche/differentiation strategy have no significant impact on changes in any performance variable. Nevertheless, correlation relationships suggest that an emphasis on this type of strategy is associated with marketing effectiveness.

Strategy shifts do not significantly affect profitability. This weaker than expected influence may be explained by the limited ability of small firms to pursue either a low cost advantage or an R&D-based advantage, indicating the importance of strategy implementation for small firms.

Business Position and Performance

Increased marketing effectiveness significantly ($p = .05$) and positively ($.44$) influences growth or share. Contrary to business policy theory, however, relative product quality does not have a significant causal effect on improved growth or share or profitability. This finding, although consistent with Jaworski and Kohli (1993), contradicts the results of Phillips, Chang, and Buzzell (1983) and Buzzell, Gale, and Sultan (1975) that are based on objective profit impact of market share data from large firms. We should note, however, that the level of perceived relative product quality in this study is significantly ($p < .01$) associated with growth or share ($.27$) and profitability ($.42$). These differences may reflect the inclusion of market orientation in our model.

As business policy theory predicts, increases in growth or share positively (.57) and significantly ($p < .01$) affect increases in profitability. This result is consistent with Buzzell's (1987) study of the impact of share on profitability. Nevertheless, the level of growth or share in 1992 is not significantly correlated with profitability in 1993, implying that growth or share may have only a short-term impact on small firm profitability. Jacobson (1988) concludes that share and profitability may be influenced by an unobserved third variable. Using his suggestion of vector autoregressive modeling, with lagged dependent and independent variables, we found that share has no significant impact on 1993 profitability, but that market orientation does have a significant impact ($.52, p < .01$).

Market Orientation, Business Position, and Profitability

Market orientation is the only variable to significantly ($p = .05$) influence (.31) the perceived level of relative product quality, leading to the acceptance of Proposition 1. In stepwise regression, market orientation is the only variable meeting the criteria to enter the model, resulting in an R^2 level of .07 compared with .22 for the full model with all variables.

Proposition 2 is also accepted. Marketing orientation significantly ($p = .05$) and positively (.24) promotes increases in marketing effectiveness. In stepwise regression, market orientation is the only variable meeting the criteria to enter the model, resulting in an R^2 level of .15 compared with an R^2 level of .40 for the full model.

Proposition 3, however, is rejected. Consistent with Jaworski and Kohli's (1993) results, market orientation does not significantly and directly influence increases in growth or share. Stepwise regression results indicate that the only variables meeting the .05 significance criterion are marketing effectiveness and product differentiation, resulting in an R^2 level of .19 compared with .33 for the full model. Market orientation therefore indirectly influences growth or share through marketing effectiveness. By way of comparison, the R^2 levels of Jaworski and Kohli's market share model (in two samples) are .06 and .11, but their model does not include organizational structure, firm strategy, or marketing effectiveness variables.

Proposition 4 is accepted. Market orientation significantly ($p < .01$) and positively (.29) improves profitability for small firms. In stepwise regression, only market orientation and growth or share meet the criterion of significance ($p = .05$), resulting in a model with an R^2 of .47 compared with .55 for the full model.

Note that Narver and Slater's (1990) study of strategic business units (SBUs) in a large forest products firm found that the impact of market orientation on profitability varies across types of products and sizes of business units. Specifically, large commodity product SBUs with low market orientation levels were more profitable than the smallest commodity product SBUs with medium levels of market orientation. In addition, Narver and Slater's results indicated that market dynamism has a significant and negative influence on profitability. On the basis of these results and our own, we conclude that market orientation is both more prevalent and more important in small firms than in large firms.

Indirect Influences on Profitability

In small firms, market orientation (but not firm structure or strategy) directly affects profitability. For a more complete picture of the determinants of profitability, we therefore must examine indirect influences. To do so, we used a procedure suggested by Duncan (1971) that uses multiplication of beta weights from path analysis regressions.

Our results reveal that marketing effectiveness (.25), product differentiation (.15), and low cost strategy (.13) all affect small firm profitability indirectly through their influence on growth or share. Formalization (.07) also indirectly affects profitability through its influence on market orientation.

What Promotes Market Orientation?

There is weak support for acceptance of Proposition 5. Of the organizational variables, only increased formalization has a significant influence (.24, $p < .05$) on the level of small firm market orientation. This may result from better implementation of customer satisfaction-oriented activities as formal procedures increase. Jaworski and Kohli (1993), in contrast, found no significant relationship between formalization and the level of market orientation. As noted previously, however, their study examines large firms, which have high levels of formalization, whereas our study focuses on small firms, which have low levels of formalization.

Although there is only weak support for the causal influence of changes in organizational structure on the level of market orientation, the significant and positive correlations between market orientation in 1993 and the level of coordinating systems and control systems in 1992 are noteworthy. Jaworski and Kohli also found a significant regression relationship between interdepartmental connectedness and market orientation. The lack of regression significance for changes in coordinating systems in our model may be due to the fact that it takes time for these systems to raise the level of market orientation in a firm.

Because increases in the use of an innovation/niche/differentiation strategy do not significantly affect the level of market orientation, we reject Proposition 6. This result, however, may reflect the small degree of change in the use of this strategy because market orientation is significantly and positively associated with the previous year's level of innovation/niche/differentiation strategy. This relationship is consistent with Narver and Slater's (1990) finding that market orientation is significantly associated with differentiation strategy.

Increases in competitive intensity and market dynamism do not significantly influence the level of market orientation, leading to our rejection of Proposition 7. Even so, the previous year's level of competitive intensity is significantly and positively associated with market orientation.

It is important to note the influence of performance feedback loops on the level of market orientation. Increases in marketing effectiveness and profitability have a significant ($p < .05$) and positive (.31 and .41, respectively) impact on market orientation. The model with performance feedback loops has an R^2 level of .36 compared with .25 for the model without performance variables.

Management Theory Versus Small Firm Realities

The weak direct influence we found between changes in market environment and changes in performance contradicts not only the expectations of industrial organization theory but also the documented variance of objective indicators across industries. The performance measures used here, however, are based on the presidents' subjective assessments of their companies' performance relative to expectations. These expectations are not influenced by industry comparisons but rather by comparisons of actual results to projected results, to previous firm performance, and to perceived performance of other firms in the industry.

In addition, the measures of industry environment characteristics are based on the presidents' subjective assessments, which are subject to bias and errors in judgment. Our results, however, do support Lado, Boyd, and Wright's (1992) argument that industrial organization theory overemphasizes the influence of the industry environment and overlooks idiosyncratic competencies, such as a market-oriented culture, that can generate a sustainable competitive advantage. In addition, small business performance may depend less on industry forces than on internal forces.

The lack of significant regression relationships fails to support the two-way influences between industry environment, strategy, and organizational structure suggested by business policy researchers. As expected, however, market dynamism is associated with an innovation or premium-pricing strategy and an organizational structure characterized by high levels of product line differentiation and coordination. Also as expected, competitive intensity is associated with a low cost strategy and a firm structure characterized by high levels of formalization and control systems.

Implications for Managers

When small firms perceive the competitive environment as hostile, some managers resort to cost control systems and price cutting. Our results suggest, however, that although a shift to a low cost strategy can generate short-term gains in market share, it guarantees neither profitability nor longer term viability. For small firms, a low cost strategy fails to provide a sustainable competitive advantage for the following reasons:

- The relative ease of copying other companies' price-oriented strategies
- The ease of understanding the impact of pricing on sales
- The relative inability of small firms to achieve low-cost producer status through economies of scale

The source of competitive advantage for small firms lies instead in developing a strong market orientation. Creating a market-oriented culture is more difficult than instituting cost-cutting norms, and it is also more difficult to understand the relationship between market orientation and performance than that between low cost efforts and performance. Nevertheless, following from Narver and Slater's (1990) finding that large businesses may be the least able to adopt a market orientation, presidents of small firms have a powerful opportunity to encourage market-oriented behaviors, given that they have a smaller number of employees and a simpler, more adaptable form of organization. A strong market-oriented culture improves performance by providing focus for small firms, which are noted for their lack of formal planning, coordinating, and control systems.

The results of this study should thus encourage small firm managers, who must constantly combat the cost advantages of larger firms, to focus on the strengths allied with a strong market orientation—innovation, flexibility, and greater value added for carefully targeted customer groups. In fact, our model indicates that market orientation is the only internal firm variable to directly influence profitability; it is also the only variable that has a significant impact on relative product quality, which is strongly related to growth or share and profitability. Moreover, market orientation is the only variable having a positive influence on marketing effectiveness and, in turn, on market growth or share.

It is therefore important to understand what promotes the presence of market orientation. Efforts to enhance formalization, coordination, and control systems—together with emphasis on an innovation/niche/differentiation strategy—should enhance levels of market-oriented norms and practices.

Directions for Future Research

This study contributes to the marketing literature by showing that market orientation is a stronger (not weaker) determinant of performance in small firms, even when the influences of strategy, structure, and business position are considered. This study also contributes to our understanding of the antecedents of market orientation in small firms.

The following are suggestions for specific ways in which future research can expand on the study summarized here:

1. Given the important distinctions between large and small firms, our results are generalizable only to small firms. We suggest that future studies of market orientation in large firms employ longitudinal data and integrated models.
2. Because our study relies on the subjective judgments of one internal critical informant, measurement of market orientation and other key variables is subject to various cognitive biases such as position bias. Future market orientation studies should use external, and perhaps more objective, informants.
3. We measured market orientation in only one year. Future studies could strengthen the causal implications by measuring this variable during several years.
4. The small sample size limits confidence in the results, especially given the number of parameters estimated in some models. Although stepwise regression indicated that parameter insignificance was not due to sample size, using larger samples would allow more confidence in the results.

Appendix 7.A: Survey Items Used to Measure Constructs

	Factor Analysis Loading	*LISREL* Square Multiple Correlation	Coefficient Alpha/Item Correlation
Market orientation			.92
Customer understanding orientation			
1. All our functions (not just marketing and sales) are responsive to, and integrated in, serving target markets. (agree/disagree)	.81	.52	.88
2. Our firm's strategy for competitive advantage is based on our thorough understanding of our customer needs. (agree/disagree)	.53	.51	.87
Customer satisfaction orientation			
3. All our managers understand how the entire business can contribute to creating customer value. (agree/disagree)	.70	.41	.88
4. Our firm responds (slowly/quickly) to negative customer satisfaction information throughout the organization.	.67	.27	.94
5. Our firm's market strategies are to a (moderate/great) extent driven by our understanding of possibilities for creating value for customers.	.64	.40	.87
6. Information on customers, marketing success, and marketing failures is communicated across functions in the firm. (agree/disagree)	.58	.33	.85
Competitor orientation			
7. How frequently do top managers discuss competitive strengths and weaknesses? (never/very frequently)	.79	.66	.92
8. How frequently do you take advantage of targeted opportunities to take advantage of competitors' weaknesses? (never/very frequently)	.77	.49	.88
9. If a major competitor were to launch an intensive campaign targeted at our customers, we would implement a response immediately. (agree/disagree)	.54	.39	.83
Performance			
(1 = much below expectations; 7 = much above expectations)			
Marketing effectiveness			.74
1. New product/service development	.85	.43	.72
2. Market development	.85	.91	.71
Growth/share			.75
3. Sales growth rate	.80	.71	.72
4. Employment growth rate	.68	.50	.66
5. Market share	.73	.58	.70

	Factor Analysis Loading	LISREL Square Multiple Correlation	Coefficient Alpha/Item Correlation
Profitability			.88
6. Operating profits	.81	.69	.79
7. Profit-to-sales ratio	.87	.70	.74
8. Cash flow from operations	.82	.64	.72
9. Return on investment	.93	.92	.87
10. Return on assets	.91	.85	.86
Relative product quality (single measure)			
11. Please rate your relative product quality on the following scale: (1 = low satisfaction; 7 = high satisfaction)			
Firm structure			
Decentralization			.87
Organization level where following decisions made: 0 = Board of directors/owner; 1 = CEO/president; 2 = Upper level dept. mgr.; 3 = midlevel dept. mgr.; 3 = First-line supervisor; 5 = Entry-level employees			
1. Determines number of workers needed	.80	.63	.83
2. Decides whether to hire entry-level worker	.81	.66	.85
3. Dismissal of a worker	.79	.62	.94
Coordination			.71
Frequency of activity or process (1 = never/rarely; 7 = frequently)			
4. Are manager committees set up to allow joint decision making among departments/work groups?	.59	.56	.70
5. Are task forces set up for collaboration on a specific project?	.56	.52	.69
6. Are product or service decisions concerning production, distribution, marketing, and R&D strategies made by different departments/work groups working together?	.69	.40	.68
7. Are capital budget decisions concerning the selection and financing of long-term investments made by different work groups or departments working together?	.80	.42	.70
Control systems			.63
Extent to which firm uses control systems (1 = never/rarely; 7 = frequently)			
8. Comprehensive management control and information system	.57	.38	.51
9. Cost centers for cost control	.83	.53	.59
10. Profit centers and profit targets	.82	.33	.52
Formalization			.73
Yes or no (1 = yes; 0 = no)			

	Factor Analysis Loading	*LISREL Square Multiple Correlation*	*Coefficient Alpha/Item Correlation*
11. Do you hand out information booklets to your employees addressing such topics as security, working conditions, etc.?	.59	.35	.59
12. A written manual of procedures and fixed rules?	.73	.49	.67
13. Written operating instructions to workers?	.81	.35	.69
14. Written job descriptions?	.63	.40	.60
Product/service differentiation			.77
Extent to which there are differences across your lines with regard to the following (1 = no difference; 7 = great differences):			
15. Customers' buying habits	.74	.40	.66
16. Nature of competition	.75	.53	.63
17. Required method of production or distribution of products/services	.74	.58	.75
Strategy			
Degree to which your firm emphasized each competitive method over past 5 years (1 = not considered; 7 = major constant emphasis):			
Low cost strategy			.72
1. Pricing below competitors	.83	.40	.70
2. Continuing, overriding concern for lowest cost per unit	.50	.32	.64
3. Products in lower-priced market segments	.65	.27	.69
Innovation/niche/differentiation strategy			.70
4. New product development	.54	.41	.66
5. Extremely strict product quality control procedures	.32	.31	.50
6. Developing and refining existing products	.52	.44	.69
7. Innovation in manufacturing process	.80	.31	.70
8. Products in higher-priced market segments	.43	.35	.55
Market environment			
Dynamism (technical/market turbulence)			.72
Frequency of factor change in industry (1 = never change; 7 = change very frequently)			
1. Production (or distribution) technique/process changes	.72	.41	.70
2. Changes in customers' needs	.71	.45	.71
3. Rate at which products/services become obsolete	.62	.28	.65
4. Nature of competitors' strategies and actions	.71	.34	.66
Competitive intensity			.69
(1 = not threatening; 7 = very threatening)			
5. The business environment as threatening the survival of your firm	.68	.35	.64
6. Tough price competition threatening	.79	.25	.69
7. Competitors' product quality or novelty	.26	.25	.51

Appendix 7.B: Correlations of Constructs

	MO	IN/DI	IN/D2	LCS1	LCS2	FORM1	FORM2	DCENT1	DCENT2	PRDIF1	PRDIF2
MO	1.00										
IN/DI	.26*	1.00									
IN/D2	.22*	.54**	1.00								
LCS1	.19	.06	-.09	1.00							
LCS2	-.09	-.16	-.04	.44**	1.00						
FORM1	.16	.15*	.22*	.00	.00	1.00					
FORM2	.38**	.16	.34**	-.03	-.01	.67**	1.00				
DCENT1	-.02	.18**	.03	.06	-.04	.18**	.06	1.00			
DCENT2	.24*	-.01	-.11	.16	.18	.07	.14	.35**	1.00		
PRDIF1	.19	.20*	.07	.05	-.07	.05	.08	-.03	-.01	1.00	
PRDIF2	.24*	-.04	.14	.03	.09	-.11	-.02	-.13	-.02	.27*	1.00
COORD1	.25*	-.01	-.12	-.13	-.06	.31**	.29**	.22**	.16	.16*	.11
COORD2	.28*	.33**	.24*	-.01	-.09	.27**	.24**	.26**	.24*	.13	.20*
CONSYS1	.28*	.31**	.27*	.03	.02	.35**	.41**	.22**	.20*	.12	.12
CONSYS2	.46**	.09	.14	.13	-.04	.30**	.34**	.15	.32**	.08	.05
DYNA1	.06	.15	.17	-.09	-.06	.02	-.09	.01	-.10	.16*	.21*
DYNA2	.24*	.20*	.30**	-.02	.01	.02	.11	-.1	.01	.18	.22*
CI1	.37**	.06	.02	.21*	.02	.13	.23*	.03	.09	.11	.17
CI2	.10	.00	-.05	.17	.26**	.00	.05	.32**	.16	.17	.16
NPS1	.10	.11	.14	.01	-.11	.18*	.15	.20*	.05	.18*	.08
NPS2	.44**	54**	.49**	.11	-.10	.24*	.25*	.03	.05	.18	-.07
RPQ2	.22	.01	-.02	.06	.03	.03	.11	-.14	.14	-.02	.18
GRWSH1	.11	-.05	-.22*	.05	-.12	.10	.08	.03	.08	-.05	.11
GRWSH2	.32**	.06	.06	-.01	-.17	.10	.13	-.04	.23*	.14	-.01
PROF1	-.10	-.08	-.12	.01	-.07	.01	-.09	.02	-.02	-.12	.06
PROF2	.38**	-.06	.01	-.02	-.19	.02	.16	-.08	.11	-.10	-.01

	COORD1	COORD2	CONSYS1	CONSYS2	DYNA1	DYNA2	CI1	CI2	NPS1	NPS2	RPQ2	GRWSH1	GRWSH2	PROF1
COORD1	1.00													
COORD2	.59**	1.00												
CONSYS1	.32**	.49**	1.00											
CONSYS2	.27**	.24*	.59**	1.00										
DYNA1	.24*	.15*	.13	-.01	1.00									
DYNA2	.25*	.14	.32**	.15	.20**	1.00								
CI1	.17*	.08	.19**	.26**	.06	.23*	1.00							
CI2	.05	.10	.09	.02	.15	-.01	.42**	1.00						
NPS1	.04	.13	.13	.11	.19*	.12	-.06	-.13	1.00					
NPS2	.23*	.29*	.27**	.40**	.10	.34**	.17	-.03	.27*	1.00				
RPQ2	.01	.24*	.09	.14	-.01	-.01	-.01	-.08	-.20	.14	1.00			
GRWSH1	.11	.10	.10	.22*	-.01	-.03	-.15	-.12	.32**	.03	-.12	1.00		
GRWSH2	.18	.08	.14	.34**	-.04	.01	-.01	-.08	.08	.36**	.27**	.21	1.00	
PROF1	.02	.23*	.14	.21	.13	.01	-.01	-.14	.13	-.02	.05	.50**	.14	1.00
PROF2	-.10	.02	.18	.32**	-.09	.05	-.25**	-.07	-.29**	-.02	.42**	.01	.59**	.22*

NOTE: Numbers after construct refer to year that data were gathered. Response base: Year 1 (1992) = 145-370 respondents; Year 2 (1993) = 79-210 respondents. CI, market competitive intensity; CONSYS, control systems; COORD, coordination in structure; DCENT, decentralization in structure; DYNA, market dynamism; FORM, formalization in structure; GRWSH, firm growth/share; IN/D, innovation/niche/differentiation strategy; LCS, low cost strategy; MO, market orientation; NPS, new product success; PRDIF, product differentiation in structure; PROF, firm profitability; RPQ, relative product quality.

*p < .05; **p < .01.

Appendix 7.C: Means and Standard Deviations for Constructs

Construct	1992 Mean	SD	1993 Mean	SD	Difference 1993–1992 Mean	SD	Difference 1993–1991 Mean	SD
Market orientation			5.48	.79				
Innovation/differentiation strategy	4.50	1.27	4.51	1.38	.21	1.26		
Low cost strategy	3.57	1.25	3.60	3.60	.19	1.36		
Formalization	.53	.37	.60	.32	.09	.28	.05	.31
Decentralization	1.65	.86	2.53	1.32	.98	1.30	.90	1.38
Product differentiation structure	3.78	1.52	4.09	1.23	.31	1.67	.22	1.76
Coordination	3.26	1.46	3.19	1.32	-.01	1.63	.22	1.65
Control systems	3.89	1.75	4.46	1.63	.48	1.51	.28	1.76
Dynamism in environment	3.51	1.10	3.84	1.00	.25	1.22	.08	1.50
Competitive intensity	3.97	1.18	4.46	1.19	.62	1.29	.75	1.31
New product success	3.96	.97	4.23	1.33	.19	1.39		
Relative product quality			5.04	1.42				
Growth/share	3.89	1.03	4.18	1.25	.21	1.43		
Profitability	3.67	1.24	4.20	1.51	.38	1.72		

NOTE: All scales are from 1 to 7, with the exception of formalization (0 = no; 1 = yes) and decentralization (0 = high; 5 = low).

References

Barney, J. (1986). Organizational culture: Can it be a source of sustained competitive advantage? *Academy of Management Review, 11,* 656-665.

Buzzell, R. D. (1981). Are there natural market structures? *Journal of Marketing, 45*(1), 42-51.

Buzzell, R. D. (1987). *The PIMS principles.* New York: Free Press.

Buzzell, R. D., Gale, B. T., & Sultan, G. M. (1975, January/February). Market share—A key to profitability. *Harvard Business Review, 53,* 97-106.

Day, G. S., & Wensley, R. (1983). Marketing theory with a strategic orientation. *Journal of Marketing, 47*(4), 79-89.

Day, G. S., & Wensley, R. (1988). Assessing advantage: A framework for diagnosing competitive superiority. *Journal of Marketing, 52*(2), 1-20.

Dennison, D. (1984). Bringing corporate culture to the bottom line. *Organizational Dynamics, 13*(2), 5-22.

Deshpandé, R., Farley, J. U., & Webster, F. E., Jr. (1993). Corporate culture, customer orientation, and innovativeness in Japanese firms: A quadrad analysis. *Journal of Marketing, 57*(1), 23-37. (See also Chapter 4)

Deshpandé, R., & Zaltman, G. (1982, February). Factors affecting the use of market research information: A path analysis. *Journal of Marketing Research, 19,* 14-31.

Duncan, O. D. (1971). Path analysis: Sociological examples. In H. M. Blalock (Ed.), *Causal models in the social sciences* (pp. 115-138). Chicago: Aldine-Atheson.

Gordon, G. G., & Tomaso, N. (1992, November). Predicting corporate performance from organizational culture. *Journal of Management Studies, 29,* 783-798.

Grinyer, P. H., Yasai-Ardekanii, M., & Al-Bazzaz, S. (1980). Strategy, structure, the environment and financial performance in 48 United Kingdom companies. *Academy of Management Journal, 23,* 193-220.

Hambrick, D. C. (1983). High profit strategies in mature capital goods industries: A contingency approach. *Academy of Management Journal, 26,* 687-707.

Hansen, G. S., & Wernerfelt, B. (1989). Determinants of firm performance: The relative importance of economic and organizational factors. *Strategic Management Journal, 10,* 399-411.

Hill, C. W. L., & Pickering, J. F. (1986). Divisionalization, decentralization, and performance in large United Kingdom companies. *Journal of Management Studies, 1,* 26-50.

Jacobson, R. (1988). Distinguishing among competing theories of the market share effect. *Journal of Marketing, 52*(4), 68-80.

Jaworski, B. J., & Kohli, A. (1993). Market orientation: Antecedents and consequences. *Journal of Marketing, 57*(3), 53-71. (See also Chapter 5)

Khandwalla, P. N. (1977). *The design of organizations.* New York: Harcourt, Brace, Jovanovich.

Kohli, A. K., & Jaworski, B. J. (1990). Market orientation: The construct, research propositions, and managerial implications. *Journal of Marketing, 54*(2), 1-18. (See also Chapter 2)

Lado, A. A., Boyd, N. G., & Wright, P. (1992). A competency-based model of sustainable competitive advantage: Toward a conceptual integration. *Journal of Management, 18,* 77-91.

Lawrence, P. R., & Lorsch, J. (1967). *Organizations and environment.* Boston: Harvard University Press.

Miles, R. E., & Snow, C. C. (1978). *Organizational strategy, structure, and process.* New York: McGraw-Hill.

Miller, D. (1988). Strategic process and content as mediators between organizational context and structure. *Academy of Management Journal, 31*(3), 544-569.

Miller, D., & Droge, C. (1986, December). Psychological and traditional determinants of structure. *Administrative Science Quarterly, 31,* 539-560.

Narver, J. C., & Slater, S. F. (1990). The effect of a market orientation on business profitability. *Journal of Marketing, 54*(4), 20-35. (See also Chapter 3)

Park, M.-H., & Mason, J. B. (1990). Toward an integrated model of determinants of business performance. *Research in Marketing, 10,* 157-201.

Pelham, A. (1993). *Mediating and moderating influences on the relationship between market orientation and performance.* Unpublished doctoral dissertation, The Pennsylvania State University, University Park.

Peters, T., & Waterman, R. H. (1982). *In search of excellence: Lessons from America's best run companies.* New York: Harper & Row.

Phillips, L. W., Chang, D. R., & Buzzell, R. D. (1983). Product quality, cost position and business performance: A test of some key hypotheses. *Journal of Marketing, 47*(2), 26-43.

Porter, M. E. (1979). How competitive forces shape strategy. *Harvard Business Review, 57,* 137-145.

Prescott, J. E. (1986). Environment as moderators of the relationship between strategy and performance. *Academy of Management Journal, 29*(2), 324-344.

Reed, R., & DeFillippi, R. (1990). Causal ambiguity, barriers to imitation, and sustainable competitive advantage. *Academy of Management Review, 15,* 88-102.

Robinson, R. B., & Pearce, J. A. (1984). Research thrusts in small firm strategic planning. *Academy of Management Review, 9,* 128-137.

Saffold, G. S., III. (1988). Culture traits, strength, and organizational performance: Moving beyond "strong" culture. *Academy of Management Review, 13*(4), 514-558.

Van de Ven, A. H., & Ferry, D. (1979). *Measurement and assessment of organization.* New York: John Wiley.

Venkatraman, N., & Prescott, J. E. (1990). Environment-strategy coalignment: An empirical test of its performance implications. *Strategic Management Journal, 11,* 1-24.

Weick, K. (1985). The significance of corporate culture. In P. J. Frost, L. F. Moore, M. R. Louis, C. Lundberg, & J. Martin (Eds.), *Organizational culture.* Beverly Hills, CA: Sage.

Zaltman, G., Duncan, R., & Holbek, J. (1973). *Innovations and organizations.* New York: John Wiley.

Market Orientation and Business Performance

An Analysis of Panel Data

John C. Narver
Robert L. Jacobson
Stanley F. Slater

The role of market orientation in improving business performance has been the subject of intense debate for more than three decades. Only in the past decade, however, have researchers empirically investigated the relationship between market orientation and business performance. Their findings provide mixed support for the long-held proposition that a business's performance is positively related to its market orientation. Even these positive findings must be viewed with skepticism because many studies have used cross-sectional databases, which cannot control for potentially unobservable, firm-specific effects. Panel data analysis—the pooling of time series and cross-sectional information—allows researchers to test and control for these effects.

This study reports the results of a panel data analysis investigating the effect of market orientation on two drivers of business performance: sales growth and return on investment (ROI). The study illuminates the issue for managers and researchers in two respects: In addition to providing insights into the relationship between market orientation and business performance, it examines the effectiveness of panel data analysis in evaluating this relationship.

195

The research sample consisted of 35 strategic business units (SBUs) in a *Fortune* 500 forest products company. In 1987 and 1991, the top management team of each SBU responded to a questionnaire dealing with the unit's market structure, environment, culture, policies, strategies, and performance in its principal market segments. The questionnaire generated self-reported measures of market orientation, sales growth, ROI, and customer retention. Using econometric techniques designed to control for unobserved business unit-specific factors, the authors found that market orientation and customer retention were significantly related to sales growth but not to ROI.

In theory, market orientation should affect both ROI and sales growth. These results suggest that this measure of market orientation taps behaviors in businesses that have a greater impact on sales growth than on ROI. Nonetheless, the findings indicate that the market-oriented behaviors measured in this study are related to business performance: The positive effect of market orientation on sales growth will increase profits as long as ROI is greater than the cost of capital. These results suggest that managers foster a market orientation in their organizations while paying close attention to the selection of target markets and the allocation of effort among competing opportunities to maximize the potential for sales growth and profitability.

The positive relationship between market orientation and sales growth reinforces the conclusions of previous research. The absence of a significant relationship between market orientation and ROI provides a challenge for future research. Analysis of more firms, for more years, with shorter intervals between observations would strengthen understanding of the impact of market orientation on ROI. In addition, emphasis should be placed on measuring behaviors in firms that more directly affect rate of return. Given the limitations of ROI as a measure of rate of return, future research should employ a different performance measure. It would be useful, for example, to link market orientation to stock return.

As the study shows, panel data analysis gives researchers the opportunity to test and isolate firm-specific factors influencing the market orientation-ROI relationship, thus yielding a truer picture of the relationship across all firms. It remains for future research to provide additional insights into market orientation's effects on performance and to develop more accurate measures of the behaviors that underlie a market orientation in firms.

For more than three decades, the role of market orientation in improving business performance has been the subject of intense debate (Kohli & Jaworski, 1990; Narver & Slater, 1990). Only recently have researchers empirically investigated the effect of a market orientation on business performance. The empirical findings provide mixed support for the long-held proposition that a business's performance is positively related to its market orientation. Resolution of this issue is critical to managers, who must weigh the benefits of being market oriented against the costs of developing a market-oriented business culture.

Narver and Slater (1990) find a positive relationship between market orientation and return on assets (ROA). Slater and Narver (1994) find, in addition, a positive relationship between market orientation and sales growth. Jaworski and Kohli (1992) find a positive relationship between market orientation and a "judgmental" measure of business performance—that is, a measure based on respondents' assessments of their performance and their performance relative to competitors. They observe no significant relationship, however, between market orientation and either of their "objective" measures of business performance—market share and return on equity. Deshpandé, Farley, and Webster (1993) find that businesses' customer orientation as reported by customers is positively related to a four-item scale of business performance (a measure that combines 3-point scale evaluations of relative profitability, size, market share, and growth). They do not detect a similar relationship between businesses' customer orientation as reported by sellers and the four-item performance scale, however. Additional analysis of the effect of market orientation on the key dimensions of business performance is clearly warranted.

All studies to date on the effect of market orientation rely on cross-sectional analysis and ordinary least squares estimation. Hausman and Taylor (1981) point out that panel data analysis—pooling time series and cross-sectional information—enables researchers to test and control for firm-specific effects—possibly unobservable—that may be correlated with the explanatory factors in the analysis. The presence of these firm-specific factors leads to biased coefficient estimates in studies that do not control for their effects, creating a serious problem for all cross-sectional studies in that, as Hausman and Taylor (p. 1377) note, cross-sectional data alone "can neither identify nor control" for such effects.

Schmalensee (1989) states that "in the long-run equilibria with which cross-sectional studies must be primarily concerned, essentially all variables that have been employed in such studies are logically endogenous" (p. 954). Because previous market orientation studies have not modeled feedback effects, to the extent that market orientation is endogenous, the findings from these studies are subject to possible simultaneous-equation bias. Noting the potential benefits of panel data, Schmalensee observes that temporal ordering (i.e., predetermined variables) allows for instrumental variable estimation and the ability to prevent simultaneous-equation bias. He points out that cross-sectional analysis is limited in this regard because "there are in general no theoretically endogenous variables that can be used as instruments" (p. 954).

These considerations, and the ability of panel data techniques to obtain more efficient estimates of the parameters than would be achieved by, for example, making use of data that averaged yearly estimates, suggest that panel data analysis can offer more accurate insights into the effect of market orientation on business performance than those supplied by previous cross-sectional research. Indeed, some studies questioned the ability of cross-sectional research to provide strategic insights. Jacobson (1990), for example, contends that the bias caused by failing to control for unobserved factors in cross-sectional research may lead to "grossly misleading" coefficient estimates.

This chapter reports the results of a panel data analysis investigating the effect of a market orientation on two drivers of business performance: sales growth and return on investment (ROI). To control for industrywide effects, both measures are reported relative to marketplace norms: Respondents report relative sales growth (market share growth) and relative ROI.[1] The study not only provides insights into the relationship between market orientation and business performance but also suggests how panel data analysis can produce a better understanding of this relationship across firms.

Our research sample consisted of 35 strategic business units (SBUs) in a *Fortune* 500 forest products company. In 1987 and 1991, we asked the top management team of each SBU to respond to a questionnaire dealing with the unit's market structure, environment, culture, policies, strategies, and performance in its principal market segments. The questionnaire generated self-reported measures of market orientation, sales growth, ROI, and customer retention.

We found that market orientation is significantly related to sales growth but not to ROI. In theory, market orientation should affect both; thus, a measure of market orientation should tap behaviors that influence each of these outcomes. Our results suggest that the measure of market orientation used in this study taps behaviors that have greater impact on sales growth than on ROI. Nonetheless, our findings indicate that the market-oriented behaviors measured in this study are related to business performance: The positive effect of market orientation on sales growth will increase profits as long as ROI is greater than the cost of capital for the business. Thus, we encourage managers to foster a market orientation in their organizations while paying close attention to the selection of target markets and the allocation of effort among competing opportunities to maximize the potential for sales growth and profitability.

We examine theoretical linkages between market orientation and sales growth and ROI. Next, we describe our study—its data sample, construct measures, modeling approach, and empirical results. We conclude with suggestions for future research.

Market Orientation and Business Performance: Theoretical Linkages

A market-oriented business culture is one in which all employees are committed to the continuous creation of superior value for customers (Narver & Slater, 1990). The orientation of the business is external in that it continuously collects and internally disseminates information about customers, competitors, and other key business influencers. A market-oriented firm draws on all functional areas to create competitive advantage. As such, market orientation is regarded as a theoretically important determinant of business performance (Day, 1990).

Narver and Slater (1990) describe market orientation as consisting of three behavioral components: a customer orientation, a competitor orientation, and an interfunctional coordination.[2] A customer orientation enables a business to continuously learn about the perceptions and needs of its current and potential target customers. A competitor orientation enables a business to continuously learn and monitor the strategies and capabilities of the businesses that are the principal alternative current or future satisfiers of the target customers' needs. Interfunctional coordination means that a business continuously applies its skills and resources to the tasks of evaluating customer and competitor information and developing and implementing superior value for the target customers. Theory suggests that the three components of market orientation are of equal importance in affecting business performance.

On the basis of the strong role that a market orientation theoretically plays in generating superior customer value, we expect market orientation to positively affect a firm's total profits by positively affecting both the firm's sales growth and its ROI. Strengthening market orientation should, all else being equal, result in favorable shifts in a firm's demand and cost curves. The shift in the demand curve provides the business with three options: (a) retain current prices with resulting unit-volume increases, (b) retain unit volume and increasing prices, or (c) exploit the advantage with both price and volume increases. The first option results in a positive relationship between market orientation and sales, the second option results in a positive relationship between market orientation and ROI, and the third option results in a positive relationship between market orientation and sales and ROI.

Similarly, favorable shifts in its cost curve provide the firm with the options of (a) retaining current prices with resulting margin (ROI) increases, (b) passing along the cost saving in terms of lower price (i.e., hold margin constant) and increasing unit sales, or (c) passing along only some of the cost saving in terms of lower price and thereby increasing both margin and volume. How firms choose to exploit the advantages created by market orientation will influence the strength of the relationship of market orientation to sales growth and ROI. Although the strength of the relationship is likely to differ among firms, as long as all firms do not engage in a strategy of either strictly holding margin constant or strictly holding unit sales constant, market orientation will be positively correlated with both sales growth and ROI.

Effects of Market Orientation on Demand

It is a commonplace notion that a customer is attracted to a seller and remains with a seller as long as the customer perceives superior value from the seller. As an organization strengthens its market orientation, it increases its opportunities to create superior customer value, which may manifest itself in (a) increases in sales to new and current customers and (b) increases in ROI. When a business does not create superior value for prospective customers, it gives them no reason to purchase its products. Also, when a business does not create superior value for current customers, it gives them no reason to continue to purchase its products. A poor alignment with prospective customers and a poor relationship with current customers reduces revenues and increases costs.

A market-oriented business, by contrast, identifies opportunities to create and sustain superior value for both prospective and current customers. Through its customer and competitor orientations, a market-oriented seller can continuously (a) identify appropriate bases for segmenting and targeting markets; (b) discover and track both the expressed and latent needs of the target customers; (c) understand who the target customers consider the principal alternative satisfiers and their strengths, weaknesses, and intentions; (d) best position its products or brands vis-à-vis the target customers; and (e) implement additional benefits for the target customers and appropriately price them to create superior value for both the customers and the business (Forbis & Mehta, 1981; Levitt, 1980). Furthermore, a market orientation facilitates a business's understanding of the factors underlying market demand (Day, 1991; Senge, 1990), which enables the business to prosper in a dynamic marketplace.

These activities enable the market-oriented firm to attract new customers and retain current customers. Through its customer orientation and competitor orientation, a market-oriented seller gains and maintains an expertise on market demand that enables it to identify the most desirable potential customers and create superior value for them. A market orientation is also critical to "relationship marketing" (Jackson, 1985; Webster, 1992). A market-oriented business understands the substantial long-term revenue and profit streams that loyal customers generate (Reichheld, 1993; Reichheld & Sasser, 1990). Webster (1992) contends that an ongoing relationship with a set of customers is a business's most important asset; on average, however, businesses lose approximately 20% of their customers every year (Hanan, 1985; Kotler, 1992; Sellers, 1989). By skillfully managing its interactions with its customers, a market-oriented business minimizes customer defections. The business can then better "grow" its current customers, thus increasing the magnitude of each customer's purchases and the business's share of each customer's purchases. Furthermore, through word of mouth and other means, these loyal customers help attract new customers to the business (Reichheld, 1993).

Effects of Market Orientation on Costs

A market orientation should favorably affect a firm's cost curve and its demand curve. A market orientation lowers a business's costs in two principal ways. First, because market-oriented businesses understand the expressed and latent needs of their current and new target customers, they continuously identify and capitalize on opportunities to add customer benefits. They streamline the non-value-adding areas of the company through outsourcing, which permits staff reductions and other efficiencies (Quinn, Doorley, & Paquette, 1990; Stalk, Evans, & Shulman, 1992). They remain efficient by staying focused on what is of the greatest expressed and latent interest to their target customers. Second, through the superior customer value and resulting sales volumes, a market-oriented business can best capture available economies of scale, volume, and scope.

The market-oriented business achieves lower short- and long-run costs principally because it learns how to (a) segment its markets given its core competencies and growth strategies, (b) identify the latent needs of both potential and current customers, (c) attract new customers, and (d) retain and increase its current customers (Day, 1990). These customer-attraction and customer-retention efficiencies directly affect the firm's marketing costs, and the increased sales volumes directly affect the firm's other operating costs.

The Study: What Is the Impact of Market Orientation on Sales Growth and ROI?

Hypotheses

The maximum profit opportunity for a business occurs when it increases demand for its products and achieves low relative costs—a position of advantage that Day (1990) calls "playing the spread." In principle, a market-oriented business is especially equipped to play the spread (Reichheld, 1993). By adding customer benefits, it can increase demand in benefit-sensitive segments, and by lowering price it can increase the quantity demanded in price-sensitive segments, all the while increasing its efficiency and capturing available economies.

The preceding arguments suggest, then, that a market orientation will enable a business to achieve superior profits within its industry. Other things being equal, a market-oriented business, relative to its competition, will achieve (a) superior sales growth and (b) superior ROI. Accordingly, we offer the following two hypotheses:

H_1: Market orientation has a positive effect on relative sales growth.

H_2: Market orientation has a positive effect on relative ROI.

By testing these two hypotheses, this study seeks to empirically assess how market orientation affects business performance. It also examines the effectiveness of panel data analysis techniques in measuring this relationship. Because a host of factors other than market orientation influence supply and demand and hence business profitability, however, it may be difficult to empirically uncover and isolate the impact of market orientation. That is, the "signal" to "noise" ratio may be inadequate given the limited number of data points in our sample (70 observations). Nonetheless, theory depicts the impact of market orientation on business success as being so powerful that strong links between market orientation and both sales growth and ROI should exist.

Data

Sample. The sample consists of 35 SBUs in a *Fortune* 500 forest products company. The SBUs are wholesalers engaged in the marketing of products that come primarily from within the corporation. They sell to several different types of customers, including building supply retailers (both independents and chains) and industrial users (e.g., cabinet manufacturers). Their competitors are mostly independent distributors (many of whom are more specialized than the sample wholesalers) and wholesalers of another *Fortune* 500 forest products company.

We sent a questionnaire to the top management team members (defined as those managers who know the SBU's strategy, performance, and policies) of each of the SBUs in 1987 and again in 1991. The top management team for each of the 35 SBUs, ranging from one to five people, was identified by the senior management of the building materials distribution division of the corporation. A senior executive estimates that during the 1987 to 1991 period, turnover among the members of the SBUs' top management teams was less than 10%. In 1987, there was a total of 121 top management team members in the 35 SBUs; 97 completed the questionnaire (a response rate of 80%). In 1991, the top management team members totaled 110; of these, 100 responded (a response rate of 91%).

The survey consisted of questions about the SBU's market structure, environment, culture, policies, strategies, and performance in its principal

Table 8.1 Descriptive Statistics (Measures Based on 7-Point Likert Scales)[a]

				Percentile	
Variable	Mean	SD	Median	10th	90th
Market orientation	4.83	.56	4.87	4.14	5.67
ΔMarket orientation	−.01	.76	.06	−.95	1.00
Customer retention rate	5.83	.77	6.00	4.50	7.00
ΔCustomer retention rate	.21	.82	.00	−.67	1.33
Relative sales growth	4.88	1.23	5.00	3.00	6.33
ΔRelative sales growth	−.21	1.61	−.17	−2.33	1.33
Relative ROI	5.04	.94	5.00	4.00	6.00
ΔRelative ROI	−0.28	1.15	0.00	−1.33	0.67

NOTE: The sample was composed of 35 business units for the years 1987 and 1991.

a. Change (Δ) reflects the difference between 1991 and 1987 values.

served market segment (PSMS). A 7-point Likert-type scale was used for each question. Because multiple respondents reported for a given SBU, the mean response for each SBU was calculated and used as the score for that SBU. This averaging of the individual respondents' scores reduces the measurement error associated with any individual response and increases the reliability of the response (Cook & Campbell, 1979).

Variable Definitions. The self-reported measures of market orientation, sales growth, return on investment, and customer retention are as follows:[3]

1. Market orientation (MO): We use the Narver and Slater (1990) measure of market orientation based on the average of an SBU's customer orientation, competitor orientation, and interfunctional coordination scores. Cronbach's alphas for customer orientation, competitor orientation, and interfunctional coordination, respectively, are .83, .80, and .67 for the 1987 data and .86, .75, and .62 for the 1991 data.

2. Relative sales growth (SG): Relative sales growth is the sales growth of the SBU relative to that of all competitors in the PSMS in the past year. The median interrater reliabilities for all SBUs for sales growth are .88 and .50 for 1987 and 1991, respectively, following James, Demaree, and Wolf (1984).

3. Relative ROI: The relative ROI is the ROI of the SBU relative to that of all competitors in the PSMS in the past year. The median interrater reliabilities for ROI are .88 and .88 for 1987 and 1991, respectively.

4. Relative customer retention (CRR): Relative customer retention is the rate at which the SBU has retained customers relative to all competitors in the PSMS in the past year. The median interrater reliabilities for customer retention are .92 and .88 for 1987 and 1991, respectively (Table 8.1).

Modeling Approach

The Random Effects Model. Our base model involves regressions of market orientation and customer retention on relative SG and relative ROI:

$$BP_{it} = \alpha_0 + \beta_1 MO_{it} + \beta_2 CRR_{it} + \varepsilon_{it} \qquad [8.1]$$

where BP_{it}, MO_{it}, and CRR_{it} are, respectively, the business performance, market orientation, and customer retention of business unit i in period t. Separate regressions are estimated for the two measures of business performance, SG and ROI.

The error term ε_{it} reflects the influence of omitted factors influencing performance. Some of the factors reflected by the error term can be posited to be specific to a particular business unit. As such, the error term in Equation 8.1 can be expressed as $\varepsilon_{it} = \mu_i + \eta_{it}$, where μ_i is an unobserved time-invariant business unit-specific factor, and η_{it} is a nonautocorrelated contemporaneous shock. This structure of the error term induces a block diagonal variance-covariance matrix and, as such, calls for the use of generalized least squares (GLS). As long as μ_i and η_{it} are uncorrelated with the explanatory factors included in the model, ordinary least squares (OLS) and GLS estimation generates consistent coefficient estimates. The reported standard errors from OLS estimation programs, however, will be biased and inconsistent. The GLS model (known as the random effects model in the analysis of panel data literature; Chamberlain, 1984; Hsiao, 1986) not only generates unbiased standard errors but also is asymptotically efficient—that is, there is minimum variance.

The Fixed Effects Model. The random effects model assumes no correlation between the explanatory factors and the unobserved firm-specific factor μ_i. Many researchers (Mundlak, 1978) have criticized the random effects specification because of the restrictiveness of this assumption. Indeed, many theories of firm performance (e.g., resource-based perspectives) emphasize the interrelatedness of invisible assets and strategic choices. The "fixed effects" model takes into account the possible correlation of strategic factors with unobservable factors that persist over time. Allowing for fixed effects of this type necessitates modeling business performance as

$$BP_{it} = \alpha_i + \beta_1 MO_{it} + \beta_2 CRR_{it} + \varepsilon_{it} \qquad [8.2]$$

Equation 8.2 differs from Equation 8.1 in that it allows for time-invariant (fixed) unobserved factors that differ across business units. The effect of these fixed factors is reflected in the business unit-specific constant α_i. To the extent that these fixed factors are correlated with the observed variables included in the model, OLS or GLS estimation of Equation 8.1 will generate biased and inconsistent coefficient estimates.

To obtain consistent estimates of the effect of the observed strategic factors, we take deviations from business unit means for each variable. That is, we estimate the model

$$(BP_{it} - \overline{BP}_i) = \beta_1(MO_{it} - \overline{MO}_i) + \beta_2(CRR_{it} - \overline{CRR}_i) + (\varepsilon_{it} - \overline{\varepsilon}_{it}) \quad [8.3]$$

where $\overline{BP}_i$, $\overline{MO}_i$, and $\overline{CRR}_i$ are the mean values of BP, MO, and CRR for business unit i.

Equation 8.3, by taking deviations from mean values, removes the effect of all time-invariant factors. Equation 8.3 assesses how business performance differs for a business unit when its strategic factors differ from their mean values. Equation 8.3 is known as a "within-group estimator" because only the variation within each group is used in forming this estimator.

The Instrumental Variable Model. Even in the absence of fixed effects correlated with the explanatory factors, omitted variable bias may be present in the estimates obtained from Equation 8.1 to the extent that explanatory factors are correlated with the contemporaneous shock η_{it}.[4] This would reflect the fact that the explanatory factors may be correlated with unobservable factors whose effect on sales growth or ROI dissipates within a year. Eliminating the possible bias caused by a correlation of the explanatory factors with these nonautocorrelated unobservable factors can be accomplished by instrumental variable estimation.

To the extent that they are autocorrelated, lagged values of the series—that is, MO_{it-1} and CRR_{it-1}—can be used as instruments.[5] Because they occur temporally prior, they cannot be influenced by the contemporaneous shock. This phase of the modeling also removes simultaneous equation bias induced by the possible effect of sales growth on market orientation or customer retention. Substituting the instrumental variable estimates into Equation 8.1 yields

$$BP_{it} = \beta_1 IVMO + \beta_2 IVCRR_{it} + \varepsilon_{it} \qquad [8.4]$$

Equation 8.4 allows for consistent coefficient estimates in the presence of nonautocorrelated unobservable effects that are correlated with the explanatory factors.

Specification Testing. Under the null hypothesis that the random effects model accurately depicts the underlying structural model, the estimates from the random effects model should not differ significantly from those obtained from the fixed effects or instrumental variable models. That is, the random effects model estimates are consistent and efficient (i.e., minimum variance) under the null hypothesis that the fixed effects and the contemporaneous shocks are uncorrelated with the explanatory factors. Under the alternative hypothesis of omitted fixed effects or contemporaneous shocks correlated with the explanatory factors included in the model, however, the random effects estimates will be biased and inconsistent. The fixed effects estimates are consistent under both the null hypothesis (although inefficient) and the alternative hypothesis of the fixed effects being correlated with the explanatory factors. The instrumental variable estimates are consistent under the null hypothesis and the alternative hypothesis of the contemporaneous shocks being correlated with the explanatory factors. As such, under the null hypothesis of no misspecification, the difference between the estimates will be insignificantly different from zero. Hausman (1978) provides a chi-square test for assessing this difference.

Empirical Results

Market Orientation and Sales Growth. Table 8.2 provides the results from GLS estimation of Equation 8.1, the random effects model, for the sales growth measure. Both MO and CRR have positive and statistically significant associations with sales growth; the estimated coefficients are .460 and .468, respectively.

Table 8.2 also reports the results from the fixed effects model (Equation 8.3). Unlike the GLS (random effects) model, the fixed effects model allows for potential correlation between the time-invariant unobservable factors and the observed strategic factors. The estimated effects for MO (.287) and CRR (.400) are positive but statistically insignificant. Because the random effects estimates are asymptotically efficient under the null hypothesis, however, the central concern is not so much the significance of the fixed effects estimates

Table 8.2 The Effect of Market Orientation and Customer Retention on Sales
Growth (Dependent Variable: Relative Sales Growth)

	Random Effect	Fixed Effect	Constrained Random Effect	Constrained Fixed Effect	Constrained Instrumental Variable
Constant	−.074 (1.256)	—	.078 (1.250)	—	−4.154 (4.193)
Customer retention	.468 (.169)	.287 (.323)	—	—	—
Market orientation	.460 (.214)	.400 (.360)	—	—	—
Customer retention + market orientation			.465 (.116)	.337 (.238)	.830 (.402)
R^2	.15	.06	.15	.06	NA
No. of observations	70	70	70	70	35[a]
MSE	.801	.601	.802	.602	1.33
Specification test		$\chi^2_2 = .45$	$\chi^2_1 = .01$	$\chi^2_1 = .38$	$\chi^2_1 = .85$

NOTE: Random effects: $SG_{it} = \alpha + \beta_1 * MO_{it} + \beta_2 * CRR_{it} + (\mu_i + \varepsilon_{it})$; fixed effects: $SG_{it} = \alpha_i + \beta_1 * MO_{it} + \beta_2 * CRR_{it} + \varepsilon_{it}$; constrained random effects: $SG_{it} = \alpha + \beta \ (MO_{it} + CRR_{it}) + (\mu_i + \varepsilon_{it})$; constrained fixed effects: $SG_{it} = \alpha_i + \beta \ (MO_{it} + CRR_{it}) + \varepsilon_{it}$; instrumental variable: $SG_{it} = \alpha + \beta * IV(MO_{it} + CRR_{it}) + \varepsilon_{it}$. Standard errors are shown in parentheses.

a. The number of observations is reduced from the other models because the first year of data for each business unit cannot be used given the use of lagged CRR + MO as an instrumental variable.

but rather the significance of their difference from the random effects models. The Hausman specification test fails to reject the null hypothesis—that is, the test statistic of .45 is less than the .05 chi-square critical value of 5.99. This finding is consistent with market orientation and customer retention not being correlated with the business unit-specific factors affecting sales growth. Another interpretation of the lack of a significant difference between the fixed effects and random effects models concerns the possible lack of existence of a fixed effect in affecting sales growth. That is, the effects of unobservable factors affecting sales growth dissipate during the 4-year period.

An interesting result from the random effects estimation concerns the similarity of the estimated coefficients depicting the effect of market orientation and customer retention. Indeed, the estimated effects appear almost identical. To obtain more efficient estimates under the hypothesis that the effects are the same, we impose this constraint. Table 8.2 reports the results of this constrained estimation, $\beta_1 = \beta_2$, for the random effects and fixed effects models, respectively. Consistent with the similarity of the coefficient estimates for random effects, there is little loss in explanatory power from moving from the random effects to the constrained random effects model. We also find that the estimated coefficient for the constrained random effects model (.465) is insignificantly different from the constrained fixed effects estimate (.337).

To test for the possible impact of contemporaneous shocks inducing omitted variable bias, we estimate the constrained instrumental variable model. Using $MO_{it-1} + CRR_{it-1}$ as an instrument, we obtained an instrumental variable estimate of $MO_{it} + CRR_{it}$.[6] Table 8.2 reports the results of this estimation. The estimated coefficient (.830) is statistically significant and larger than the estimate obtained from the random effects (GLS) estimator. The difference is statistically insignificant, however: The Hausman specification test statistic of .85 is less than the .05 chi-square critical value of 5.99.[7] Thus, we cannot reject the assumption underlying the use of the random effects estimator.

Because the instrumental variable estimate is a linear function of $MO_{it-1} + CRR_{it-1}$, this result could be reinterpreted as establishing that MO + CRR leads sales growth, thus suggesting the possibility of carryover effects. To obtain insights into possible carryover effects, we regressed current and lagged market orientation and customer retention on sales growth. That is, we estimated the model

$$SG_{it} = \alpha_0 + \delta_1(MO_{it} + CRR_{it}) + \delta_2(MO_{it-1} + CRR_{it-1}) + \delta_3(SG_{it-1}) + \varepsilon_{it}$$

The estimated coefficients (standard errors) were as follows: $\delta_1 = .41$ (.234), $\delta_2 = .20$ (.218), and $\delta_3 = -.05$ (.195). The small and insignificant coefficient for δ_3 suggests that the autocorrelation in yearly sales growth, if it exists, dissipates within 4 years. The positive estimate for δ_2 suggests the possible presence of carryover effects. With a t statistic of .917, however, any interpretation—for example, geometric decay—would be highly speculative. Clearly, future research should obtain annual data and test for carryover effects. Of particular interest would be to determine if a lagged effect was greater than the contemporaneous association.

Market Orientation and ROI. Table 8.3 provides the results from GLS estimation of Equation 8.1, the random effects model, for the ROI measure. The coefficients for MO and CRR are both positive (.306 and .100, respectively). Although neither effect is significant at the 5% level, the results suggest that market orientation has a positive impact on ROI.

To test for the presence of SBU-specific factors, Table 8.3 reports the results of the fixed effects estimation. The Hausman specification test statistic

Table 8.3 The Effect of Market Orientation and Customer Retention on ROI
(Dependent Variable: Relative ROI)

	Random Effect	Fixed Effect
Constant	2.98	—
	(1.11)	
Customer retention	.100	−.375
	(.156)	(.234)
Market orientation	.306	.061
	(.210)	(.260)
R^2	.05	.07
No. of observations	70	70
MSE	.69	.31
Specification test		$\chi^2_2 = 7.68$

NOTE: Random effects: $ROI_{it} = \alpha + \beta_1 * MO_{it} + \beta_2 * CRR_{it} + (\mu_i + \varepsilon_{it})$; fixed effects: $ROI_{it} = \alpha_i + \beta_1 * MO_{it} + \beta_2 * CRR_{it} + \varepsilon_{it}$. Standard errors are indicated in parentheses.

of 7.68 (compared with the .05 chi-square critical value of 5.99) allows us to reject the null hypothesis of the random effects model and suggests the applicability of a fixed effects model. The estimated effect of market orientation on ROI in the fixed effects estimation is small and insignificantly different from zero—that is, an estimated coefficient of .06 with a standard error of .26.[8] Thus, after allowing for firm-specific fixed factors, we do not find evidence of a significant association of market orientation with ROI.

Conclusions and Directions for Future Research

The results of using panel data to investigate the relationship between market orientation and performance partly support and partly conflict earlier findings based on cross-sectional analysis. We find that both market orientation and customer retention are positively related to a business's sales growth. Indeed, our analysis shows the effects of market orientation and customer retention on sales growth to be virtually identical. We find that neither market orientation nor customer retention is significantly positively related to ROI.[9]

In theory, a business's market orientation should affect both ROI and sales growth. Thus, a market orientation measure must tap behaviors that influence each of these outcomes. The results of this study suggest that our measure of market orientation taps behaviors that are more closely related to sales growth than to ROI.[10] Even if this is the case, our results suggest that the market orientation measure used in the study is nevertheless related to business performance. That is, because we do not find a negative effect of market orientation on ROI, market orientation's positive effect on sales growth will increase total profits as long as ROI is greater than the cost of capital for the business.[11] Still, because it is common for increases in ROI to generate higher profits than increases in sales (Alberts, 1989), a market-oriented business should be concerned with ROI. Measures of market orientation should thus capture behaviors that affect ROI.

Future research must further assess the empirical relationship (or the lack thereof) between market orientation and ROI. Our analysis could be strengthened to better deal with such problems as low statistical power, inadequacies in modeling the unobserved factors, and potential measurement error in the data and the constructs. Although the signal-to-noise ratio appears sufficiently strong to detect a relationship for the sales growth model, our statistical tests have low power given the small size of our sample. Analysis of more firms for more years would help alleviate this problem. Furthermore, having data of higher frequency—that is, with intervals of less than 4 years—is likely to yield more powerful instrumental variable estimates. In particular, a data interval of 1 year would yield more observations but be sufficiently long to allow for changes in market orientation.

Having more time series information would not only generate a larger sample but also allow for the estimation of models involving other types of unobservable factors besides fixed effects. For example, a minimum of three time periods is required to estimate an instrumental variable/fixed effects model, one that allows not only for firm-specific effects but also for the potential correlation between market orientation and the contemporaneous shocks influencing ROI. The modeling could also address the role played by autocorrelated unobservables—factors that persist longer than 1 year but that dissipate over time. The cooperation of firms would be critical to executing a more meaningful longitudinal study.

Additional research involving different and improved measures is also warranted. In particular, given the weak linkage between past measures of market orientation and ROI, emphasis should be placed on measuring behaviors that more directly affect rate of return. Moreover, given the widely recognized limitations of ROI as a measure of rate of return (Fisher & McGowan, 1983), future research should employ a different performance measure. Because alternative accounting measures have many of the same deficiencies (if not more) as ROI, it would be useful to link market orientation to stock return. Such analysis could assess how changes in market orientation influence stock market participants' expectations of future cash flows.

The positive relationship that we found between market orientation and sales growth reinforces and strengthens the conclusions of previous research. The lack of a relationship between market orientation and ROI provides a challenge for future research. Although additional cross-sectional analysis of the market orientation-ROI relationship may be suggestive, research using panel data is required to effectively test and isolate the underlying relationships. Further research using panel data is needed not only to provide additional insights into how market orientation affects business performance but also to assist in the development of measures that more accurately tap the management behaviors underlying market orientation.

Appendix 8.A: Market Orientation Questionnaire

Market Orientation Questionnaire Items [On the actual instrument, some items are worded negatively to avoid a response bias and the labels "Custo" (customer), "Compo" (competitor), and "Coord" (coordination) do not appear].*

In answering, use the following response scale and place the most appropriate number in the blank space to the left of each statement. Please respond to each statement.

Not at all 1	To a very slight extent 2	To a small extent 3	To a moderate extent 4	To a considerable extent 5	To a great extent 6	To an extreme extent 7

In our business—

Compo _____ Our salespeople regularly share information within our business concerning competitors' strategies.

Custo _____ Our business objectives are driven primarily by customer satisfaction.

Compo _____ We rapidly respond to competitive actions that threaten us.

Custo _____ We constantly monitor our level of commitment and orientation to serving customers' needs.

Coord	_____	Our top managers from every function regularly visit our current and prospective customers.
Coord	_____	We freely communicate information about our successful and unsuccessful customer experiences across all business functions.
Custo	_____	Our strategy for competitive advantage is based on our understanding of customers' needs.
Coord	_____	All of our business functions (e.g., marketing/sales, manufacturing, R&D, finance/accounting, etc.) are integrated in serving the needs of our target markets.
Custo	_____	Our business strategies are driven by our beliefs about how we can create greater value for customers.
Custo	_____	We measure customer satisfaction systematically and frequently.
Custo	_____	We give close attention to after-sales service.
Compo	_____	Top management regularly discusses competitors' strengths and strategies.
Coord	_____	All of our managers understand how everyone in our business can contribute to creating customer value.
Compo	_____	We target customers where we have an opportunity for competitive advantage.

	*Custo	Item from customer orientation subscale
	Compo	Item from competitor orientation subscale
	Coord	Item from interfunctional coordination subscale

Sales Growth and Customer Retention

Rate how well your business has performed relative to all other competitors in your principal served market segment (PSMS) over the past year.

1	2	3	4	5	6	7
<10%	11–25%	26–40%	41–55%	56–70%	71–85%	86–100%

Example: If you believe that your sales growth is greater than that of approximately 60% of all competitors in your PSMS, rate yourself a 5 for sales growth.

	Rating
Customer retention	_____
Sales growth	_____
Return on investment*	_____

*For this study, we consider CROI, ROI, ROA, and RONA to be equivalent.

Notes

1. Sales growth and ROI are two of the most commonly used business performance indicators by both managers and researchers (Hofer, 1983; Venkatraman & Ramanujam, 1986). The joint impact of sales and ROI on profits can be seen by first noting that business profits depend on (a) the spread between ROI and the cost of capital and (b) the amount of capital invested. That is, profit = invested capital $*$ (ROI $-$ k), where k is the risk-adjusted cost of capital. Restating the amount of capital invested as sales $*$ capital intensity (where capital intensity = invested capital/sales) yields the following: profits = sales $*$ capital intensity $*$ (ROI $-$ k). As such, given capital intensity and the cost of capital, sales and ROI jointly determine firm profits. Total profitability will increase with increases in ROI and, as long as the firm has a positive ROI to cost-of-capital spread, with increases in sales growth. Empirically, studies have shown that movements in both measures are associated with stock return. That is, stock market participants perceive both measures to contain information about current and future business performance. An extensive literature in accounting (Lev, 1989) documents a positive association of ROI with stock return. Although fewer studies have investigated the stock market reaction to sales growth, evidence suggests a significant positive association (although less than that of ROI). Nerlove (1968) and Stano (1976), for example, find that not only is sales growth positively correlated with stock return but also the association exists even when earnings growth is included in the analysis. That is, market participants perceive sales growth to contain information about future term business performance that is incremental to that depicted by earnings.

2. See, for example, Kohli and Jaworski (1990) for another operationalization of the market orientation construct.

3. Appendix 8.A supplies the questions used in constructing the measures. Table 8.1 provides descriptive statistics for the variables and the difference between the 1991 and 1987 values.

4. Instrumental variable estimation can also be undertaken in the presence of a fixed effect. This estimation, however, is infeasible with our data sample because it requires the use of variables of order 2 and higher—that is, observations for period $t - 2$ and prior—as instrumental variables. Because our sample does not include time series data of this order, we can test for this type of bias only if the hypothesis of fixed effects was rejected.

5. Because our data are measured at a 4-year increment, one increment in our analysis is 4 years—that is, for the 1991 data period $t - 1 = 1987$.

6. The regression of $MO_{it-1} + CRR_{it-1}$ on $MO_{it} + CRR_{it}$ yielded a coefficient of .41. This 4-year autocorrelation is consistent with a first-order yearly autocorrelation of .8—that is, $.8^4 = .4096$.

7. Due to the use of lagged values as an instrumental variable, only the data for 1991 are available for analysis and, as such, necessitate a comparison with the OLS estimate for 1991. We also estimated an instrumental variable model with separate estimates for CRR and MO. We were unable to reject the hypothesis that contemporaneous shocks are not present—that is, the assumption of the random effects model. The correlation of the instrumental variable estimates in this unconstrained model—that is, both are strongly related to lagged CRR—makes it difficult to separate the effects and limits the power of the test.

8. As discussed previously, having found evidence of a fixed effect, the limited time series information in our data sample precludes the estimating models that allow for correlation between the contemporaneous shocks affecting ROI and the explanatory factors.

9. Our analysis focused on the direct effects of market orientation on business performance. Indirect effects may also be present to the extent that market orientation affects customer

retention, which in turn affects the business performance measures. Empirically, however, we find little association between market orientation and customer retention. A fixed effects model of customer retention yields a small and statistically insignificant effect for market orientation—that is, a coefficient of −.0016 with a *t* statistic of .19.

10. Work by Slater and Narver (1993) provides further support for this conclusion. On the basis of a cross-sectional study of 228 Colorado businesses, they report a significant effect (.34) of market orientation on sales growth but find a small (.03) and statistically insignificant effect of market orientation on ROI.

11. Of course, we are limited in attaching any interpretation to the estimated effect of market orientation on ROI given the small *t* statistic and our inability to carry out additional specification tests (e.g., instrumental variable estimation).

References

Alberts, W. W. (1989). The experience curve doctrine reconsidered. *Journal of Marketing, 53*(3), 36-49.

Chamberlain, G. (1984). Panel data. In Z. Griliches & M. Intriligator (Eds.), *Handbook of econometrics* (pp. 1247-1318). Amsterdam: North Holland.

Cook, T. D., & Campbell, D. T. (1979). *Quasi-experimentation: Design & analysis issues for field settings.* Boston: Houghton Mifflin.

Day, G. S. (1990). *Market driven strategy.* New York: Free Press.

Day, G. S. (1991). *Learning about markets* (Report No. 91-117). Cambridge, MA: Marketing Science Institute.

Deshpandé, R., Farley, J. U., & Webster, F. E., Jr. (1993). Corporate culture, customer orientation, and innovativeness in Japanese firms: A quadrad analysis. *Journal of Marketing, 57*(1), 23-37. (See also Chapter 4)

Fisher, F. M., & McGowan, J. J. (1983, March). On the misuse of accounting rates of return to infer monopoly profits. *American Economic Review, 73,* 82-97.

Forbis, J. L., & Mehta, N. T. (1981, May/June). Value-based strategies for industrial products. *Business Horizons, 24,* 32-42.

Hanan, M. (1985). *Consultative selling* (3rd ed.). New York: AMACOM.

Hausman, J. A. (1978). Specification tests in econometrics. *Econometrica, 46,* 1251-1270.

Hausman, J. A., & Taylor, W. E. (1981). Panel data and unobservable individual effects. *Econometrica, 49,* 1377-1398.

Hofer, C. W. (1983). ROVA: A new measure for assessing organizational performance. In R. Lamb (Ed.), *Advances in strategic management 2* (pp. 43-55). New York: JAI.

Hsiao, C. (1986). *Analysis of panel data.* Cambridge, UK: Cambridge University Press.

Jackson, B. B. (1985). *Winning and keeping industrial customers.* Lexington, MA: Lexington Books.

Jacobson, R. (1990). Unobservable effects and business performance. *Marketing Science, 9,* 74-85.

James, L. R., Demaree, R. G., & Wolf, G. (1984, February). Estimating within-group interrater reliability with and without response bias. *Journal of Applied Psychology, 69,* 85-98.

Jaworski, B. J., & Kohli, A. K. (1992). *Market orientation: Antecedents and consequences* (Report No. 92-104). Cambridge, MA: Marketing Science Institute. (See also Chapter 5)

Kohli, A. K., & Jaworski, B. J. (1990). Market orientation: The construct, research propositions, and management implications. *Journal of Marketing, 54*(2), 1-18. (See also Chapter 2)

Kotler, P. (1992, September/October). Marketing's new paradigm: What's really happening out there. *Planning Review, 20,* 50-52.

Lev, B. (1989). On the usefulness of earnings and earnings research: Lessons and directions from two decades of empirical research. *Journal of Accounting Research, 27*(Suppl.), 153-192.

Levitt, T. (1980, January/February). Marketing success through differentiation—of anything. *Harvard Business Review, 58,* 83-91.

Mundlak, Y. (1978). On the pooling of time series and cross section data. *Econometrica, 46,* 69-85.

Narver, J. C., & Slater, S. F. (1990). The effect of a market orientation on business profitability. *Journal of Marketing, 54*(4), 20-35. (See also Chapter 3)

Nerlove, M. (1968, August). Factors affecting differences among rates of return on investments in individual common stocks. *Review of Economics and Statistics,* 312-331.

Quinn, J. B., Doorley, T. L., & Paquette, P. C. (1990, March/April). Beyond products: Service-based strategy. *Harvard Business Review, 68,* 2-8.

Reichheld, F. F. (1993, March/April). Loyalty-based management. *Harvard Business Review, 71,* 64-73.

Reichheld, F. F., & Sasser, W. E., Jr. (1990, September/October). Zero defections: Quality comes to services. *Harvard Business Review, 68,* 105-111.

Schmalensee, R. (1989). Inter-industry studies of structure and performance. In R. Schmalensee & R. D. Willig (Eds.), *Handbook of industrial organization* (Vol. 2, pp. 952-1009). Amsterdam: Elsevier.

Sellers, P. (1989, March 13). Getting customers to love you. *Fortune,* 38-49.

Senge, P. M. (1990, Fall). The leader's new work: Building learning organizations. *Sloan Management Review, 32,* 7-23.

Slater, S. F., & Narver, J. C. (1993). *The strategic profile of a market-oriented business* [Working paper]. Colorado Springs: University of Colorado-Colorado Springs, College of Business Administration.

Slater, S. F., & Narver, J. C. (1994). Does competitive environment moderate the market orientation-performance relationship? *Journal of Marketing, 58,* 46-55. (See also Chapter 6)

Stalk, G., Evans, P., & Shulman, L. E. (1992, March/April). Competing on capabilities: The new rules of corporate strategy. *Harvard Business Review, 70,* 57-69.

Stano, M. (1976, Autumn). Monopoly power, ownership control, and corporate performance. *Bell Journal of Economics,* 672-679.

Venkatraman, N., & Ramanujam, V. (1986, October). Measurement of business performance in strategy research: A comparison of approaches. *Academy of Management Review, 11,* 801-814.

Webster, F. E., Jr. (1992). The changing role of marketing in the corporation. *Journal of Marketing, 56*(4), 1-17.

Additional Reading

Boulding, W., & Staelin, R. (1990). Environment, market share, and market power. *Management Science, 36*(10), 1160-1178.

Ruekert, R. W. (1992, August). Developing a market orientation: An organizational strategy perspective. *International Journal of Research in Marketing, 9,* 225-245.

Understanding Market Orientation

A Prospectively Designed
Meta-Analysis of Three Market
Orientation Scales

Rohit Deshpandé
John U. Farley

In this study, Deshpandé and Farley synthesized existing measurements of market orientation to provide a parsimonious and predictive tool with which to measure this important strategic construct. The study is based on the work of Narver and Slater, Kohli and Jaworski, and Deshpandé, Farley, and Webster, who, in the late 1980s, developed three different but syntactically similar scales that measured the extent of a firm's market orientation. Since then, many studies have found that market orientation is associated with better performance.

The purpose of the study is twofold. First, it provides a tested scale by which practitioners can assess market orientation. Second, by taking stock of accumulated knowledge regarding market orientation early in the development of this field, the study aims to direct researchers' attention toward potentially fruitful research options.

Using a multinational sample of 82 marketing executives from 27 firms, the authors assessed how the scales relate to one another, to various validity measures, and to performance. Then, synthesizing these measurements, they developed a new 10-item managerially oriented scale to assess a firm's market orientation.

In addition, as a result of this scale development, they were able to more parsimoniously define market orientation as "the set of cross-functional processes and activities directed at creating and satisfying customers through continuous needs assessment" (p. 228).

There is a clear and encouraging movement afoot in marketing to attempt to draw generalizations from existing bodies of work. The impetus for such work comes from a number of sources, not the least of which is managers' impatience with specialized and frequently arcane research that does not seem broadly applicable. Examples of work in the direction of such synthesis include a special issue of *Marketing Science* (1995) dealing with empirical generalizations in marketing and a similar issue of *Management Science* (1994) dealing with cross-national generalizations of management science applications, including several in the marketing area.

Meta-Analysis in Marketing

Meta-analysis has offered a useful approach for generalizing about advertising (Assmus, Farley, & Lehmann, 1984) and price elasticities (Tellis, 1988) as well as parameters from diffusion models (Sultan, Farley, & Lehmann, 1990, 1996) and buyer behavior models (Farley, Lehmann, & Ryan, 1982a, 1982b). (See Farley, Lehmann, and Sawyer [1995] for an attempt to generalize on a set of underlying meta-analyses.) Because no consensus has been reached on the design of studies in the field, however, draconian statistical methods are often required for a meta-analysis to hold constant a whole range of differences in interstudy design factors.

Meta-analyses in marketing have typically been applied to relatively mature fields with 100 to 200 existing studies. One conclusion that has emerged from this stream of work, however, is that it would be very useful to attempt to make partial generalizations early in the development of a field that appears to have the potential to generate a large volume of work in a fairly short time period. Such "prospective" meta-analyses help shape the field by directing researchers' attention toward research options that really add knowledge and away from options that essentially repeat known and reliable results. The measurement of market orientation is a topic with such potential; it has received considerable research interest in the past decade and, prompted by its managerial relevance, will continue to have top priority status at the Marketing Science Institute (MSI).

The State of Empirical Measurement of Market Orientation

In the late 1980s, more or less without knowledge of each others' work, three sets of researchers developed measurements of market orientation:

Narver and Slater (N-S) developed a 15-item factor-weighted scale, which they used as one of nine different measures in explaining return on investment (ROI). The other measures included buyer and seller power, concentration and ease of entry, market growth, technological change, and firm size and growth. The scale was tested, along with the other measurements, on split samples from 371 self-administered questionnaires from top managers of 140 strategic business units (SBUs) of a single corporation. Their results were reported in *Journal of Marketing* (Narver & Slater, 1990), in which the authors found differential effects (positive and significant) of market orientation for commodity and noncommodity businesses.

Kohli, Jaworski, and Kumar (K-J-K) published MARKOR, a freestanding 20-item scale in *Journal of Marketing Research* (Kohli, Jaworski, & Kumar, 1993). This particular empirical study did not attempt to explain a dependent variable or use other explanatory factors. Kohli and Jaworski (1990), however, had previously established a conceptual path model of factors affecting market orientation. Their scale was constructed using nonlinear factor analysis of matched samples of senior marketing and nonmarketing executives from 222 SBUs, including firms that were members of the MSI.

Deshpandé, Farley, and Webster (D-F-W) developed a customer orientation scale as part of a broader study of the impact of corporate culture, innovation, and market orientation on firm performance. Their 9-item scale was developed from a list of 30 items, along with measures of item salience, using results from a study of 138 Japanese executives published in *Journal of Marketing* (Deshpandé, Farley, & Webster, 1993). Personal interviews with double dyads of respondents from pairs of customer and supplier firms allowed assessment of interrater reliabilities at the firm level.

Each of the scales was used in later substantive research. Deshpandé, Farley, and Webster (1995) expanded their research for international comparison. The N-S scale was used in Slater and Narver (1994) in an analysis of whether the competitive environment moderates the market orientation-performance relationship. Selnes, Jaworski, and Kohli (1996) also conducted an across-country comparison with the K-J-K scale, adding a series of antecedent and performance measures.

As work on market orientation expanded, researchers and managers (in part via MSI research priorities) became interested in the extent to which the three scales were complementary—that is, the extent to which similar substantive conclusions would have been supported by interchanging or synthesizing the scales. At the same time, research on the implementation of market orientation became a priority of the MSI.

The "Designed" Meta-Analysis

The purpose of this chapter is to examine interscale and intrascale characteristics of these three market orientation scales. Our goal is not to judge which are better or worse but rather to determine how they compare under similar conditions. To our knowledge, this is the first time that such a comparison of these three scales has been attempted. To this end, we solicited the help of marketing executives from 27 major firms that are members of MSI.

The meta-analysis was, in effect, designed prospectively, in contrast to the more traditional role of meta-analysis—to form generalizations about estimates of important quantities that have been measured or estimated on different populations in different circumstances using different methods. As the marketing field recognized the magnitude of the systematic differences in results, attention of meta-analysis shifted from simple averaging to complex analyses of covariance that simultaneously estimated the size of these systematic differences. It was later documented that some effects are very hard to separate—that is, they are nearly nested in a sort of "natural" experimental design (Farley et al., 1995). A prospective meta-analysis helps remedy this problem.

Using this design, of course, we can perform conventional reliability and validity analysis of the behavior of the three scales. This design also allows more direct comparison of the various methods. Furthermore, because it offers the ability to examine industry and geographic differences and to examine how the three scales interrelate, this design allows us to examine two of the four (Farley & Lehmann, 1986) basic elements of meta-analytic variability: research environment and measurement.

The Study

Sample

Our sample is composed of 82 marketing executives from 27 participating companies, which represented 45% of the MSI 1995 membership. The sample of companies was assembled from participants in an MSI session on market orientation in Boston (9 American companies) and attendees at MSI meetings in Berlin (8 European companies) and in San Diego (10 American companies). Included are respondents from business units in a comprehensive cross section of nine industry categories, including retailing and wholesaling, financial and other services, and manufacturing of consumer nondurables and durables, industrial capital goods, and components and consumables.

Individual companies were asked to submit three or four independently completed questionnaires that contained all 44 items in the three scales (i.e., 15 N-S, 9 D-F-W, and 20 K-J-K items), two performance scales, and some demographics. Responses averaged three per SBU, with no firm having more than one SBU represented in the sample. This allowed us to examine within-company and SBU reliabilities. Participants were promised an assessment of their own firm's market orientation based on a new composite scale assembled from elements of the three existing scales. The full text of the three scales is provided in Appendix 9.A.

Reliability and Validity of the Scales

We first examine various aspects of reliability and validity of the individual scales. In all cases of statistical testing, we use a significance level of .05.

1. *Reliability:* The following are the respective Cronbach alphas of the three scales:

	This study	*Published in the original study*
N-S	.90	.81
D-F-W	.72	.71
K-J-K	.51	*NA*[a]
All combined	.90	*NA*

a. *NA*, not applicable.

Selnes et al. (1996) reported reliability measures (Cronbach alphas) of .89 for the K-J-K scales in both the United States and Scandinavia.

2. *Validity:* Our questionnaire also included a validity check that Kohli et al. (1993) used. It is a constant sum scale to measure similarity of the responding firm to one that is sales oriented against one that is market oriented. All three scales correlated significantly with this validity check for market orientation (and symmetrically negatively correlated with sales orientation): N-S, .36; D-F-W, .50; K-J-K, .40.

3. *Interrater within-company reliability:* Twenty of the 27 companies provided three or more responses, allowing comparison of interrater reliabilities of the scales. The within-company standard deviations of the K-J-K and D-F-W scales are significantly smaller than the overall variability of the sample, indicating a high degree of intracompany reliability in self-assessment of market orientation. The N-S scale has smaller within-company variability but not significantly so.

4. *Covariates:* Kohli et al. (1993) also developed three covariate measures to represent competitive conditions: competitive intensity, technological turbulence, and market turbulence. All three market orientation scales were negatively and significantly correlated with competitive intensity and positively but insignificantly correlated with technological and market turbulence.

5. *Discriminant validity:* To test discriminant validity of the scales, we included a set of measures from an organizational climate scale that were also used by Deshpandé et al. (1993). The correlations with the three market orientation scales are generally insignificant and have no systematic pattern.

Market Orientation Scales

	N-S	D-F-W	K-J-K
Our organization is characterized by competitiveness and a high degree of goal achievement.	.10	.13	.05
Our organization is characterized by order, rules and regulations, and smooth operations.	.00	.23	.33
In our organization, there is a strong tendency toward high-return, high-risk investments.	.32	.08	.04

6. *Predictive validity:* To test for predictive validity, we examined the correlation of the scales with performance. Two scales based on self-reports were used to measure performance—one based on Narver and Slater (1990) and the other on Deshpandé et al. (1993) (Appendix 9.B). In each case, the authors commented on the difficulty in securing desegregated financial information for comparison, especially internationally. Narver and Slater used a series of four subjectively estimated quantitative financial return measures, whereas Deshpandé et al. used a four-element scale adapted from the profit impact of market share study. The Cronbach alpha for the N-S scale was .71 and for the D-F-W scale .75. The correlation between the two performance scales was .45. All three scales were consistently correlated with both performance measures.

	Performance Scale	
Market Orientation Scale	*N-S*	*D-F-W*
N-S	.39	.54
D-F-W	.35	.67
K-J-K	.44	.30

Selnes et al. (1996) found a positive correlation between the K-J-K scale and a subjective performance measure in the United States and Sweden.

Synthesis of the Three Scales: Meta-Analytic Scaling

The three scales perform quite similarly in terms of reliability and of predictive and discriminant validity, and the general pattern of results is similar for personal interviews and self-administered questionnaires. In this section, we can generalize in three ways that require measurement of all scales on the same subjects. First, we examine the intercorrelations among the scales. Second, we examine the substantive implications of the scales in terms of international and interindustry differences in performance. Third, we attempt to develop from the 44 items a more compact summary scale that would be easier to use and that preserves as much of the aggregate information as possible.

1. *Correlation of the Scales.* Not surprisingly, given the results in the previous section, the scales are also highly correlated with one another:

	N-S	D-F-W
N-S		.65
K-J-K	.55	.64

We can compare the squares of these correlations with the eta square measures resulting from the analysis of variance in which between-firm sums of squares are compared to within-firm sums of squares, the latter representing interrater reliabilities:

Scale	Eta Square
N-S	.48
D-F-W	.56
K-J-K	.45

In comparison, the correlation of the scales with one another represents the majority of the reliable within-firm information available in the scales.

To this extent, the scales appear interchangeable. Although they can also be used together, we have found that they are somewhat redundant, which makes the task of using all three rather tedious.

In our work with managers on general issues related to market orientation, however, we were strongly advised to seek a smaller set of items that constitute a more parsimonious measurement device based on the three scales. Concepts such as market orientation, once developed, are often only part of a larger study, and parsimony in measurement of each item is very useful (Hulland, 1995). For example, Deshpandé et al. (1995) used 8 items to measure organizational climate; these were derived using factor analysis from a 56-item battery of measures used earlier in a study of corporate performance (Capon, Farley, & Hoenig, 1994). The whole set of organizational climate measures was simply too large and unwieldy to use in a multiconcept, multinational questionnaire, in which organizational climate was only 1 of 10 different concepts being measured. Furthermore, some items are superior to others in terms of scale characteristics and ability to predict performance.

2. *Scale Synthesis.* The synthesis of the items into a smaller number proceeded as follows: The 44 individual items from the three original scales (15 from N-S, 9 from D-F-W, and 20 from K-J-K) were submitted to a factor analysis. The first factor significantly separated from others on a screen test of eigenvalues and explained more than 40% of the cumulative variance from the major factors. Items loading highly on this factor were then examined for low nonresponses (indicating the item was easy for manager respondents to understand). Because the objective was to develop a short scale, the 10 items with the highest loadings on the first factor were used in the summary scale. These 10 items did not appear to have nonresponse problems.

This process resulted in a scale of 10 items reported in Appendix 9.C. The items appear to have intuitive integrity in that they all deal with "customer focus" notions of market orientation (i.e., items dealing with separable, albeit related, issues, such as competitive intelligence, competitor orientation, and human resource drivers of market orientation, did not enter the scale). Finally, this 10-item summary scale was examined for reliability. Inter-item correlations, and consequently Cronbach's alpha coefficient, were extremely robust (the latter being .89).

As a check on the validity of the procedure, we compared the average correlations of the 10 individual items in the summary scale with those of the 34 items not in the scale with the two performance measures. The average correlation of the 10 summary scale items with both performance measures was higher than the average of the other 34 items—significantly so in the case of the N-S measure.

Generalizability: Geography and Industry

Meta-analysis typically seeks qualitative generalizations (good) and quantitative generalizations (even better). It is not necessarily harmful that scales of the type we are discussing are different across research environments (e.g., industries or parts of the globe). For example, there are good reasons to expect that scales that measure a construct such as organizational culture will be linked to cultural characteristics of a country, and they are indeed linked (Deshpandé et al., 1995). Market orientation, however, is an element of marketing that takes on a sort of universal characteristic—that is, the theoretical underpinnings should be valid in all settings. Furthermore, lack of interindustry or internation differences in means may extend the arena of comparability in ways useful to management. In this case, the results reported previously are quite robust with regard to both geography and industry.

1. *Geography.* Of our sample of 82 respondents in 27 companies, 17 people in 8 companies are European. They represent six different western European industrial countries. There are no significant differences between the means of American and European firms on any of the three original market orientation scales, on the new synthesizing scale, or on either of the performance scales.

    Regressions with the two performance measures as dependent variables specified different intercepts and slopes for the European observations. None of the European slope differentials were significantly different from the overall slopes for all observations, all of which were positive and significant. The insignificant slope differentials were also small in absolute value, averaging about 8% of the overall slope relating performance and market orientation for the various measures.

2. *Industry.* Industry was classified on the basis of self-report into the nine categories described earlier. There was no significant difference among

industries in any of the market orientation scales or any of the performance scales.

Discussion and Conclusions

We examined the usefulness of the principles of meta-analyses to consolidate knowledge in a field in which different measurement methods have been developed for nearly similar constructs. The application combines three different scales measuring market orientation that were developed at about the same time and more or less independently. The basic idea is to construct a kind of integrative study that allows simultaneous application of the various measurement approaches on a set of units, within which are some multiple raters. Multiple locations allow assessment of geography.

Overall, the three scales measuring market orientation, although developed more or less independently, show remarkable similarity in terms of reliability and show internal and external validity in this test, which used a multifirm, multinational sample of 82 marketing executives from 27 firms that are members of MSI. It is reasonable to conclude that the methodology is robust and that the substantive conclusions reached using the scales are sustainable under other measurement regimes and with other samples. For example, besides the general within-sample consistencies shown in this study, Deshpandé et al. (1995) have shown alphas of approximately the same size for their market orientation and performance scales in Asia, North America, and Europe. This helps ameliorate concern expressed originally by all three groups that the original scales, each developed on single-country samples, might not "internationalize" well.

We also developed a more parsimonious and managerially oriented scale for use in future applications, particularly in broader studies in which time is short.

Methodologically, we found that a prospectively designed meta-analysis can be very useful in helping "take stock" of a developing research field in terms of quantitative generalizations. It appears that the measurement issues related to the concept of market orientation are under control both conceptually and across international and interindustry research environments.

The basic power of a prospectively designed meta-analysis of the type reported here is that a group of related measurements on the same sample allows direct comparison of alternative measurement techniques. It also allows tests leading to a synthesis of particularly "good" items into a more parsimonious and compact scale, and it allows direct examination of whether substantive results are uniquely dependent on a particular measurement method. The prospective approach thus controls troublesome interstudy differences plaguing many meta-analyses.

We note that the new, abbreviated 10-item market orientation scale shown in Appendix 9.C has inevitably lost some of the information contained in the original 44 items from the N-S, K-J-K, and D-F-W scales. The required parsimony from using only 10 items has two notable substantive implications: The new scale does not deal with market orientation as a "culture" (i.e., a set of shared values and beliefs about the central importance of the customer) but rather focuses on "activities" (i.e., a set of behaviors and processes related to continuous assessing and serving customer needs), and the new scale does not deal with market orientation as covering noncustomer-related activities (e.g., collecting intelligence on competitors) but rather, as noted earlier, with cross-functional activities devoted to satisfying target market needs. These are two issues for which there has been confusion over the definition and measurement of market orientation. The current scale-development activity has helped us better understand the essence of the concept of market orientation. Hence, we can now define market orientation as *the set of cross-functional processes and activities directed at creating and satisfying customers through continuous needs assessment.* We believe that this inductively derived definition helps move us forward toward the next stage of utilizing this scale in broader assessment efforts devoted to implementing market orientation as part of the strategic intent of a firm.

Appendix 9.A: Market Orientation Scales: N-S, D-F-W, and K-J-K

I. A. (N-S Scale) In answering, please use the following response scale and place the most appropriate number to the left of each statement. Please respond to each statement.

Not at all	To a very slight extent	To a small extent	To a moderate extent	To a considerable extent	To a great extent	To an extreme extent
1	2	3	4	5	6	7

In our strategic business unit —

_____ 1. Our salespeople regularly share information within our business concerning competitors' strategies.

_____ 2. Our business objectives are driven primarily by customer satisfaction.

_____ 3. We rapidly respond to competitive actions that threaten us.

_____ 4. We constantly monitor our level of commitment and orientation to serving customers' needs.

_____ 5. Our top managers from every function regularly visit our current and prospective customers.

_____ 6. We freely communicate information about our successful and unsuccessful customer experiences across all business functions.

_____ 7. Our strategy for competitive advantage is based on our understanding of customers' needs.

_____ 8. All of our business functions (e.g., marketing/sales, manufacturing, R&D, finance/accounting, etc.) are integrated in serving the needs of our target markets.

_____ 9. Our business strategies are driven by our beliefs about how we can create greater value for customers.

_____ 10. We measure customer satisfaction systematically and frequently.

_____ 11. We give close attention to after-sales service.

_____ 12. Top management regularly discusses competitors' strengths and strategies.

_____ 13. All of our managers understand how everyone in our business can contribute to creating customer value.

_____ 14. We target customers where we have an opportunity for competitive advantage.

_____ 15. We share resources with other business units.

B. (D-F-W Scale) The statements below describe norms that operate in businesses. Please indicate your extent of agreement about how well the statements describe the actual norms in your business.

Instructions: Please answer in the context of your specific product/market or service/market business. (Circle one number for each line.)

	Strongly Disagree	Disagree	Neither Agree nor Disagree	Agree	Strongly Agree
	1	2	3	4	5
1. We have routine or regular measures of customer service.	1	2	3	4	5
2. Our product and service development is based on good market and customer information.	1	2	3	4	5
3. We know our competitors well.	1	2	3	4	5
4. We have a good sense of how our customers value our products and services.	1	2	3	4	5
5. We are more customer focused than our competitors.	1	2	3	4	5
6. We compete primarily based on product or service differentiation.	1	2	3	4	5
7. The customer's interest should always come first, ahead of the owners.	1	2	3	4	5
8. Our products/services are the best in the business.	1	2	3	4	5
9. I believe this business exists primarily to serve customers.	1	2	3	4	5

C. (K-J-K Scale) In responding to the following questions, please focus on your strategic business unit (SBU) rather than the corporation as a whole. If a question is not applicable, please leave a blank.

	Strongly Disagree				Strongly Agree
1. In this business unit, we meet with customers at least once a year to find out what products or services they will need in the future.	1	2	3	4	5
2. In this business unit, we do a lot of in-house market research.	1	2	3	4	5
3. We are slow to detect changes in our customers' product preferences. (R)	1	2	3	4	5
4. We poll end-users at least once a year to assess the quality of our products and services.	1	2	3	4	5

	Strongly Disagree				Strongly Agree
5. We are slow to detect fundamental shifts in our industry (e.g., competition, technology, regulation). (R)	1	2	3	4	5
6. We periodically review the likely effect of changes in our business environment (e.g., regulation) on customers.	1	2	3	4	5
7. We have interdepartmental meetings at least once a quarter to discuss market trends and developments.	1	2	3	4	5
8. Marketing personnel in our business unit spend time discussing customers' future needs with other functional departments.	1	2	3	4	5
9. When something important happens to a major customer or market, the whole business unit knows about it in a short period.	1	2	3	4	5
10. Data on customer satisfaction are disseminated at all levels in this business unit on a regular basis.	1	2	3	4	5
11. When one department finds out something important about competitors, it is slow to alert other departments. (R)	1	2	3	4	5
12. It takes us forever to decide how to respond to our competitors' price changes. (R)	1	2	3	4	5
13. For one reason or another we tend to ignore changes in our customers' product or service needs. (R)	1	2	3	4	5
14. We periodically review our product development efforts to ensure that they are in line with what customers want.	1	2	3	4	5
15. Several departments get together periodically to plan a response to changes taking place in our business environment.	1	2	3	4	5
16. If a major competitor were to launch an intensive campaign targeted at our customers, we would implement a response immediately	1	2	3	4	5
17. The activities of the different departments in this business unit are well coordinated.	1	2	3	4	5
18. Customer complaints fall on deaf ears in this business unit. (R)	1	2	3	4	5
19. Even if we came up with a great marketing plan, we probably would not be able to implement it in a timely fashion. (R)	1	2	3	4	5
20. When we find that customers would like us to modify a product or service, the departments involved make concerted efforts to do so.	1	2	3	4	5

R, reverse scored.

Appendix 9.B: Measures of Performance

This section includes several measures of business unit performance. Please give your own best estimate rather than attempting to ascertain an exact value from other sources.

A. (N-S Scale) Sales growth and customer retention. Rate how well your business unit has performed relative to all other competitors in your principal served market segment (PSMS) over the past year.

1	2	3	4	5	6	7
<10%	11–25%	26–40%	41–55%	56–70%	71–85%	86–100%

Example: If you believe that your sales growth is greater than that of approximately 60% of all competitors in your PSMS, rate yourself a 5 for sales growth.

Customer retention	_____
Sales growth	_____
Return on investment*	_____
Return on sales	_____

* For this study, we consider CROI, ROI, ROA, and RONA to be equivalent.

B. (D-F-W Scale) Please circle the appropriate answer. Relative to our business unit's largest competitor, we:

	(1)	*(2)*	*(3)*	*(4)*	*(5)*
(a)	Are much less profitable	Are less profitable	Are about equally profitable	Are more profitable	Are significantly more profitable
(b)(R)	Are much larger	Are larger	Are about the same size	Are smaller	Are much smaller
(c)(R)	Have a much larger market share	Have a larger market share	About the same market share	Have a smaller market share	Have a much smaller market share
(d)	Are growing much more slowly	Are growing more slowly	Are growing at about the same rate	Are growing faster	Are growing much faster

R, reverse scored.

Appendix 9.C: Summary Scale for Market Orientation

The statements below describe norms that operate in businesses. Please indicate your extent of agreement about how well the statements describe the actual norms in your business.

Instructions: Please answer in the context of your strategic business unit. (Circle one number for each line.)

	Strongly Disagree	Disagree	Neither Agree nor Disagree	Agree	Strongly Agree
	1	*2*	*3*	*4*	*5*
1. Our business objectives are driven primarily by customer satisfaction.	1	2	3	4	5
2. We constantly monitor our level of commitment and orientation to serving customer needs.	1	2	3	4	5
3. We freely communicate information about our successful and unsuccessful customer experiences across all business functions.	1	2	3	4	5
4. Our strategy for competitive advantage is based on our understanding of customers' needs.	1	2	3	4	5
5. We measure customer satisfaction systematically and frequently.	1	2	3	4	5
6. We have routine or regular measures of customer service.	1	2	3	4	5
7. We are more customer focused than our competitors.	1	2	3	4	5
8. I believe this business exists primarily to serve customers.	1	2	3	4	5
9. We poll end-users at least once a year to assess the quality of our products and services.	1	2	3	4	5
10. Data on customer satisfaction are disseminated at all levels in this business unit on a regular basis.	1	2	3	4	5

References

Assmus, G. J., Farley, J. U., & Lehmann, D. R. (1984, February). How advertising affects sales: Meta-analysis of econometric results. *Journal of Marketing Research, 21,* 65-74.

Capon, N., Farley, J. U., & Hoenig, S. (1994). *Why some firms perform better than others* [Working manuscript]. New York: Columbia University.

Deshpandé, R., Farley, J. U., & Webster, F. E., Jr. (1993). Corporate culture, customer orientation, and innovativeness in Japanese firms: A quadrad analysis. *Journal of Marketing, 57*(1), 23-37. (See also Chapter 4)

Deshpandé, R., Farley, J. U., & Webster, F. E., Jr. (1995). *A five-country comparison of how corporate culture and climate, customer orientation, and innovativeness affect business performance* [Working paper]. Hanover, NH: Dartmouth College, Amos Tuck School.

Farley, J. U., & Lehmann, D. R. (1986). *Generalizing about market response models: Meta-analysis in marketing.* Lexington, MA: Lexington Books.

Farley, J. U., Lehmann, D. R., & Ryan, M. J. (1982a, October). Generalizing from imperfect replication. *Journal of Business, 54,* 597-610.

Farley, J. U., Lehmann, D. R., & Ryan, M. J. (1982b, Spring). Pattern in parameters of buyer behavior models: Generalization from sparse replication. *Marketing Science, 1,* 181-204.

Farley, J. U., Lehmann, D. R., & Sawyer, A. (1995). Empirical marketing generalization using meta-analysis. *Marketing Science, 14*(3), G36-G46.

Hulland, J. (1995). *Market orientation and market learning systems: An environment-strategy-performance perspective* [Working paper]. London, Ontario, Canada: Western Business School.

Kohli, A. K., & Jaworski, B. J. (1990). Market orientation: The construct, research propositions, and managerial implications. *Journal of Marketing, 54*(2), 1-18. (See also Chapter 2)

Kohli, A. K., Jaworski, B. J., & Kumar, A. (1993, November). MARKOR: A measure of market orientation. *Journal of Marketing Research, 30,* 467-477.

Management Science focused issue: Is management science international? (1994, January). *Management Science, 40* [Special issue].

Marketing Science special issue on empirical generalizations in marketing. (1995). *Marketing Science, 14*(3, Part 2) [Special issue].

Narver, J., & Slater, S. F. (1990). The effect of a market orientation on business profitability. *Journal of Marketing, 54*(4), 20-35. (See also Chapter 3)

Selnes, F., Jaworski, B. J., & Kohli, A. K. (1996). Market orientation in United States and Scandinavian countries: A cross-cultural study. *Scandinavian Journal of Management, 12*(2), 139-157.

Slater, S. F., & Narver, J. C. (1994). Does competitive environment moderate the market orientation-performance relationship? *Journal of Marketing, 58*(1), 46-55. (See also Chapter 6)

Sultan, F., Farley, J. U., & Lehmann, D. R. (1990, February). Meta-analysis of application of diffusion models. *Journal of Marketing Research, 27,* 70-77.

Sultan, F., Farley, J. U., & Lehmann, D. R. (1996, May). Reflections on a meta-analysis of application of diffusion models. *Journal of Marketing Research, 33,* 247-249.

Tellis, G. J. (1988, November). The price elasticity of selective demand: A meta-analysis of econometric models of sales. *Journal of Marketing Research, 25,* 331-342.

Additional Reading

Farley, J. U., & Lehmann, D. R. (1994, January). Cross-national "laws" and differences in market response. *Management Science, 40,* 111-122.

Market Oriented Is Not Enough

Build a Learning Organization

Stanley F. Slater
John C. Narver

Numerous executives and scholars have suggested that in competitive markets learning may be the only source of sustainable competitive advantage. Learning organizations continuously acquire, process, and disseminate throughout the organization knowledge about markets, products, technologies, and business processes. This knowledge is based on information from customers, suppliers, competitors, and other sources. Through complex communication and coordination processes, these organizations reach a shared interpretation of the information that enables them to act swiftly and decisively to exploit opportunities and confront problems. In their ability to anticipate and act on opportunities in turbulent and fragmenting markets, these organizations are outstanding.

Organizations that can consistently develop and act on new knowledge share a common set of key management practices. Market orientation has rightfully received much attention as the foundation of this configuration of management practices. Market orientation, however, is only one component of a learning architecture. Learning organizations must also be entrepreneurial: They must be risk taking, experimental, and aggressive in their

237

efforts to develop and apply knowledge. Furthermore, they must be led by individuals with vision and the ability to develop and empower people throughout the organization.

To enhance information sharing and empower those with information, learning organizations have flexible structures that make extensive use of teams and informal coordinating devices. To develop productive learning partners, they do not construct rigid boundaries around themselves. They focus their planning and analysis efforts through strategic subsystems that are guided by a comprehensive strategic vision. Most important, they recognize that it is the synergy among the components that leads to learning and superior performance and provides the basis for a competitive advantage that is very difficult for competitors to imitate.

This chapter describes how organizations develop new knowledge and change their behavior to improve performance. It describes the key practices of learning organizations and concludes with recommendations for how researchers can contribute to an understanding of the successful development of a learning organization.

The importance of a market orientation has resurfaced as an issue important to managers and scholars alike (Day, 1990, 1992; Shapiro, 1988). For the first time, a comprehensive theory of the antecedents to and consequences of a market orientation has been developed (Kohli & Jaworski, 1990), and a body of research illustrating the relationship between market orientation and performance has emerged (Jaworski & Kohli, 1993; Narver & Slater, 1990; Ruekert, 1992; Slater & Narver, 1994). Market orientation and market-driven management have taken a central role in discussions about marketing management and strategy (Day, 1992).

Market orientation, however, is only one facet of a more comprehensive theory of organization, the learning organization. Learning organizations continuously acquire, process, and disseminate throughout the organization knowledge about markets, products, technologies, and business processes. This knowledge is based on information from customers, suppliers, competitors, and other sources. Through complex communication and coordination processes, these organizations reach a shared interpretation of information that enables them to act swiftly and decisively to exploit opportunities and defuse problems. These organizations stand out in their ability to anticipate and act on opportunities in turbulent and fragmenting markets.

In this commentary, we (a) describe the process through which organizations develop new knowledge and change their behavior to reflect the better understanding of their customers and markets, (b) explain how knowledge-driven behavior change creates and sustains competitive advantage during periods of high uncertainty, and (c) propose organizational practices that promote organizational learning. We conclude with recommendations for how researchers can contribute to our understanding of the successful development of a learning organization.

Organizational Learning

Although organizational learning has been discussed in the managerial literature for more than 15 years (Argyris, 1977), scholars have not reached a consensus on its definition (Garvin, 1993) because organizational learning is a complex, multidimensional construct occurring at different cognitive levels— adaptive and generative (Argyris, 1977, 1991; Senge, 1990)—and potentially encompassing multiple subprocesses (Garvin, 1993; Huber, 1991; Sinkula, 1994). In its most basic definition, organizational learning is the development of new knowledge or insights that have the potential to influence behavior (Fiol & Lyles, 1985; Huber, 1991; Simon, 1969; Sinkula, 1994). Others argue that meaningful learning requires behavior change because behavior change is essential to any type of organizational improvement (Garvin, 1993). This more stringent test eliminates organizations that are adept at creating or acquiring new knowledge but unable to apply this knowledge to their own activities and organizations whose behavior may be influenced indirectly by new knowledge.

From a managerial perspective, the fundamental assumption is that learning will improve future performance (Fiol & Lyles, 1985; Garvin, 1993; Senge, 1990). Performance improvement requires behavior change whether it is directly or indirectly stimulated by new knowledge. Thus, debating the precise definition of organizational learning is less important than recognizing that knowledge development, behavior change, and performance improvement are desirable goals that all businesses competing in dynamic and turbulent environments must pursue. Next, we describe the difference between adaptive and generative learning and discuss knowledge development and behavior change.

Levels of Organizational Learning

Adaptive learning is the most basic form of learning. It takes place within a set of recognized and unrecognized constraints that reflect the organization's assumptions about its environment and about itself. For example, Prahalad and Bettis (1986) argue that businesses can be effectively managed using a dominant general management logic that focuses the conceptualization of the business and guides the development of core capabilities. An unintended consequence, however, is that the dominant logic or traditional core capabilities, left unquestioned, may become "core rigidities" that can inhibit innovation (Leonard-Barton, 1992). Furthermore, Hamel and Prahalad (1991, p. 83) describe the "tyranny of the served market," in which narrow business charters cut short the search for unconventional business opportunities. In the examples of both "dominant logic" and "served market," it is clear how conceiving the company from a narrow perspective significantly reduces the range of opportunities that managers might pursue and the different ways they might pursue them. These restrictions limit organizational learning to the adaptive variety, which is usually sequential, incremental, and focused on issues or opportunities within the organization's traditional scope of activities.

Generative learning takes place when the organization is willing to question long-held beliefs about mission, customers, capabilities, or strategy. It requires the development of a new way of looking at the world based on an understanding of the systems and relationships that link key issues and events. Argyris (1991, p. 100) suggests that before organizations can develop new learning routines, organizational members must reflect critically on their biases, identify how they often contribute to the organization's myopic perspective, and then change their frames of reference so that they can contribute to generative learning.

The key challenge is to learn how the very way in which they perceive of the organization and its internal and external relationships can be a problem in its own right. For example, Stalk (1988), observing that time is the key linkage in many organizational systems, explains how companies, mostly Japanese, that recognized these relationships gained a strong competitive advantage by reducing their new products' time to market and improving

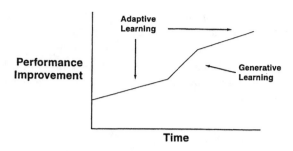

Figure 10.1. A Dynamic View of Learning

product quality, thus enhancing value for their customers. In contrast, their competitors focused on optimizing activities that took place within traditional functional areas. This is an example of how some companies examined their business practices and redefined the way they conducted their business, whereas others focused on making functions, presumably the home to the organization's core capability, more efficient. The latter approach is characteristic of adaptive learning and is quite typical of businesses with strong functional biases, which become learning boundaries. As time-based strategies show, generative learning is frame breaking and is more likely to sustain the business's competitive advantage.

Sustained generative learning is an elusive goal, however. Although Wal-Mart redefined the discount retail industry through its focus on logistics and information technology, it has sustained its competitive advantage through continued incremental investments and system improvements (Stalk, Evans, & Shulman, 1992). Toyota achieved the position of offering the highest quality automobiles in the world through its development of the "lean production" system (Womack, Jones, & Roos, 1990). Toyota has seen its quality advantage erode, however, as competitors learn and introduce lean production methods into their own facilities.

Like the development of scientific knowledge, which Kuhn (1970, p. 208) describes as "a succession of tradition-bound periods punctuated by noncumulative (i.e., revolutionary) breaks," generative learning is most likely to occur irregularly and unexpectedly, as illustrated in Figure 10.1. This is consistent with Miller and Friesen's (1980) finding that organizations tend to experience periods of momentum during which change is stable and predictable and periods of revolution during which significant reorientations in strategy and structure take place. Bhide (1986) argues that opportunities to gain a lasting advantage through a blockbuster strategic move are exceedingly rare. Thus, revolutionary periods of generative learning may provide a window of competitive advantage that may be kept open only through continuous improvement. Eventually, that window will begin to close as the knowledge about the innovation diffuses to competitors.

Knowledge Development

Knowledge development is a three-stage process consisting of information acquisition, information dissemination, and shared interpretation. Information may be acquired through direct experience, from the experiences of others, and from organizational memory. The clearest illustration of acquiring knowledge from experience is the learning curve or experience curve, which shows the effect of cumulative production and user experience on productivity in manufacturing (Alberts, 1989). Other examples of learning from experience include the use of large-scale demonstration projects and small-scale market experiments (Garvin, 1993). Hamel and Prahalad (1991, p. 89) describe the strategies of Sony, Matsushita, Nissan, and Toshiba as being based on "a higher rate of market experimentation and learning."

Learning from others encompasses such common practices as benchmarking, working with lead customers, forming joint ventures, networks, and strategic alliances (Kanter, 1989; Webster, 1992), and providing continuing education or training. Effective managers establish numerous credible internal and external sources to obtain objective information about their enterprise and its surrounding environments (Wrapp, 1967). They search beyond their organization's formal information systems, fearing them to be too historical, tradition bound, or extrapolative to expose fundamental shifts in the market or the organization (Quinn, 1978). To avoid the adaptive learning trap, executives who aggressively seek new potential threats or opportunities make sure their networks include people who view the world quite differently from the dominating culture of the organization. For example, Coca-Cola undertook a "secret and unorthodox" study that solicited advice from "ten unconventional thinkers," including Peter Drucker, Ted Levitt, and Arthur Nielsen, in an attempt to radically reorient its advertising campaign to distinguish itself from Pepsi-Cola (Sellers, 1993, p. 156). Alternatively, some companies incorporate devil's advocates into their planning processes to accomplish the same goal (Quinn, 1991, p. 801).

Learning organizations recognize that the random, chaotic nature of market and technological change cuts across organizational and institutional lines. These companies tap into multiple outside sources of technology and into their customers' capabilities. In industries such as electronics, customers provide much information about markets, products, and technologies. Information from lead customers is particularly valuable to accurately anticipate where new opportunities will develop (Garvin, 1993; von Hippel, 1986). At Hewlett-Packard, 3M, Sony, and Raychem, engineers frequently introduce radically new products through small teams that work closely with lead customers (Quinn, 1985). This activity is complemented by a reduced emphasis on traditional market research for innovative products because such research misses paradigm shifts and encourages adaptive learning (Prokesch, 1993). In the computer industry, microprocessor suppliers and software developers supply many creative insights, whereas in other industries, such as biotechnology, universities strongly support the development of new knowledge.

If it were not for organizational memory, learning would have a short half-life due to personnel turnover and the passage of time (Levitt & March, 1988). It is essential that important knowledge be codified or recorded in operating procedures, white papers, mission statements, organizational stories, or routines. The extent to which these memories are used and are useful should determine how long the memory should persist. It must be recognized, however, that these memories may constrain generative learning or even encourage ineffective learning if they focus the organization inappropriately (Dickson, 1992). In this situation, a core capability can become a "competency trap" (Leonard-Barton, 1992; Levitt & March, 1988), which occurs when new procedures or capabilities may be more effective than old ones but the organization is unwilling or unable to reject the capability it has invested in so heavily. IBM found itself in this situation in the 1980s when it maintained its focus on and commitment to mainframe computers, the core business that had made it very successful, even as the market was moving to distributed data processing systems (Loomis, 1993). An experienced consultant (Martin, 1993) describes this as a situation in which "corporations have created a world in which managers not only cannot see what is salient in their markets, they have gradually become impervious to learning" (p. 82). In this situation, the organization must promote active unlearning (Schein, 1990). As John Seely Brown (1991), the chief scientist of the Xerox Palo Alto Research Center, explains, "Unlearning is critical in these chaotic times because so many of our hard-earned nuggets of knowledge, intuitions, and just plain opinions depend on assumptions about the world that are simply no longer true" (p. 192).

The parts of the process that distinguish organizational learning from personal learning are information dissemination and accomplishment of a shared (organizational) interpretation of the information. Quinn (1992, p. 254) noted, "A unique characteristic of knowledge is that it is one of the few assets that grows most—usually exponentially—when shared." Effective dissemination, or sharing, increases information value when all organizational players who might be affected by it can see each piece of information in its broader context and can feed back questions, amplifications, or modifications, which provide new insights to the sender. This process has been extensively studied in the product development literature (Cooper & Kleinschmidt, 1991; Gupta, Raj, & Wilemon, 1985, 1986; Ruekert & Walker, 1987). To drive new products from concept to launch more rapidly and with fewer mistakes, Gupta et al. (1986, p. 7) conclude that "all functional interfaces are important in the product development process." Effective interfacing is accomplished through greater emphasis on "multifunctional activities, . . . multifunctional discussions, and information exchange" (Cooper & Kleinschmidt, 1991, p. 140). When organizations remove the functional barriers that impede the flow of information from development to manufacturing to sales and marketing, they improve the organization's ability to make rapid decisions and execute them effectively. An increasingly common approach to encourage information sharing in the development process is to send people from different functions on customer visits. Not only does this approach stimulate real-time information sharing but also it generally increases the quality of the information gathered (McQuarrie & McIntyre, 1992).

The final stage of knowledge development is shared interpretation of the information. If there is no consensus on what the information means and its implications for the business, organizational learning has not occurred (Day, 1991, p. 2). Dess and Origer (1987, p. 327), in their extensive review of the consensus literature, find that high-performing firms in dynamic and complex markets strive for consensus to ensure more effective strategy implementation. Prior to achieving consensus, however, "organizations competing within an industry experiencing high growth may benefit from a relatively high level of disagreement in assessing the relative importance of company objectives and competitive methods" (Dess, 1987, p. 274). The result of disagreement is a closer inspection of the validity of different assumptions and alternatives. Thus, high performance in high-velocity environments requires balancing the need for rapid decision making with the need to carefully consider the ramifications of alternative action plans through effective conflict-resolution processes (Bourgeois & Eisenhardt, 1988; Eisenhardt, 1989).

Effective conflict resolution may require the use of structured processes for surfacing disagreement; allowing disagreement to surface informally may lead to emotional confrontation and create long-term rifts among key members of the management team (Cosier & Schwenk, 1990). By exposing new information to different interpretations through programmed techniques such as dialectical inquiry and devil's advocacy (Cosier & Schwenk, 1990; Schwenk, 1989) and by developing alternative action plans for constructive discussion (Eisenhardt, 1989), new insights leading to generative learning may be developed in a positive atmosphere.

Conflict resolution is further enhanced by developing group norms that encourage the open sharing of information and that remove constraints on information and communication flows (Kanter, 1989, p. 113; Woodman, Sawyer, & Griffin, 1993). To ensure that all information is considered, businesses must provide forums for information exchange and discussion. This communication may occur through liaison positions, integrator roles, matrix organizations, face-to-face contact in meetings and on task forces, or by utilizing information technology to create organizational bulletin boards on topics such as competitive activity or technology development. The more uncertain the problem or opportunity, the more desirable it is to have higher frequency and informality in communication patterns (Gupta & Govindarajan, 1991; Jaworski, 1988).

Figure 10.2 illustrates the knowledge development process and the learning boundary that separates generative knowledge development from adaptive knowledge development. Figure 10.2 also includes behavior change as an element in the learning process. Although some argue that meaningful learning has occurred only when there is behavior change (Garvin, 1993), it is possible that new knowledge confirms what was already suspected or changes managerial perspectives (Menon & Varadarajan, 1992). Consequently, behavior may not change, but change may be more confidently pursued as a result of the new knowledge, or the stage may be set for some future behavior change to occur (Sinkula, 1994). Whether behavior change actually is part of the learning process or is a separate and distinct activity is less important than recognizing that in the long term behavior change is an essential link between knowledge development and performance improvement (Fiol & Lyles, 1985).

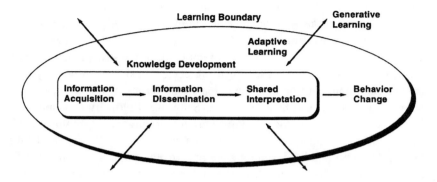

Figure 10.2. The Process of Organizational Learning

NOTE: Adaptive learning occurs when knowledge development is constrained by the learning boundary—strongly held beliefs about the organization and its environment. For generative learning to occur, the organization must extend itself beyond the learning boundary, challenging those assumptions to reveal new insights.

Behavior Change

Behavior change is the link between knowledge development and performance improvement, the ultimate objective of organizational learning. There are three ways that knowledge can be used to change organizational behavior (Menon & Varadarajan, 1992). Action-oriented use is the direct application of knowledge to solve a problem. Knowledge-enhancing use means that the knowledge influences managerial perspectives on problems but is less likely to directly change behavior. Finally, knowledge may be developed for affective use—that is, to increase satisfaction or decrease dissonance with a decision. Thus, Garvin (1993) might argue that organizational learning has not occurred when knowledge development results in knowledge-enhancing use or affective use. A new frame of reference, however, may provide the foundation for revolutionary behavior change (i.e., generative learning) at some point in the future. Consequently, we believe that it may be imprudent to expect direct and immediate behavior change based on new knowledge. These types of knowledge use form a continuum, from direct to indirect, of the effects of knowledge development on behavior change.

It is the organization's culture, the pattern of shared values and beliefs that provide individuals with norms for behavior (Deshpandé & Webster,

1989), that enables and stimulates behavior change. The culture of the organization is revealed through its systems, structure, and leadership style. We argue that learning is most likely to occur and produce behavior change in an organization characterized by a strong market orientation, an entrepreneurial culture, a facilitative style of leadership, an organic structure, and a hybrid approach to planning. Before elaborating on the nature and importance of these characteristics, we consider the final link in the learning process—the translation of learning into competitive advantage and superior performance.

Organizational Culture and Competitive Advantage

Can a specific type of culture, a learning culture, be a source of competitive advantage? The following is a frequently paraphrased sentiment: "Learning may be the only source of sustainable competitive advantage" (De Geus, 1988; Dickson, 1992; Nonaka, 1991; Stata, 1989). Supporting this contention are several recent studies of corporate culture (Deshpandé, Farley, & Webster, 1993; Jaworski & Kohli, 1993; Kotter & Heskett, 1992; Narver & Slater, 1990; Ruekert, 1992; Slater & Narver, 1994) that show a positive relationship between culture (particularly a market-driven culture) and different measures of organizational performance. What are the necessary conditions for culture to produce competitive advantage and superior performance?

A resource or competency is a basis for sustained competitive advantage when it provides value to customers and is difficult to imitate (Barney, 1991; Day & Wensley, 1988). A culture whose values and behavioral norms encourage improvements in effectiveness or efficiency (Day & Wensley, 1988, p. 7) satisfies the first requirement, and one whose social complexity is difficult to understand and emulate satisfies the second requirement (Barney, 1986, 1991). A learning culture clearly is valuable to a firm's customers because this learning is directed toward understanding and effectively satisfying the customers' current and latent needs through new products, services, and ways of doing business (Dickson, 1992). This should lead to "positional sources of advantage" (Day & Wensley, 1988, p. 7), such as greater new product success, superior customer retention, and higher customer-defined quality. As we describe the characteristics of a learning organization in the next section, its complexity and its difficulty for competitors to imitate will become apparent.

The Learning Organization

An extensive managerial literature is emerging that suggests management practices that facilitate organizational learning. Suggested practices include high-involvement strategic planning (De Geus, 1988; Stata, 1989), systems thinking or problem solving (Garvin, 1993; McGill, Slocum, & Lei, 1992; Senge, 1990; Stata, 1989), developmental leaders (Senge, 1990; Stata, 1989), a rigorous measurement system (Garvin, 1993), creativity and experimentation (Garvin, 1993; McGill et al., 1992; Nonaka, 1991), and an open organizational architecture (McGill et al., 1992; Stata, 1989). Although these writings make strong recommendations concerning appropriate managerial action, they lack a well-developed theoretical foundation. Also, regarding some practices, such as the role and nature of strategic planning in the learning organization (De Geus [1988] vs. Prokesch [1993]) and the value of standardized processes for transferring knowledge (Garvin [1993] vs. Stata [1989]), there is considerable disagreement. We believe this illustrates a serious shortcoming in our understanding of the learning organization that is due to (a) the paucity of theoretically grounded arguments for the management practices that facilitate organizational learning, (b) the lack of operational definitions for the management practice constructs, and (c) the absence of research that identifies the most appropriate areas for management attention. Our current objective is to stimulate research by offering a theory of the organizational characteristics of the learning organization and by suggesting appropriate research methods to initiate a test of the theory.

A Strong Market Orientation

> Organizations that are well educated about their markets stand out in their ability to rapidly sense and act on events in volatile and fragmenting markets.
>
> —Day (1991, p. 1)

> Even small improvements in learning about the marketplace and in making creative use of market information can have a major effect in eliciting more favorable responses to the firm's offerings.
>
> —Barabba and Zaltman (1991, p. ix)

Market orientation is the foundation of the learning organization and, per Kohli and Jaworski's (1990, p. 6) definition, strongly parallels the content of the learning process described previously: "Market orientation is the organizationwide generation of market intelligence pertaining to current and future needs, dissemination of the intelligence across departments, and organizationwide responsiveness to it." Narver and Slater's (1990) discussion has much in common with Kohli and Jaworski's, although they also explicitly consider the development and sharing of information about competitors. Narver and Slater's definition is more normative in that they describe market orientation as the culture that provides norms for behavior that lead to the creation of superior value for buyers.

Our purpose is to highlight the elements of a market orientation that are essential to organizational learning. Readers are referred to Shapiro (1988), Kohli and Jaworski (1990), and Narver and Slater (1990) for a comprehensive discussion of the domain of market orientation. Sinkula (1994) argues that market-based learning is essential to the learning organization. Basically, through its external emphasis on obtaining information about customers and competitors, the market-driven business is well positioned to anticipate the emerging needs of its customers and to respond by producing innovative new products and services, thus providing the basis for competitive advantage. Moreover, because it strongly emphasizes interfunctional teaming, sharing of information, and consensus on the meaning of the information, the market-driven business will have an advantage in both the speed and the effectiveness of its responsiveness to opportunities and threats.

Being market oriented, however, is no panacea. The "tyranny of the served market" (Hamel & Prahalad, 1991, p. 83) poses a great danger for many businesses that perceive themselves to be market driven. They focus on the same customers and competitors to the point of ignoring emerging markets or competitors or both. Another concern is that, according to common definitions (Kohli & Jaworski, 1990; Narver & Slater, 1990; Shapiro, 1988), market orientation means focusing on customers and competitors. This exclusive focus ignores numerous potential learning partners: suppliers, businesses in entirely different industries, consultants, universities, government agencies, and others possessing valuable knowledge (Dickson, 1992; Kanter, 1989; Webster, 1992). A narrow definition of market orientation will thus lead, at best, to adaptive learning. For a market orientation to be a powerful foundation for a learning organization and to provide the opportunity for generative learning, its scope must be expanded to include all stakeholders and constituencies that possess, or are developing, knowledge that has the potential to contribute to the creation of superior customer value.

An Entrepreneurial Culture

> This is the entrepreneurial role: to gather, evaluate, and utilize information. Resources flow toward the firms that are most competent in using information.
>
> —*Jacobson (1992, p. 788)*

> We are committed to identifying potential corporate entrepreneurs, training them, and developing their ideas into new businesses.
>
> —*Raymond Smith, chief executive officer (CEO) of*
> *Bell Atlantic Corporation (as quoted in Kanter, 1991, p. 127)*

Corporate entrepreneurship involves the creation of new businesses within the existing business and the renewal or revival of ongoing businesses that have become stagnant or in need of transformation (Schendel, 1990, p. 2). These objectives may be accomplished through the development of new products or the reformulation of existing ones, the creation of new manufacturing methods or distribution channels, or the discovery of new approaches to management or competitive strategy (Guth & Ginsberg, 1990; Stevenson & Jarillo, 1990). Schumpeter (1934, 1942) observed that entrepreneurial firms outcompete other firms and can earn excess profits in the short term. The entrepreneur's innovations, however, eventually will be imitated, and profits will return to their normal level. The entrepreneur must use the profits from the earlier innovation to pursue additional innovations. Successful innovations occur when entrepreneurs recognize a gap between what the market needs and what it is offered and successfully direct resources toward filling that need. Although some of these opportunities may be uncovered through chance, firms with a history of successful innovation have effective systems for collecting and evaluating information that leads to the identification of opportunities (Jacobson, 1992).

Successful entrepreneurial efforts are thus the product of learning organizations. It is the culture that values entrepreneurship and innovation, however, that fosters the environment in which continuous learning is most likely to take place (Quinn, 1985; Sykes & Block, 1989). Entrepreneurial cultures are often characterized as valuing traits such as high tolerance for risk (Sykes & Block, 1989), proactiveness (Miller & Friesen, 1982; Naman & Slevin,

1993), receptivity to innovation (Burgelman, 1985; Kanter, 1989), and active resistance to bureaucracy (Kanter, 1989; Mintzberg, 1991; Quinn, 1985). These are traits that are strongly associated with acquiring knowledge through experience, challenging assumptions to create generative learning, and rapidly developing new behaviors to leverage learning.

For example, a fundamental entrepreneurial activity is not only to create products ahead of competitors but also to create them ahead of their explicit desire by customers through a focus on customers' latent needs (Brown, 1991; Hamel & Prahalad, 1991). This activity, of course, is risky, particularly when competitors often copy product innovations in 9 to 15 months (Ghemawat, 1986). To minimize risk and maximize learning, successful innovators frequently undertake low-cost market experiments (Hamel & Prahalad, 1991; Kanter, 1989) or experiment through ongoing quality or cost-reduction programs (Garvin, 1993). To ensure understanding of the causes of success or failure, managers subject these activities to systematic analysis (Garvin, 1993; Hamel & Prahalad, 1991), such as the "Five Why's" (Womack et al., 1990, p. 57) or Deming's "Plan-Do-Check-Act" process (Garvin, 1993).

Another powerful entrepreneurial trait is a resistance to accepting the status quo or traditional view of products, markets, and business processes. Canon's development of its revolutionary minicopier came from a team discussion over a few beers that led to a comparison of how a copier drum resembles an aluminum beer can. By exploring this analogy, the development team was able to design a process technology that could manufacture a low-cost aluminum copier drum (Nonaka, 1991). In 1984, Convex Computer was being squeezed between Digital Equipment Corporation, which owned the minicomputer market, and Cray, which owned the supercomputer market. Instead of going head-to-head with either of the leaders, Convex created a new niche, the "mini-supercomputer," which had a price-performance range between the two major categories and was highly attractive to a specific market segment (McKenna, 1991). Of course, the challenge is to create an environment in which entrepreneurship can flourish.

A New Style of Leadership

> Leaders must shift their orientation from controlling subordinates' behavior to changing their behavior by facilitating their interactions and development.
>
> —*Ray Stata, CEO of Analog Devices Incorporated*
> *(as quoted in "Letters to the Editor," 1993, p. 190)*

The transformational leader changes the social warp and woof of reality.
—*Bass (1985, p. 24)*

American business has had a long obsession with the leader as forceful commander. Perhaps Harold Geneen, the former CEO of ITT, who almost single-handedly ran a highly diversified, global conglomerate to the enrichment of his shareholders, best typified this management style (Pascale & Athos, 1981). After his retirement, however, the empire crumbled, and his successor, who tried to emulate his style, could not cope with the business's extraordinary complexity. In contrast, Jack Welch, the CEO of General Electric (GE), has succeeded in empowering his management and executive staff to manage their own businesses and has handed over substantial power to "process champions" (Stewart, 1992, p. 475). Welch noted (as quoted in Stewart, 1992, p. 474), "We've got to take out the boss element." Raymond Smith (as quoted in Kanter, 1991, p. 126) explains that Bell Atlantic is moving from a leadership style "in which people are handed procedures to follow mindlessly to one that helps them make tough choices." This is how Smith intends to create his corporate entrepreneurs.

The fact is that one does not have to be the CEO of a multinational enterprise to confront dynamic complexity on a continuing basis. It is foolish to believe that the CEO must or can make all strategic decisions. A complex environment calls for transformational or facilitative leaders who can raise the awareness of colleagues, clients, and others about issues of importance. They arouse or alter the strength of values that may have been dormant or subverted. They motivate people to do more than what has been expected of them. By changing the "warp and woof of reality," they encourage organizational members to break through learning boundaries (Bass, 1985).

Of course, many of the traditional leadership tasks are as relevant today as ever. Clearly, the leader must establish a motivating vision for the organization. The power of a well-crafted vision is that it, like the organization's culture, establishes norms of behavior and provides guidance for the type of knowledge to be pursued. Thomas Wajnert, the CEO of AT&T Capital corporation, explains (as quoted in "Letters to the Editor," 1993, p. 196), "Effective learning is purposeful and should be related explicitly to an organization's mission. Unless learning efforts are guided by clear purposes, the organization risks [becoming] skilled at many things, but expert at none." CEO of Corning Jamie Houghton (as quoted in "Letters to the Editor," 1993, p. 200) was able to move the corporation only by going to the organization "year after year with the same story, the same resolve, and the same personal commitment."

As reflected in Stata's (1989) comments, leaders must focus on developing the people around them. This has numerous implications for the leader's style. First, it means abandoning the role of expert whose job it is to teach subordinates the correct way to do things. Instead, the leader acts as a coach, helping to surface assumptions and understand patterns and relationships among people, organizations, and events. By understanding the nature of these systematic relationships, subordinates make better decisions with less interference from top management (Senge, 1990).

Facilitative leaders are adept at motivating people to want to learn. Senge (as cited in Meen & Keough, 1992) suggests that their objective is to create a "demand pull" system in which people in the organization want to learn more. To accomplish this objective, recognized learning organizations, such as Motorola, GE, and Banc One, have established their own in-house "universities." Leaders in learning organizations expect employees to use company time to pursue knowledge that is outside of the immediate scope of their work. They encourage lateral, cross-functional transfers that enable employees to learn and develop new skills (Nonaka, 1991).

Facilitative leaders are frequent and effective communicators within and outside of the organization. They constantly articulate and reinforce the organization's vision through their speech and actions. They share information about business trends and competitors' activities. They freely provide operational information about productivity, inventory, and quality so that problems can be quickly identified and successes shared. They keep the workforce informed about the company's overall performance.

Finally, leaders must take a key role in "unlearning" traditional but detrimental practices. By surfacing and challenging their own assumptions and mental models, they encourage employees to do the same. General Electric uses "Workout" sessions to "challenge every single piece of conventional wisdom, every book, every rule." In these sessions, executives, including CEO Welch, take the floor of GE's management development center to respond to tough questions from managers who are taking classes at the center. This practice has created an environment in which difficult issues can be raised without fear of retribution and executives must respond with plans and solutions (Potts, 1992). John Seely Brown (1991, p. 110), director of the Xerox Palo Alto Research Center, focuses on how the corporation rejects certain ideas so that it does not erect obstacles to innovations that emanate from out-side the traditional processes.

A Flexible, Organic Structure

> We want an organization that can evolve, that can modify itself as tech-nology, skills, competitors, and the entire business change.
> —*Paul Allaire, CEO of the Xerox Corporation*
> *(as quoted in Howard, 1992, p. 109)*

> Boundarylessness is an open, trusting, sharing of ideas. A willingness to listen, debate, and then take the best ideas and get on with it.
> —*Jack Welch, CEO of GE*
> *(as quoted in "Jack Welch's Lessons," 1993, p. 29)*

Burns and Stalker (1961) first suggested that high-performing firms, competing in complex and dynamic industries, adopt an "organic form"—an organizational architecture that is decentralized, with fluid, ambiguous job responsibilities and extensive lateral communication processes. Members of these organizations, both internal and external, recognize their interde-pendence and are willing to cooperate and share information to sustain the effectiveness of the organization (Miles & Snow, 1992). The necessity of ef-fective information sharing in the learning organization demands that system-atic or structural constraints on information flows be dismantled (Woodman et al., 1993). On the basis of an extensive review, Gupta and Govindarajan (1991, p. 778) conclude that high environmental uncertainty requires high frequency and informality in communication patterns among organizational units for effective diffusion of knowledge (Ruekert, Walker, & Roering, 1985).

Mintzberg (1991, p. 732) suggests grouping experts into functional units for housekeeping purposes but deploying them in project teams for specific tasks and relying on teams, task forces, and integrating managers to encourage mutual adjustment within and between the teams. Under these conditions, information and decision processes flow flexibly and informally to promote innovation and creativity. Because standardization and bureau-cratic routines no longer serve as coordinating mechanisms, coordination becomes the responsibility of experts rather than individuals with power or authority. Consequently, the organization must make use of an extensive set of liaison devices, such as cross-unit committees, integrator roles, and matrix structures (Gupta & Govindarajan, 1991, p. 777), to encourage informal co-ordination and mutual adjustment. The downside to this organizational form is the frustration that may arise from the fluidity, ambiguity, and uncertainty of the work environment. Furthermore, the need for frequent and extensive communication exacts a high price in the extent of individual involvement, the anxiety created, and length of time required to reach a decision (Mintzberg, 1991, p. 745).

A recent study of high-technology firms in Silicon Valley (Bahrami, 1992) illustrates how the nature of the organic structure continues to evolve. These firms rely on a stable substrate of formal structure supplemented by an overlay of temporary project teams and multifunctional groups, with the effect of achieving the efficiency of a functional organization and the market effectiveness of a divisional form (Miles & Snow, 1992). The temporary teams engage in a wide range of activities: new product development, strategic assessments, and formation of new management processes. They also make extensive use of information technology, such as electronic mail and shared databases, which has reduced the need for the traditional middle-management role of information conduit. The benefits include rapid awareness of and response to competitive and market change, more effective information sharing, and a reduction in the lag between decision and action.

Another critical dimension of the learning organization's architecture is its linkages with external "learning partners." As Webster (1992, p. 1) notes, "New organization forms, including strategic partnerships and networks, are replacing simple market-based transactions." The implications of this philosophical shift are particularly profound for learning organizations. Essentially, we are moving away from Porter's (1980) model in which the strength of competitive forces dictates strategic choice to the recognition that the power of collaborative forces also influences firm strategy and performance (Kanter, 1989). To a large degree, organizational learning is an interdependent activity. Organizations learn from customers, distributors, suppliers, alliance partners, universities, and others. To the extent that we treat these information exchanges as "independent transactions," we limit the value of the exchange. Conversely, the development of long-term, stable relationships (Miles & Snow, 1992; Ruekert et al., 1985, p. 22) with "learning partners" leads to information sharing that benefits both partners. Learning-driven companies such as Ford Motor Company, the most admired U.S. auto manufacturer (Welsh, 1994), Analog Devices, and Corning make extensive use of cooperative relationships (Kanter, 1989). Bahrami (1992) found that high-technology companies have been at the forefront of utilizing strategic partnerships. To maximize the value of these relationships, many firms have access to their partners' internal information systems, assign employees to a strategic partner for a specific project, and collaborate extensively on new product development projects.

Planning in the Learning Organization

Long-term planning weds companies to approaches and technologies too early, which is deadly in our marketplace.
—*Ed McCracken, CEO of Silicon Graphics*
(as quoted in Prokesch, 1993, p. 137)

Our approach to planning as a learning process has greatly facilitated our ability to forge a consensus for change among those who must make it happen.
—*Ray Stata, CEO of Analog Devices (1989, p. 68)*

The role of planning in the learning organization is not clearly understood. Although the traditional rational-comprehensive model of strategy formulation (Braybrooke & Lindblom, 1970) has been criticized for its questionable assumptions of rationality (Cyert & March, 1963) and cognitive capacity (Simon, 1957) even under stable conditions, the model is clearly unrealistic under turbulent conditions. The extreme alternative is to allow strategy to emerge in response to an evolving environment (Mintzberg, 1987). Whereas the rational-comprehensive model is formal and proactive, the emergent model appears to be informal and reactive.

Hart (1992), in his review of the strategy-making process literature, concluded that in complex, heterogeneous environments, an iterative participative approach is necessary to gain adequate knowledge and commitment from key stakeholders. Given its focus on managing stakeholder relationships and organizational learning, this approach, Hart concluded, most effectively supports an analyzer strategy (Miles & Snow, 1978) aimed at incremental product or service improvement. Hart also concluded, however, that innovation-oriented, prospector businesses develop strategy through a process of bottom-up intrapreneurship in which the role of top management is to encourage experimentation and nurture the development of ideas with the highest potential. Thus, Mintzberg (1987) and Hart (1992) seem to agree that learning-based strategies are most effectively formed, not formulated, through an unstructured, emergent process that top managers encourage but are somewhat removed from. We strongly believe that this perspective oversimplifies and understates the contribution that an appropriate planning system can make in a learning organization.

Much like the organic architecture that has a stable foundation and a flexible, responsive overlay of informal, ad hoc processes, planning in a learning organization also has a dual nature. At its foundation are three distinguishing features. The first piece of the foundation is a motivating vision, grounded in a sound understanding of the market, that is continuously communicated throughout the organization (Day, 1990, p. 15; "Letters to the Editor," 1993). Closely related is the necessity for an integrating theme, supportive of the business's competitive advantage efforts, that focuses learning and strategy development (Hamel & Prahalad, 1989; "Letters to the Editor," 1993). The final piece of the foundation is its ability to adapt specialized planning subsystems to the evolving needs of the business (Quinn, 1978) and to integrate the results of these planning activities into a strategic plan for the business.

An example of a critical planning subsystem that is highly dependent on organizational learning is the new product development process. Companies at the leading edge of product development, such as 3M, Hewlett-Packard, and Canon, work in handpicked, multidisciplinary teams from concept development to product introduction. Instead of waiting for one phase of the development process to be completed before moving to the next phase, some parts of the process are conducted in parallel. Although the team may be forced to reconsider prior decisions based on recent information, the process continues as a sequence of iterative experiments. Team members maintain constant access to market and technological information, learn by doing through frequent experimentation, and actively share knowledge throughout the organization and specifically with other new product development teams (Takeuchi & Nonaka, 1986). The same type of approach may be applied to planning subsystems concerned with quality improvement or acquisitions. Analog Devices formed 15 corporatewide product, market, and technology task forces that produced nine initiatives for change that became the company's strategic plan (Stata, 1989, p. 67). Thus, the value of the "top management planning system" is not as a source of innovative ideas regarding products, markets, or technologies; instead, it plays a powerful role in guiding the rather independent and chaotic activities of a wide variety of seemingly unrelated systems to produce a coherent organizational strategy (Quinn, 1985; Stata, 1989). The effectiveness of the planning process is a direct function of the top management team's ability to integrate the decisions generated by the subsystems (Eisenhardt, 1989).

The Motivating Influence of Environment

> Where markets shift, technologies proliferate, competitors multiply, and products become obsolete almost overnight, successful companies are those that consistently create new knowledge, disseminate it widely throughout the organization, and quickly embody it in new technologies and products.
>
> —*Nonaka (1991, p. 96)*

So far, we have focused on internal influences on organizational learning. A discussion of influences on organizational learning would be incomplete, however, without consideration of the effect of the competitive environment. The managerial literature (Garvin, 1993; Hamel & Prahalad, 1991; Nonaka, 1991; Stata, 1989) stresses the powerful motivation of a dynamic, hostile environment on the development of a learning organization. Fiol and Lyles (1985, p. 805) concur, stating that "a certain amount of [environmental] stress is a necessity if learning is to occur." Environmental hostility stimulates both the processes that comprise organizational learning and the development of the appropriate architecture to facilitate learning.

In some organizations, however, environmental complexity that threatens organizational performance may cause paralysis because it makes it too difficult for decision makers and learners to map their environment (March & Olsen, 1975). As Martin (1993, p. 84) explains, "People in corporate crisis are in no frame of mind to learn new facts of life." Furthermore, environmental change makes learning by experience less valuable because this experience may not be generalizable very far into the future (March, 1991). An inability to learn and adapt in changing conditions forced companies such as GM, IBM, and Sears into well-publicized predicaments in the early 1990s (Loomis, 1993).

Effective organizations are "loosely coupled" (Pfeffer & Salancik, 1978; Weick, 1979) with their environments in the sense that there is a

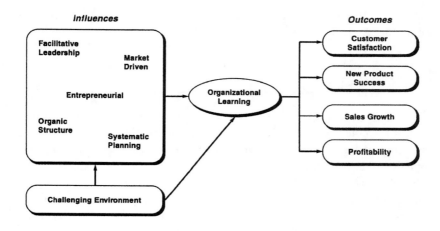

Figure 10.3. The Learning Organization

"buffer" between organization and environment that enables them to avoid a reactionary response to every event. We view a learning culture as just such a buffer. The buffering is accomplished in at least three ways. First, learning, particularly generative learning, is anticipatory and reduces the frequency and magnitude of major shocks. Second, because learning organizations have close and extensive relationships with customers, suppliers, and other key constituencies, there is a cooperative spirit that facilitates mutual adjustment when the unexpected occurs. Finally, because of its flexible, organic structure, the learning organization can quickly reconfigure its architecture and reallocate its resources to focus on the emergent opportunity or threat. Consequently, we concur with Nonaka (1991) and others that in a dynamic and hostile environment, creation of a learning organization is the only alternative that will lead to the development of competitive advantage.

Figure 10.3 illustrates our conception of the architecture of a learning organization. It is important to recognize that organizational learning is the product of synergies among the described management practices. By itself, an organic structure may result in inefficiency and disarray. Market orientation without an entrepreneurial drive may focus the organization's efforts too narrowly and, at best, produce adaptive learning. Thus, in isolation, the contribution of any one or two of these organizational features may be minor. A learning architecture satisfies the requirements for competitive advantage in that it is well positioned to provide superior value to customers, is complex to develop, and is difficult to imitate.

Conclusions

If we accept the proposition that learning organizations are best positioned to achieve competitive advantage, the development of a clear understanding of the processes of organizational learning and the management practices that facilitate or hinder it should be a high priority (Adams, 1993). The relevant literature is broad, drawing on work from sociology, psychology, and anthropology as well as from the business disciplines. Integrating this diverse work and establishing an agenda for research on organizational learning and the learning organization is a monumental task. Because we are primarily interested in marketing strategy and marketing management, we restrict our comments to these areas.

First, we see the need for both fine-grained and coarse-grained research. Coarse-grained research would focus on testing broader theories of the learning organization such as the framework of management practices that we have presented in this chapter. This line of research might be extended to consider environmental moderators of the relationships or whether different learning styles are appropriate for different strategy types. The major challenge in this research stream will be to develop a valid measure of organizational learning. We have taken the first step in this process by specifying the domain of the construct (Churchill, 1979). The next step is the development of scales to capture the dimensions of organizational learning (for examples of this process in a related area, see Jaworski & Kohli [1993] and Narver & Slater [1990]). Alternatively, one might use indirect measures of learning, such as patent activity, new product introductions, or sales growth, as surrogates. Because many of the organizational constructs discussed have operational measures (e.g., market orientation [Narver & Slater, 1990] and organic structure [Miller, 1987]), testing of this type of framework through survey research, as suggested by Deshpandé and Webster (1989), could proceed rapidly once appropriate measures of organizational learning were established.

Fine-grained research focused on understanding individual and group learning processes is also critical. Numerous writers (Argyris, 1991; Levitt & March, 1988) have pointed out obstacles to learning and behavior change. Research on strategies for overcoming obstacles to learning and for reaching consensus without sacrificing constructive disagreement would help improve the quality of organizational learning. Sujan, Weitz, and Kumar (1993) employed survey methodology to study the effect of a learning orientation on salesperson selling effectiveness. Schein (1990) argues that clinical studies undertaken while the researcher is actually working in the organization would have greater external validity than the experimental designs used to study these phenomena in the past (Schweiger, Sandberg, & Ragan, 1986).

There remains an important role for ethnographic studies focused on specific issues in single organizations (Deshpandé & Webster, 1989). For example, Corning Incorporated derives almost 50% of its revenues from alliances and joint ventures (Kanter, Stein, & Jick, 1992, p. 192). An ethnographic study focused on mechanisms for learning from these relationships would be highly valuable.

We agree with the many scholars and executives who have expressed the sentiment that organizational learning may be the only sustainable source of competitive advantage. The research challenge is to develop knowledge about specific management practices and how they should be configured to provide solid guidance to managers in their efforts to build learning organizations.

References

Adams, M. (1993). *Seeing differently: Improving the ability of organizations to anticipate and respond to the constantly changing needs of customers and markets* (Report No. 93-103). Cambridge, MA: Marketing Science Institute.

Alberts, W. W. (1989). The experience curve doctrine reconsidered. *Journal of Marketing, 53*(3), 36-49.

Argyris, C. (1977, September/October). Double loop learning in organizations. *Harvard Business Review,* 115-125.

Argyris, C. (1991, May/June). Teaching smart people how to learn. *Harvard Business Review, 69,* 99-109.

Bahrami, H. (1992, Summer). The emerging flexible organization: Perspectives from Silicon Valley. *California Management Review,* 34-52.

Barabba, V. P., & Zaltman, G. (1991). *Hearing the voice of the market: Competitive advantage through creative use of market information.* Boston: Harvard Business School Press.

Barney, J. (1986). Organizational culture: Can it be a source of sustained competitive advantage? *Academy of Management Review, 11,* 656-665.

Barney, J. (1991). Firm resources and sustained competitive advantage. *Journal of Management, 17,* 99-120.

Bass, B. M. (1985). *Leadership and performance beyond expectations.* New York: Free Press.

Bhide, A. (1986, September/October). Hustle as strategy. *Harvard Business Review, 64,* 59-65.

Bourgeois, L. J., & Eisenhardt, K. (1988). Strategic decision processes in high velocity environments: Four cases in the microcomputer industry. *Management Science, 34,* 816-835.

Braybrooke, D., & Lindblom, C. E. (1970). *A strategy of decision: Policy evaluation as a social process.* New York: Free Press.

Brown, J. S. (1991, January/February). Research that reinvents the corporation. *Harvard Business Review, 69,* 102-111.

Burgelman, R. A. (1985, January/March). Managing the new venture division: Research findings and implications for strategic management. *Strategic Management Journal, 5,* 39-54.

Burns, T., & Stalker, G. M. (1961). *The management of innovation.* London: Tavistock.

Churchill, G. A., Jr. (1979, February). A paradigm for developing better measures of marketing concepts. *Journal of Marketing Research, 26,* 64-73.

Cooper, R. G., & Kleinschmidt, E. J. (1991). New product processes at leading industrial firms. *Industrial Marketing Management, 20,* 137-147.

Cosier, R. A., & Schwenk, C. R. (1990). Agreement and thinking alike: Ingredients for poor decisions. *Academy of Management Executive, 4,* 69-74.

Cyert, R., & March, J. (1963). *A behavioral theory of the firm.* New York: Prentice Hall.

Day, G. S. (1990). *Market driven strategy; Processes for creating value.* New York: Free Press.

Day, G. S. (1991). *Learning about markets* (Report No. 91-117). Cambridge, MA: Marketing Science Institute.

Day, G. S. (1992, Fall). Marketing's contribution to the strategy dialogue. *Journal of the Academy of Marketing Science, 20,* 323-329.

Day, G. S., & Wensley, R. (1988). Assessing advantage: A framework for diagnosing competitive superiority. *Journal of Marketing, 52*(2), 1-20.

De Geus, A. P. (1988, March/April). Planning as learning. *Harvard Business Review, 66,* 70-74.

Deshpandé, R., Farley, J. U., & Webster, F. E., Jr. (1993). Corporate culture, customer orientation, and innovativeness in Japanese firms: A quadrad analysis. *Journal of Marketing, 57*(1), 23-37. (See also Chapter 4)

Deshpandé, R., & Webster, F. E., Jr. (1989). Organizational culture and marketing: Defining the research agenda. *Journal of Marketing, 53*(1), 3-15.

Dess, G. G. (1987, May/June). Consensus on strategy formulation and organizational performance: Competitors in a fragmented industry. *Strategic Management Journal, 8,* 259-277.

Dess, G. G., & Origer, N. K. (1987, April). Environment, structure, and consensus in strategy formulation: A conceptual integration. *Academy of Management Review, 12,* 313-330.

Dickson, P. R. (1992). Toward a general theory of competitive rationality. *Journal of Marketing, 56,* 69-83.

Eisenhardt, K. M. (1989, September). Making fast strategic decisions in high-velocity environments. *Academy of Management Journal, 32,* 543-576.

Fiol, C. M., & Lyles, M. A. (1985). Organizational learning. *Academy of Management Review, 10*(4), 803-813.

Garvin, D. A. (1993, July/August). Building a learning organization. *Harvard Business Review, 71,* 78-91.

Ghemawat, P. (1986, September/October). Sustainable advantage. *Harvard Business Review, 64,* 53-58.

Gupta, A. K., & Govindarajan, V. (1991). Knowledge flows and the structure of control within multinational corporations. *Academy of Management Review, 16*(4), 768-792.

Gupta, A. K., Raj, S. P., & Wilemon, D. (1985). R&D and marketing dialogue in high-tech firms. *Industrial Marketing Management, 14,* 289-300.

Gupta, A. K., Raj, S. P., & Wilemon, D. (1986). A model for studying R&D—Marketing interface in the product innovation process. *Journal of Marketing, 50*(2), 7-17.

Guth, W. D., & Ginsberg, A. (1990, Summer). Guest editors' introduction: Corporate entrepreneurship. *Strategic Management Journal, 11,* 5-15.

Hamel, G., & Prahalad, C. K. (1989, May/June). Strategic intent. *Harvard Business Review, 67,* 63-76.

Hamel, G., & Prahalad, C. K. (1991, July/August). Corporate imagination and expeditionary marketing. *Harvard Business Review, 69,* 81-92.

Hart, S. L. (1992, April). An integrative framework for strategy-making processes. *Academy of Management Review, 17,* 327-351.

Howard, R. (1992, September/October). The CEO as organizational architect: An interview with Xerox's Paul Allaire. *Harvard Business Review, 70,* 106-121.

Huber, G. P. (1991, February). Organizational learning: The contributing processes and the literatures. *Organization Science, 2,* 88-115.

Jack Welch's lessons for success. (1993). *Leadership Lessons,* 24-29. (Reprinted from *Fortune, 127*(2), January 25, 1993)

Jacobson, R. (1992). The "Austrian" school of strategy. *Academy of Management Review, 17*(4), 782-807.

Jaworski, B. J. (1988). Toward a theory of marketing control: Environmental context, control types, and consequences. *Journal of Marketing, 52*(3), 23-39.

Jaworski, B. J., & Kohli, A. K. (1993). Market orientation: Antecedents and consequences. *Journal of Marketing, 57*(3), 53-70. (See also Chapter 5)

Kanter, R. M. (1989). *When giants learn to dance.* New York: Touchstone.

Kanter, R. M. (1991, January/February). Championing change: An interview with Bell Atlantic's CEO Raymond Smith. *Harvard Business Review, 69,* 118-130.

Kanter, R. M., Stein, B. A., & Jick, T. D. (1992). *The challenge of organizational change: How companies experience it and leaders guide it.* New York: Free Press.

Kohli, A. K., & Jaworski, B. J. (1990). Market orientation: The construct, research propositions, and managerial implications. *Journal of Marketing, 54*(2), 1-18. (See also Chapter 2)

Kotter, J. P., & Heskett, J. L. (1992). *Corporate culture and performance.* New York: Free Press.

Kuhn, T. (1970). *The structure of scientific revolutions* (2nd ed.). Chicago: University of Chicago Press.

Leonard-Barton, D. (1992). Core capabilities and core rigidities: A paradox in managing new product development. *Strategic Management Journal, 13,* 111-125.

Letters to the Editor. (1993, September/October). *Harvard Business Review, 71,* 190-200.

Levitt, B., & March, J. G. (1988). Organizational learning. *Annual Review of Sociology, 14,* 319-340.

Loomis, C. J. (1993, May 9). Dinosaurs? *Fortune, 127,* 36-42.

March, J. G. (1991). Exploration and exploitation in organizational learning. *Organization Science, 2,* 71-87.

March, J. G., & Olsen, J. P. (1975). The uncertainty of the past: Organizational learning under ambiguity. *European Journal of Political Research, 3,* 147-171.

Martin, R. (1993, November/December). Changing the mind of the corporation. *Harvard Business Review, 71,* 81-94.

McGill, M. E., Slocum, J. W., Jr., & Lei, D. (1992, Summer). Management practices in learning organizations. *Organizational Dynamics,* 5-17.

McKenna, R. (1991, January/February). Marketing is everything. *Harvard Business Review, 69,* 65-79.

McQuarrie, E. F., & McIntyre, S. H. (1992). *The customer visit: An emerging practice in business-to-business marketing* (Report No. 92-114). Cambridge, MA: Marketing Science Institute.

Meen, D. E., & Keough, M. (1992). Creating the learning organization. *McKinsey Quarterly, 1,* 58-86.

Menon, A., & Varadarajan, P. R. (1992). A model of marketing knowledge use within firms. *Journal of Marketing, 56*(4), 53-71.

Miles, R. E., & Snow, C. C. (1978). *Organizational strategy, structure, and process.* New York: McGraw-Hill.

Miles, R. E., & Snow, C. C. (1992, Summer). Causes of failure in network organizations. *California Management Review,* 53-72.

Miller, D. (1987, January/February). The structural and environmental correlates of business strategy. *Strategic Management Journal, 8,* 55-76.

Miller, D., & Friesen, P. H. (1980). Momentum and revolution in organizational adaptation. *Academy of Management Journal, 23*(4), 591-614.

Miller, D., & Friesen, P. H. (1982). Innovation in conservative and entrepreneurial firms: Two models of strategic momentum. *Strategic Management Journal, 3,* 1-25.

Mintzberg, H. (1987). Crafting strategy. *Harvard Business Review, 65*(5), 66-75.

Mintzberg, H. (1991). The innovative organization. In H. Mintzberg & J. B. Quinn (Eds.), *The strategy process: Concepts, contexts, cases* (2nd ed., pp. 731-746). Englewood Cliffs, NJ: Prentice Hall.

Naman, J. L., & Slevin, D. P. (1993). Entrepreneurship and the concept of fit: A model and empirical tests. *Strategic Management Journal, 14,* 137-153.

Narver, J. C., & Slater, S. F. (1990). The effect of a market orientation on business profitability. *Journal of Marketing, 54*(4), 20-35. (See also Chapter 3)

Nonaka, I. (1991, November/December). The knowledge-creating company. *Harvard Business Review, 69,* 96-104.

Pascale, R. T., & Athos, A. G. (1981). *The art of Japanese management.* New York: Warner.

Pfeffer, J., & Salancik, G. R. (1978). *The external control of organizations: A resource dependent perspective.* New York: Harper & Row.

Porter, M. E. (1980). *Competitive strategy: Techniques for analyzing industries and competitors.* New York: Free Press.

Potts, M. (1992). Toward a boundary-less firm at General Electric. In R. M. Kanter, B. A. Stein, & T. D. Jick (Eds.), *The challenge of organizational change* (pp. 450-455). New York: Free Press.

Prahalad, C. K., & Bettis, R. (1986). The dominant logic: A new linkage between diversity and performance. *Strategic Management Journal, 7,* 485-501.

Prokesch, S. E. (1993, November/December). Mastering chaos at the high-tech frontier: An interview with Silicon Graphic's Ed McCracken. *Harvard Business Review, 71,* 134-144.

Quinn, J. B. (1978). Strategic change: Logical incrementalism. *Sloan Management Review, 20,* 7-21.

Quinn, J. B. (1985, May/June). Managing innovation: Controlled chaos. *Harvard Business Review, 63,* 73-84.

Quinn, J. B. (1991). Managing strategies incrementally. In H. Mintzberg & J. B. Quinn (Eds.), *The strategy process: Concepts, contexts, cases* (2nd ed., pp. 800-807). Englewood Cliffs, NJ: Prentice Hall.

Quinn, J. B. (1992). *Intelligent enterprise.* New York: Free Press.

Ruekert, R. W. (1992). Developing a market orientation: An organizational strategy perspective. *International Journal of Research in Marketing, 9,* 225-245.

Ruekert, R. W., & Walker, O. C., Jr. (1987). Interactions between marketing and R&D departments in implementing different business strategies. *Strategic Management Journal, 8,* 233-248.

Ruekert, R. W., Walker, O. C., Jr., & Roering, K. J. (1985). The organization of marketing activities: A contingency theory of structure and performance. *Journal of Marketing, 49*(1), 13-25.

Schein, E. H. (1990, February). Organizational culture. *American Psychologist, 45,* 109-119.

Schein, E. H. (1993, Winter). How can organizations learn faster? The challenge of entering the green room. *Sloan Management Review,* 85-92.

Schendel, D. (1990, Summer). Introduction to the special issue on corporate entrepreneurship. *Strategic Management Journal, 11,* 1-3.

Schumpeter, J. A. (1934). *The theory of economic development.* Cambridge, MA: Harvard University Press.

Schumpeter, J. A. (1942). *Capitalism, socialism and democracy.* New York: Harpers.

Schweiger, D. M., Sandberg, W. R., & Ragan, J. W. (1986). Group approaches for improving strategic decision making: A comparative analysis of dialectical inquiry, devil's advocacy, and consensus. *Academy of Management Journal, 29,* 51-71.

Schwenk, C. R. (1989). A meta-analysis on the comparative effectiveness of devil's advocacy and dialectical inquiry. *Strategic Management Journal, 10,* 303-306.

Sellers, P. (1993, November 15). Do you need your ad agency? *Fortune,* 147-164.

Senge, P. M. (1990, Fall). The leader's new work: Building learning organizations. *Sloan Management Review,* 7-23.

Shapiro, B. P. (1988, November/December). What the hell is "market oriented"? *Harvard Business Review, 66,* 119-125.

Simon, H. (1957). *Administrative behavior.* New York: Free Press.

Simon, H. (1969). *Sciences of the artificial.* Cambridge: MIT Press.

Sinkula, J. M. (1994). Market information processing and organizational learning. *Journal of Marketing, 58*(1), 35-45.

Slater, S. F., & Narver, J. C. (1994). Does competitive environment moderate the market orientation performance relationship? *Journal of Marketing, 58*(1), 46-55. (See also Chapter 6)

Stalk, G. (1988, July/August). Time—The next source of competitive advantage. *Harvard Business Review, 66,* 41-51.

Stalk, G., Evans, P., & Shulman, L. E. (1992, March/April). Competing on capabilities: The new rules of corporate strategy. *Harvard Business Review, 70,* 57-69.

Stata, R. (1989, Spring). Organizational learning—The key to management innovation. *Sloan Management Review,* 63-74.

Stevenson, H. H., & Jarillo, J. C. (1990, Summer). A paradigm of entrepreneurship: Entrepreneurial management. *Strategic Management Journal, 11,* 17-27.

Stewart, T. A. (1992). GE keeps those ideas coming. In R. M. Kanter, B. A. Stein, & T. D. Jick (Eds.), *The challenge of organizational change* (pp. 474-482). New York: Free Press.

Sujan, H., Weitz, B., & Kumar, N. (1993). *Learning orientation, working smart, and effective selling* (Report No. 93-119). Cambridge, MA: Marketing Science Institute.

Sykes, H. B., & Block, Z. (1989). Corporate venturing obstacles: Sources and solutions. *Journal of Business Venturing, 4,* 159-167.

Takeuchi, H., & Nonaka, I. (1986, January/February). The new new product development game. *Harvard Business Review, 64,* 137-146.

von Hippel, E. (1986, July). Lead users: A source of novel product concepts. *Management Science, 32,* 791-805.

Webster, F. E., Jr. (1992). The changing role of marketing in the corporation. *Journal of Marketing, 56*(4), 1-17.

Weick, K. E. (1979). *Social psychology of organizing.* Reading, MA: Addison-Wesley.

Welsh, T. (1994, February 7). Best and worst corporate reputations. *Fortune,* 58-76.

Womack, J. P., Jones, D. T., & Roos, D. (1990). *The machine that changed the world: The story of lean production.* New York: HarperCollins.

Woodman, R. W., Sawyer, J. E., & Griffin, R. W. (1993). Toward a theory of organizational creativity. *Academy of Management Review, 18*(2), 293-321.

Wrapp, H. E. (1967, September/October). Good managers don't make policy decisions. *Harvard Business Review,* 91-99.

Additional Reading

Dougherty, D. (1990, Summer). Understanding new markets for new products. *Strategic Management Journal, 11,* 59-78.

Sykes, H. B. (1986). The anatomy of a corporate venturing program. *Journal of Business Venturing, 1,* 275-293.

The Influence of Market Orientation on Channel Relationships

A Dyadic Examination

Judy A. Siguaw
Penny M. Simpson
Thomas L. Baker

Many companies have sought to alter channels of distribution to achieve the strategic gains necessary to compete in challenging global markets. At the same time, marketers have advocated adoption of the marketing concept and a market orientation to enhance competitive positioning. A meshing of the two concepts—using a market orientation to alter the channel of distribution relationship—may provide companies with a viable way of creating a sustainable competitive advantage and enhancing organizational performance.

It has been determined from market orientation research that market-oriented behaviors positively affect various corporate measures such as profitability, employees' attitudes, and salesperson orientations. In this study, Siguaw, Simpson, and Baker examine the influence of market orientation on key factors that may influence the performance of the channel, most notably trust, cooperation, and commitment. Using 179 matched sets of questionnaires from a national sample of distributor members of the National Association of Wholesalers and their key suppliers, they found that the direct effects of market orientation on trust, cooperation, and performance were significant.

Their findings lend strong support to the importance of a market orientation in a channel relationship to strengthen the relationship and to enhance organizational performance. Furthermore, this study highlights additional benefits to both parties in the channel dyad of seeking to fulfill customer needs. A mutually held market orientation allows channel members to better serve shifting market needs within the context of strategic partners pursuing the same goals. These market-oriented actions also strengthen channel alliances.

Mutual trust has been found to be more crucial to the formation of strong channel relationships than contractual agreements or techniques. To facilitate the creation of trusting channel relationships, firms should adopt market-oriented behaviors. This research clearly indicates that market orientation has a positive and significant effect on the level of trust in the dyadic relationship and, thereby, indirectly influences cooperation and commitment. Consequently, the practice of market-oriented behaviors is a critical means of building and reinforcing trust in the channel relationship to keep channels intact and to reduce channel tensions.

Market orientation also has a positive direct and indirect effect on channel performance. Because better performance is the ultimate goal of business, a strong market orientation appears to be a critical element for all firms.

The challenges presented by foreign competition and maturing domestic markets have created tensions between manufacturers and other channel members that demand a satisfactory resolution (Frazier & Antia, 1995; Webster, 1992). Given the significant and broad effects of market orientation identified in prior research, one viable strategy for easing these strained channel relationships, while countering future environmental threats, may be the adoption of market-oriented behaviors. A high level of market orientation within a channel relationship would incorporate the advantages of corporate alliances but still allow the economies created by the performance of specialized, independent firms (Anderson & Weitz, 1992).

The importance of market orientation to the marketing discipline is evidenced by the number of recent research studies incorporating the market orientation construct (Cadogan & Diamantopoulos, 1995; Day, 1994; Kohli, Jaworski, & Kumar, 1993). To date, this research has indicated that market-oriented behaviors have positive effects on profitability (Ruekert, 1992; Slater & Narver, 1994; Webster, 1992), employees' attitudes (Jaworski & Kohli, 1993), and salesperson orientations (Siguaw, Brown, & Widing, 1994). This research, however, has ignored the potential impact of market orientation on channel relationships and the ramifications of market-oriented behaviors within a dyadic relationship. The lack of attention devoted to the study of market orientation within a channel relationship context is regrettable given the sweeping effects of the firm's market-oriented actions and the established importance of good channel relationships (Kumar, Scheer, & Steenkamp, 1995).

The empirical research undertaken and described here involves an analysis of the interrelationships of market orientation and other channel relationship elements within the dyad formed by the manufacturer and distributor. We provide a brief discussion of market orientation and the importance of dyadic research. Then an iterative model is presented that depicts the hypothesized direct and indirect relationships between the market orientation of the dyad and the levels of trust, cooperation, commitment, and performance found within the manufacturer-distributor relationship. The roles of selected mediating variables—shared values, communication, relationship benefits, relationship duration, and relationship termination costs—are also included in the posited conceptualization. Data collected from 179 manufacturer-distributor dyads are used to test the hypothesized relationships via three-stage least squares regression and partial correlations, and the results are provided. We conclude with a discussion incorporating an overview of the study and managerial implications designed to assist the practitioner in evaluating the selection and pursuit of a specific company orientation.

Background and Definition of Market Orientation

Before presenting the conceptual development of the proposed model and the corresponding research propositions, a discussion of the market orientation construct is provided due to the mixed operationalizations presented in the literature (Dreher, 1993). For the most part, definitions of market orientation have been developed from conceptualizations of the marketing concept; therefore, much of the variation in definitions may be attributed to the diverse manner in which the marketing concept has been defined over time. Initially, King (1965) defined the marketing concept as "a managerial philosophy concerned with mobilization, utilization, and control of total corporate effort for the purpose of helping consumers solve selected problems in ways compatible with planned enhancement of the profit position of the firm" (p. 85). Consistent with King (1965), Barksdale and Darden (1971) and McNamara (1972) identified three components of the marketing concept: (a) the customer as a focal point for business activities, (b) the necessity of integrating marketing activities across functions, and (c) the need for a profit orientation. These balanced conceptualizations, however, were opposed by other scholars. For example, Bell and Emory (1971) argued that profit is a consequence of customer orientation; therefore, customer orientation should take precedence over profit orientation. Conversely, Houston (1986) argued that profit should be the reason for adopting a customer orientation: "Satisfaction of the market's demand is important to the extent that doing so yields profits" (p. 85).

Day and Wensley (1983) contended that all the earlier conceptualizations of the marketing concept failed to adequately address the need for a competitor orientation. They cautioned that the three-pillar marketing concept is appropriate for a static market, but the dynamic nature of today's marketplace requires the firm to also consider competitive offerings and strategies.

By the late 1980s, the term *market orientation* was being used synonymously with *marketing concept* (Shapiro, 1988; Webster, 1988), and the governing determinants of a market orientation were identified as market information collection and usage. Indeed, Shapiro (1988, p. 120) noted that an organization has a market orientation only if "[i]nformation on all important buying influences permeates every corporate function," whereas Selnes and Wesenberg (1993, p. 23) explained market orientation as a "response to market information."

In accordance with this informational focal point for market orientation, Kohli and Jaworski (1990) conceptualized market orientation as the implementation of the marketing concept and developed a measure (Kohli et al., 1993) that focused on the firm's activities and behaviors regarding customer needs, competitive information, market intelligence, and the sharing of such knowledge across organizational functions. A profitability component was not incorporated into this conceptualization of market orientation.

Narver and Slater (1990) offered a somewhat different view of market orientation, suggesting that market orientation consists of three behavioral components (customer orientation, competitor orientation, and interfunctional coordination) and two decision criteria (long-term focus and profitability). Congruent with recent beliefs regarding the linkage between market orientation and market information, Narver and Slater proposed that the behavioral components comprise "the activities of market information acquisition and dissemination and the coordinated creation of customer value" (p. 21).

For the purposes of this study, we adopt a balanced view of market orientation that features concepts that have been synthesized from the literature. Thus, we define market orientation as the set of behaviors emanating from the organization's leadership whose primary objective is to acquire and use market information for the purpose of satisfying customer needs through superior organizational performance on an ongoing basis (Jaworski & Kohli, 1993; Kohli & Jaworski, 1990; Narver & Slater, 1990; Slater, Narver, & Aaby, 1994).

Importance of Dyadic Research

Much of the emerging research involving channels issues has centered on the dyadic relationship between firms (Anderson & Narus, 1990; Anderson & Weitz, 1992; Ganesan, 1994)—a stream of study that has been labeled of "paramount interest" (Anderson, Håkansson, & Johanson, 1994). Collecting dyadic data from both suppliers and distributors within a channel relationship has been strongly encouraged by researchers to facilitate academic and practitioner understanding of relationship development, management, and maintenance (Weitz & Jap, 1995). In the current study, we recognize that the relevant level of analysis is with the dyad that is formed and the relationship developed between participants in the channel rather than with the individual organizations. Indeed, Baker and Hawes (1993) note that "a channel dyad can be thought of as an 'organization' because the success of each organization is dependent on the success of the other" (p. 85). Thus, we emphasize that the framework and hypotheses presented in this study focus on the dyadic relationship rather than on the individual behaviors and attitudes of the supplier and distributor.

Conceptual Framework and Hypotheses

The model to be developed and tested in this chapter is presented in Figure 11.1. The model is circular to depict the ongoing, iterative relationship

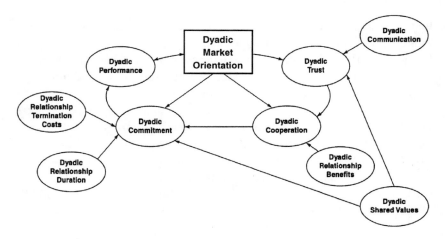

Figure 11.1. Proposed Effects of Market Orientation on Channel of Distribution Relationship Variables

or process that is characteristic of manufacturer-supplier relationships; this nonrecursive process has been defined and supported in previous studies (Anderson & Weitz, 1992). In the proposed model, market orientation is hypothesized to directly impact the other major constructs of interest (trust, cooperation, commitment, and performance). In addition, market orientation implicitly is hypothesized to indirectly affect the relationships between trust, cooperation, commitment, and performance via the proposed direct effect of market orientation on trust. Although the posited model implies a cycle that occurs over time, the empirical data presented here investigate the hypothesized relationships at one point in time and thus provide a static perspective. Support for the use of cross-sectional data to examine channel relationships is derived from Weitz and Jap (1995), who noted that such relationships typically develop incrementally.

Although the focus of this study is on the relationships between market orientation, trust, cooperation, commitment, and performance, secondary relationships involving the constructs of communication, shared values, relationship duration, relationship benefits, and relationship termination costs are also investigated to assist with model specification. Admittedly, the list of mediating constructs included in this model is necessarily limited, and other relevant variables may be omitted; those mediating variables well substantiated in the literature, however, are incorporated to avoid an omission of specification error. After presenting a discussion of our conceptualization of the market orientation of the dyad, we present the hypotheses relative to the primary variables in the model followed by the hypotheses relating the secondary variables to the primary ones.

Market Orientation of the Dyad

The market orientation of the channel dyad is posited to consist of the distributor's market orientation and the supplier's market orientation as well as the distributor's perception of the supplier's market orientation and the supplier's perception of the distributor's market orientation. That is, the level of market orientation within the dyad will be determined by the actual market-oriented behaviors of both participants and by how each party perceives the other party's market orientation. Through their verbal and nonverbal communication, distributors and suppliers presumably reveal their actual market orientation to each other, which may not necessarily be the intended market orientation (for a discussion of commitment behavior, see Anderson & Weitz, 1992). Interpretation of this behavior will, in turn, be affected by each party's own market-oriented behaviors. Each participant in the channel relationship must perceive the other participant's market orientation as meeting or exceeding its own or the market orientation of any alternative party or both before the latter participant will be perceived as market-oriented (for similar effects for other relationship variables, see Anderson et al., 1994). Thus, the market orientation of the dyad will be high only if actual and perceived behaviors of each party are highly market oriented.

Primary Relationships

Market Orientation and Trust. Trust has been called a "fundamental relationship model building block" (Wilson, 1995, p. 337) and involves confidence that the other party will behave in a fair, noncoercive, concerned manner (Carnevale & Wechsler, 1992; Cook & Wall, 1980; Hrebiniak, 1971; Rotter, 1967). Carnevale and Wechsler noted, "The development of trust in a relationship is reciprocal, so that individuals [or firms] respond in kind to the trust or mistrust directed toward them" (p. 473). Other studies have also supported this progression of trust in a relationship (Becker, 1987; Garfinkel, 1964; Golembiewski & McConkie, 1975; Luhman, 1979). Thus, as greater trust is placed in the supplier, the distributor presumably responds in a manner meant to encourage the supplier to place greater trust in the distributor and vice versa. One form of trust is identification based; this manifestation of trust is defined by Shapiro, Sheppard, and Cheraskin (1992, p. 371) as "the highest order of trust [which] assumes that one party has fully internalized the other's preferences." By definition, a market-oriented organization collects information concerning customer needs and strives to meet these needs in a competitive fashion, thereby internalizing its customers' preferences. Prior research has also indicated that individuals trust organizations that allow open communication and the opportunity to participate (Carnevale & Wechsler, 1992). Because communication between customers and the firm regarding needs, services, and products is an integral part of market orientation and because market orientation permits customer input into the production process, which in turn increases joint identification, distributors of a market-oriented supplier should have greater trust in the supplying organization. Furthermore, the basis of a market orientation is the gathering and utilization of information to satisfy customer needs. These corporate actions demonstrate concern and noncoerciveness and thus increase trust in the relationship. These arguments suggest that a high level of market orientation within the dyad should increase the level of trust within the dyad. Therefore, the market orientation of the dyad is hypothesized to influence the level of dyadic trust, which is a function of the degree of trust between two parties.

H_1: The greater the market orientation of the dyad, the greater the level of trust within the dyadic relationship.

Trust and Cooperation. Trust within the dyad is hypothesized to positively influence cooperative behavior in which parties unite to accomplish shared goals (Anderson & Narus, 1990). We suggest that trust is an attitude or frame of mind, whereas cooperation is the behavioral result of this attitude. This conceptualization is consistent with that of Morgan and Hunt (1994, p. 24), who argued that " 'willingness to rely' should be viewed as an outcome . . . of trust," where willingness to rely is the behavioral intention of trust. The relationship between cooperation and trust may actually be bidirectional, but "the initiation of the relationship is based on a certain level of 'beginning' trust" (Neilson & Wilson, 1994, p. 6). Hence, initial feelings of trust lead to cooperative efforts, which, if satisfactory, in turn lead to increased levels of trust that then increase efforts to cooperate. Although the direction of causation is open for discussion, the proposed relationship, which indicates that trust must be present to gain cooperative behavior, has been previously supported in the social science and marketing literature (Deutsch, 1960; Loomis, 1959; Morgan & Hunt, 1994; Pruitt, 1981).

H_2: The greater the level of trust within the dyad, the greater the cooperation demonstrated within the dyadic relationship.

Cooperation and Commitment. Commitment has previously been determined to be an outcome of trust (Achrol, 1991; Moorman, Zaltman, & Deshpandé, 1992; Morgan & Hunt, 1994); similarly, a recent study posited commitment as a critical consequence of cooperation (Anderson et al., 1994). We believe that the appropriate linkage among these variables is trust → cooperation → commitment.

In this study, commitment is measured as a psychological attachment (Angle & Lawson, 1993; Porter, Steers, Mowday, & Boulian, 1974). Cooperation is hypothesized to directly influence commitment, where commitment is defined as "an exchange partner *believing* [italics added] that an ongoing relationship with another is so important as to warrant maximum efforts at maintaining it" (Morgan & Hunt, 1994, p. 23). We do not believe that commitment can be achieved without initial cooperative efforts serving as a behavioral intent (outward expression) of the trust between the two parties. That is, some form of cooperation (as a behavioral expression of trust) must exist between two parties prior to the parties believing that they are committed to the relationship. This posited relationship between cooperation and commitment is contrary to the view of Morgan and Hunt (1994), who indicated support for their contention that "[a] partner committed to the relationship will cooperate with another member because of a desire to make the relationship work" (p. 26). Although committed partners will certainly seek to continue cooperating with one another after commitment is established, cooperation must exist first. Therefore, we believe that the placement of cooperation between trust and commitment is logical and theoretically sound. Accordingly,

H_3: The greater the cooperation of the dyad, the greater the commitment within the dyadic relationship.

Commitment and Performance. Commitment to a relationship is thought to result in a higher performance level ("And Now," 1986; Stern & El-Ansary, 1990) and provide advantages (e.g., greater satisfaction of customer needs and greater access to market information or critical resources) not found in traditional channels (Anderson & Weitz, 1992; Buchanan, 1992; Hickson, Hinnings, Lee, Schneck, & Pennings, 1971). Only partial empirical support for this perspective has been reported in the literature, however. Kumar, Hibbard, and Stern (1994) determined that affective relationship commitment results in better organizational performance, whereas calculative and moral commitment resulted in lower performance. Heide and Stump (1995) indicated that relationship continuity (measured as the expectation that the relationship would continue in the future) had a positive effect on performance only when conditions of high uncertainty and specific assets were involved; otherwise, continuity had a low or negative influence on performance. Similarly, Buchanan (1992) reported that the level of dependence between trade partners had a significant effect on performance under conditions of high uncertainty. Although previous research has provided equivocal results regarding the relationship between commitment and performance, we expect that the commitment construct we have included in our framework will affect performance in a manner similar to that of the affective relationship commitment construct tested by Kumar et al. (1994). That is, persistent behavior designed to sustain the dyadic relationship will benefit the performance of both parties within the dyad. Thus, we propose the following:

H_4: The greater the commitment of the dyad, the greater the
performance of the dyad.

Performance and Market Orientation. Our model is completed by linking performance and market orientation. Firms that recognize the direct and indirect effects of market orientation on performance would likely pursue higher levels of market-oriented behaviors to attain increased performance goals; that is, higher levels of performance are hypothesized to encourage behaviors that will result in greater levels of market orientation. The hypothesized association between performance and market orientation is approximately equivalent to the finding that higher profits will increase the probability of continuing a business relationship (Gladstein, 1984). Therefore, we propose that the greater the benefits (e.g., higher market share and profits) indirectly derived from the practice of market-oriented behaviors through the trust-cooperation-commitment linkage, the more likely is a firm to increase its efforts at developing and maintaining such an orientation. Hence,

H_5: The greater the performance of the dyad, the greater the practice of market-oriented behaviors within the dyadic relationship.

Market Orientation and Cooperation. In the conceptualized model, market orientation is posited to positively and directly affect cooperation. Although an association between market orientation and cooperation has not been previously proposed in the literature, by definition channel members that are market-oriented are seeking to provide a superior value to meet the needs of their customers. Therefore, market-oriented channel members have a common goal of serving customers, and when these parties exert efforts to achieve this common goal they are engaging in cooperative behaviors (Anderson & Narus, 1990). Accordingly,

H_6: The greater the market orientation of the dyad, the greater the level of cooperation within the dyadic relationship.

Market Orientation and Commitment. Few studies have examined the relationship between market orientation and commitment posited in our model. A strong association between market orientation and organizational commitment of employees has been empirically tested and supported (Jaworski & Kohli, 1993; Siguaw et al., 1994); the linkage between market orientation and commitment to the channel relationship, however, has not been explicitly examined in prior studies, although variables closely related to channel commitment have been investigated. For example, Kohli and Jaworski (1990) conceptualized a causal relationship between market orientation and "repeat business from customers," whereas Narver and Slater (1990) empirically tested and found support for an association between market orientation and customer retention. The theoretical underpinnings thus suggest a positive relationship between market orientation and commitment; consequently, we assert the following:

H_7: The greater the market orientation of the dyad, the greater the level of commitment within the dyadic relationship.

Market Orientation and Performance. In the hypothesized model, market orientation is posited to have a direct and positive effect on channel performance. Although this relationship has frequently been assumed to exist (Houston, 1986; Webster, 1988), empirical evidence provides only equivocal support. Narver and Slater (1990) found that "market orientation is an important determinant of profitability" (p. 32). Their finding is consistent with studies by Lusch and Laczniak (1987), Ruekert (1992), and Webster (1992). Other researchers have reported that market orientation is significantly related to judgmental performance measures but not necessarily to objective measures, such as market share, sales growth, and profit margin (Diamantopoulos & Hart, 1993; Jaworski & Kohli, 1993). In their discussion, Jaworski and Kohli conjectured that certain objective measures (e.g., market share) may not be good indicators of performance or that a lagged effect of market orientation on these variables may occur. Although some inconsistencies in findings exist, the weight of evidence appears to support a linkage between market orientation and performance; thus, the proposed model is specified to test the following hypothesis:

H_8: The greater the market orientation of the dyad, the greater the performance within the dyadic relationship.

Secondary Relationships

Communication. Although we propose that market orientation should lead to increased trust within the relationship, communication between channel members will also influence trust. Anderson and Narus (1990) define communication as "the formal as well as informal sharing of meaningful and timely information between firms" (p. 44). Communication has routinely been cited in the literature as a positive influence on trust (Dwyer, Schurr, & Oh, 1987; Mellinger, 1956; Morgan & Hunt, 1994), and increased interaction has been determined to specifically strengthen dyadic trust (Samter & Burleson, 1984). Therefore,

H_9: The greater the communication between the supplier and distributor, the greater the perceptions of trust within the relationship.

Shared Values. Shared business values are measured as the degree to which two channel members believe in the utilization of the same business practices (Hunt, Wood, & Chonko, 1989). The absence of a common culture composed of similar business values makes the maintenance of the relationship very difficult (Wilson, 1995). For example, one channel member may believe in utilizing questionable practices to increase sales, whereas the other believes that long-term rewards will only be achieved through ethical behaviors. Consequently, although the two parties may be involved in an exchange transaction or series of exchange transactions, they are reluctant to trust and commit to an exchange relationship due to fundamental differences in the way they practice business. In this case, the parties recognize that a further meshing of the two organizations would be difficult because of differences in their basic business values. Prior research has indicated that channel members with congruent values will have greater trust in and commitment to the relationship (Morgan & Hunt, 1994). Thus,

$H_{10:}$ The greater the similarity in shared values within a dyad, the greater the perceptions of trust between these channel members.

$H_{11:}$ The greater the similarity in shared values within a dyad, the greater the perceptions of commitment between these channel members.

Relationship Benefits. Although trust is hypothesized to increase cooperation, cooperation is also posited to be influenced by the benefits of the dyadic relationship. Cooperation is necessary to derive the potential benefits of the dyadic relationship (Anderson & Weitz, 1992). Buchanan (1992, p. 67) notes that if trade partners value one another's resources, "they are unlikely to act opportunistically." In other words, channel members are more likely to undertake cooperative behaviors together when one or both parties perceive benefits of the required effort.

$H_{12:}$ The greater the perceived benefits of the relationship, the greater the cooperation within the dyad.

Relationship Termination Costs and Relationship Duration. Commitment is hypothesized to be influenced by two additional factors—relationship termination costs and the duration of the business relationship. Relationship termination costs are those expenses that would be incurred or investments that would be lost if the relationship ended. High switching costs may increase a party's "interest in maintaining a quality relationship" (Dwyer et al., 1987, p. 14), whereas low termination costs may encourage the dissatisfied party to exit the relationship (Buchanan, 1992).

The duration of the business association is hypothesized to influence commitment within the relationship. Although relationship longevity does not sufficiently capture relationship commitment, duration of a relationship likely influences commitment (Kelley, 1983). That is, the longer the business association has endured between the two parties, the more likely the parties are to feel committed to the relationship.

H_{13}: The greater the relationship termination costs, the greater the commitment between these channel members.

H_{14}: The greater the duration of the business association, the greater the commitment between these channel members.

Methods

Data Collection

To test the hypotheses generated from the model presented in Figure 11.1, data were collected from matching manufacturer and distributor dyads. Names of distributors were culled from the membership rosters of associations affiliated with the National Association of Wholesalers; these associations included Associated Equipment Distributors, Fluid Power Distributors Association, International Wholesale Furniture Association, National Electronic Distributors Association, National Fastener Distributors Association, National Welding Supply Association, and Power Transmission Distributors Association. Each distributor was first contacted by telephone to secure cooperation in the study and to obtain the name of a person with the distributor's primary supplier who was most knowledgeable about the relationship. Coded questionnaires were mailed to all informants along with a cover letter on university stationery explaining the coding system (to match the manufacturer-distributor dyad), the purpose of the study, and the confidentiality of responses.

Surveys were returned to the researchers via preaddressed, postage-paid envelopes enclosed with the questionnaires. One follow-up mailing with a duplicate questionnaire and cover letter was sent to nonrespondents.

A total of 1,127 supplier-distributor dyads received questionnaires. The two mailings resulted in responses from 453 distributors and 380 manufacturers for an overall response rate of 36.95%. Of these respondents, 179 matched sets of questionnaires (a total of 358) were received from distributors and their corresponding manufacturers. These matched responses provided the data used in the subsequent analysis.

Measures

All constructs included in this research, with the exception of relationship duration, were measured using multi-item scales drawn from prior studies (see Appendix 11.A for scale development and properties). The scales used to measure the constructs were exactly the same for both the distributors and the suppliers, with the exception of minor changes in wording to reflect the perspective of the party receiving the questionnaire. For example, an item on the communication scale sent to the suppliers read, "We hesitate to give this distributorship too much information," whereas the same item on the scale sent to the distributors read, "We hesitate to give this supplier too much information." The response categories for each scale were anchored by 1 (strongly disagree) and 7 (strongly agree), with the exception of the market orientation, commitment, and performance scales. Although these scales were also measured using 7-point response categories, the wording of the response alternatives was slightly altered to better fit the wording of the scale items.

All measures were determined by averaging the responses to each item in a particular scale. These mean dyadic responses were used to test the model; distributor and supplier responses, however, were compared to determine the extent of agreement between the two groups. As Table 11.1 indicates, there were significant differences in the responses of the two groups on almost every construct (market orientation, relationship benefits, and commitment were exceptions); these diverse perceptions on the part of channel members raise interesting questions for future research. Furthermore, these differences tend to bias the results of the model toward insignificance. The means, standard deviations, Cronbach's alphas, and construct intercorrelations for the constructs are presented in Table 11.2.

Table 11.1 Assessment of Agreement and Disagreement Between Suppliers' and Distributors' Responses

Variable	Distributor Mean	Supplier Mean	F	p
Market orientation	5.13	5.08	.44	.51
Trust	5.45	5.69	4.95	.03
Relationship termination costs	4.95	4.36	24.66	.00
Relationship benefits	4.29	4.42	.95	.33
Communication	4.71	5.17	17.55	.00
Shared values	6.51	6.65	3.02	.08
Cooperation	5.36	5.58	4.48	.04
Commitment	5.59	5.70	2.05	.15
Performance	4.64	5.34	26.46	.00

Table 11.2 Means, Standard Deviations, Cronbach's Alphas, and Correlations of Measures

				Variable									
Variable	Mean	SD	Cronbach's Alpha	D1	D2	D3	D4	D5	D6	D7	D8	D9	D10
D1	5.10	.70	a	1.00									
D2	5.57	1.03	.95	.61	1.00								
D3	4.66	1.15	.88	.29	.13	1.00							
D4	4.49	1.20	.75	.49	.48	.49	1.00						
D5	4.94	1.06	.82	.48	.53	.39	.62	1.00					
D6	7.58	.75	a	.27	.31	.12	.23	.24	1.00				
D7	5.47	.98	.83	.48	.66	.22	.38	.51	.22	1.00			
D8	6.18	.86	.90	.49	.59	.46	.51	.52	.31	.55	1.00		
D9	5.04	1.65	.92	.19	.20	−.03*	.15	.13	.13	.18	.14	1.00	
D10	8.41	13.73	a	.06*	.02*	.17	.13	.04*	.11	.02*	.13	.01*	1.00

NOTE: D1, marketing orientation (DYADMO); D2, trust (DYADTRST); D3, relationship termination costs (DYADCOST); D4, relationship benefits (DYADBENF); D5, communication (DYADCOMM); D6, shared values (DYADVALU); D7, cooperation (DYADCOOP); D8, commitment (DYADCOMT); D9, performance (DYADPERF); D10, relationship duration (DYADDUR).

a. Alpha value was unable to be calculated.

*$p > .05$.

Analysis

The iterative model, representing Hypotheses 1 through 5 and 9 through 14, was tested using three-stage least squares regression. This technique has been used to test other similarly structured (i.e., nonrecursive) models that have been reported in the marketing literature (Anderson & Weitz, 1992). The hypotheses can be represented by the following system of equations:

$$DYADTRST = \beta_{10} + \beta_{11}DYADMO + \beta_{12}DYADCOM + \beta_{13}DYADVALU \qquad [11.1]$$

$$DYADCOOP = \beta_{20} + \beta_{21}DYADTRST + \beta_{22}DYADBENF \qquad [11.2]$$

$$DYADCOMT = \beta_{30} + \beta_{31}DYADCOOP + \beta_{32}DYADCOST + \beta_{33}DYADVALU + \beta_{34}DYADDUR \qquad [11.3]$$

$$DYADPERF = \beta_{40} + \beta_{41}DYADCOMT \qquad [11.4]$$

$$DYADMO = \beta_{50} + \beta_{51}DYADPERF \qquad [11.5]$$

For parsimonious reasons and to avoid the increased level of multi-collinearity that would be introduced into the system of equations, the direct effects of market orientation on cooperation, commitment, and performance, represented by Hypotheses 6 through 8, were tested using partial correlation analysis. This method of analysis allows the determination of the relationship between two variables while controlling for the effects of other variables.

Results

Three-Stage Least Squares

This section presents the results of the tests of the iterative model, H_1 through H_5 and H_9 through $H_{14,}$ which are summarized in Table 11.3. The system of equations used to test these hypotheses has a system-weighted R^2 of .39.

Table 11.3 Results of Three-Stage Least Squares Regression Analysis

Endogenous Variable	Hypothesized Influence	Hypothesis Tested	Estimated Coefficient (Standardized)	t	p
Trust	Market orientation	H_1	$\beta_{11} = .66$	8.86	.0001
	Communication	H_9	$\beta_{12} = .28$	5.61	.0001
	Shared values	H_{10}	$\beta_{13} = .17$	2.97	.0032
Cooperation	Trust	H_2	$\beta_{21} = .63$	14.58	.0001
	Relationship benefits	H_{12}	$\beta_{22} = .04$	1.13	.2600
Commitment	Cooperation	H_3	$\beta_{31} = .42$	11.20	.0001
	Relationship termination costs	H_{13}	$\beta_{32} = .26$	8.43	.0001
	Shared values	H_{11}	$\beta_{33} = .16$	3.37	.0009
	Relationship duration	H_{14}	$\beta_{34} = .00$	.98	.3299
Performance	Commitment	H_4	$\beta_{41} = .40$	3.35	.0009
Market orientation	Performance	H_5	$\beta_{51} = .10$	4.40	.0001

Sample size = 179 dyads (a total of 358 respondents).

Trust. Equation 11.1 tests the hypothesized effects of market orientation, communication, and shared values on trust; strong support was found for all three hypotheses (H_1, H_9, and H_{10}). H_1 proposed that the level of market orientation in the relationship has a positive effect on the level of trust in the relationship. As shown in Table 11.3, the regression coefficient is positive and highly significant ($\beta_{11} = .66$, $p < .01$). The findings also indicate that the level of communication in the relationship has a significant and positive effect on the level of trust in the relationship ($\beta_{12} = .28$, $p < .01$). Finally, the regression coefficient provides strong support for H_{10}, which proposed that the greater the degree of shared values, the higher the level of trust in the relationship ($\beta_{13} = .17$, $p < .01$).

Cooperation. The estimated values of Equation 11.2 provide tests of the effects of trust and relationship benefits on cooperation (H_2 and H_{12}). The positive relationship posited between the level of trust in the relationship and the level of cooperation (H_2) receives strong support ($\beta_{21} = .63$, $p < .01$). The results indicate, however, that the benefits resulting from a relationship do not have a significant impact on the level of dyadic cooperation (H_{12}) because the regression coefficient, although in the predicted direction, is not significant ($\beta_{22} = .04$, $p = .26$).

Commitment. Equation 11.3 provides tests of the hypotheses that co-operation (H_3), shared values (H_{11}), relationship duration (H_{14}), and relationship termination costs (H_{13}) are all positively related to each partner's degree of commitment to the dyadic relationship. As proposed, there is a strong positive relationship between cooperation and commitment ($\beta_{31} = .42$, $p < .01$). In addition, Table 11.3 shows that both shared values and relationship termination costs are significantly and positively related to commitment. This finding indicates that firms have a tendency to be committed to other firms that are like themselves (shared values) and when costs associated with finding an alternative trading partner are high as predicted by research on the effect of transaction-specific assets (Heide & John, 1988). Interestingly, the amount of time the relationship between the two firms has been in place (DYADDUR) did not have a significant influence on cooperation between the firms ($\beta_{34} = .00$, $p > .05$).

Performance. The fourth equation provides a test of H_4, which proposes that commitment will result in a higher degree of performance. The regression coefficient is significant and positive, which provides support for the hypothesis ($\beta_{41} = .40$, $p < .01$).

Market Orientation. The model presented in Figure 11.1 proposes that there is a nonrecursive relationship between the variables included in the model such that if partners in dyadic relationships attribute part of their performance to the direct and indirect effects of market orientation, higher levels of performance should then lead to higher levels of market orientation (H_5). As Table 11.3 indicates, performance is positively and significantly related to market orientation ($\beta_{51} = .10$, $p < .01$).

Partial Correlation Analysis

The results of the partial correlation analysis used to test the direct effects of market orientation on cooperation, commitment, and performance (H_6-H_8) are presented in this section and summarized in Table 11.4.

Table 11.4 Results of Partial Correlation Analysis

Correlation Pair	Hypothesis Tested	Partial Correlation Coefficient	p
Market orientation and cooperation[a]	H_6	.10	.06
Market orientation and commitment[b]	H_7	.02	.75
Market orientation and performance[c]	H_8	.14	.02

a. Correlation was calculated while controlling for trust, communication, relationship benefits, and shared values.

b. Correlation was calculated while controlling for trust, cooperation, communication, relationship benefits, shared values, relationship termination costs, and relationship duration.

c. Correlation was calculated while controlling for trust, cooperation, commitment, communication, relationship benefits, shared values, relationship termination costs, and relationship duration.

H_6 proposes that market orientation directly and positively impacts the degree of cooperation in the dyadic relationship. The partial correlation coefficient between market orientation and cooperation was calculated, controlling for each of the variables that were hypothesized to enter the model prior to cooperation (i.e., trust, communication, relationship benefits, and shared values). Table 11.4 indicates that the coefficient, .10 ($p = .06$), was marginally significant, indicating that there is some direct impact of market orientation on cooperation. To conduct the test for H_7, the partial correlations coefficient between market orientation and commitment was calculated while controlling for the effects of trust, cooperation, communication, relationship benefits, shared values, relationship duration, and relationship termination costs. The coefficient, .02 ($p = .75$), was not significant, indicating that there is no direct relationship between market orientation and commitment when controlling for the effects of the other variables specified in the model. Finally, to conduct the test for H_8, the partial correlation coefficient between market orientation and performance was calculated while controlling for all the other variables specified in the model. In this case, the coefficient, .14 ($p = .02$), was significant, indicating that market orientation influences performance even when the effects of the other variables in the model are controlled.

Discussion and Conclusions

Although marketers have recognized the potential significance of a market orientation, empirical research examining its effects is still in its

Table 11.5 Summary of Findings

Hypothesis	Conclusion
H_1: The greater the market orientation of the dyad, the greater the level of trust within the dyadic relationship.	Supported
H_2: The greater the level of trust within the dyad, the greater the cooperation demonstrated within the dyadic relationship.	Supported
H_3: The greater the cooperation of the dyad, the greater the commitment within the dyadic relationship.	Supported
H_4: The greater the commitment of the dyad, the greater the performance of the dyad.	Supported
H_5: The greater the performance of the dyad, the greater the practice of market-oriented behaviors within the dyadic relationship.	Supported
H_6: The greater the market orientation of the dyad, the greater the level of cooperation within the dyadic relationship.	Marginally supported
H_7: The greater the market orientation of the dyad, the greater the level of commitment within the dyadic relationship.	Not supported
H_8: The greater the market orientation of the dyad, the greater the performance within the dyadic relationship.	Supported
H_9: The greater the communication between the supplier and distributor, the greater the perceptions of trust within the relationship.	Supported
H_{10}: The greater the similarity in shared values within a dyad, the greater the perceptions of trust between these channel members.	Supported
H_{11}: The greater the similarity in shared values within a dyad, the greater the perceptions of commitment between these channel members.	Supported
H_{12}: The greater the perceived benefits of the relationship, the greater the cooperation within the dyad.	Not supported
H_{13}: The greater the relationship termination costs, the greater the commitment between these channel members.	Supported
H_{14}: The greater the duration of the business association, the greater the commitment between these channel members.	Not supported

infancy. This study models and supports the effects of market orientation in the channel relationship using a dyadic framework, substantially adding to the emerging stream of literature regarding the importance of adopting a market orientation. Furthermore, previous research models incorporating the key constructs used in this study have mostly been recursive models and, consequently, have not examined how the outcome variable (performance) may in turn affect the source variable (market orientation). Three-stage least squares regression and partial correlation analysis were used to find support for the proposed model (see Table 11. 5 for summary of findings). Overall, the model suggests that market orientation is a way of instilling and promoting trust in a channel relationship, which then leads to greater cooperation and commitment. Greater relationship commitment ultimately results in enhanced organizational performance, which then works to further improve market orientation; thus, the cycle continues.

The direct effects of market orientation on cooperation and commitment were not completely supported because neither relationship was significant at the .05 level. The findings indicated, however, that market orientation does have a direct effect on performance; thus, the supported model depicts a bidirectional relationship between market orientation and performance.

Consistent with Morgan and Hunt (1994), our study found support for the posited relationship between trust and cooperation: The more channel members believe that they can trust one another, the more they are willing to cooperate with each other. Contrary to Morgan and Hunt, however, who found that trust and commitment lead to cooperation, we found that cooperation leads to commitment. This ordering is somewhat substantiated by Skinner, Gassenheimer, and Kelley (1992), who determined that cooperation led to satisfaction, and by Macneil (1978), who indicated that cooperation enhanced solidarity in channel relationships.

The attitudinal measure, commitment, was found in our study to affect the ultimate measure of a business—performance. This finding is especially significant because the linkage has been subjected to only limited empirical research (Heide & Stump, 1995; Kumar et al., 1994). Finally, performance was found to significantly impact market orientation, completing the iterative cycle. This study found that a high level of performance directly increases the level of market orientation that the firm pursues.

The model examined in this study also included secondary variables that may strengthen the association of the primary variables examined. Communication and shared values were determined to have a significant effect on trust in the channel dyadic relationship in our study, lending support to previous findings (Morgan & Hunt, 1994). Our analyses also substantiated prior findings that shared values (Morgan & Hunt, 1994) and relationship termination costs (Anderson & Weitz, 1992; Morgan & Hunt, 1994) have a significant impact on commitment to the channel relationship.

Our findings indicate that the explicit communication of relationship benefits is not necessary to elicit cooperation in the channel. In addition, relationship duration is less influential in determining commitment than expected. As Ganesan (1994) noted, long-term orientation (or a belief that the exchange relationship will continue into the future) is apparently a better indicator of closeness in relationship than length of the relationship.

Managerial Implications

Recent studies have detailed two prominent trends in channel relationships. One trend indicates a deterioration of channel relationships as global competition has encouraged manufacturers to use dual channels of distribution and reduce investments in their traditional channels while requiring greater channel investments (and thus risk) on the part of distributors (Arthur Anderson & Company, 1995; Frazier & Antia, 1995). There appears to be a trend toward developing strong relational exchanges to offset competitive thrusts and augment long-term stability, however (Nevin, 1995; Weitz & Jap, 1995). This study examines the utilization of market orientation as a strategic means of ensuring strong channel ties to enhance organizational performance and counter environmental threats. Strong channel alliances "can lead to a competitive positional advantage by enabling the alliance partners to perform various value chain activities at a lower cost and/or in a way that leads to differentiation" (Varadarajan & Cunningham, 1995, p. 292). Furthermore, Fites (1996) notes that "the global winners over the next 10 to 20 years are going to be the companies with the best distribution organizations that also provide superb customer support" (p. 86).

Market-oriented suppliers and distributors have associations equivalent to corporate alliances, which should provide a competitive advantage capable of thwarting environmental threats to either organization. Strong strategic partnerships between manufacturers and their distributors merge the goals of each firm, allowing for rapid channel adjustments to meet the challenges of global competition and changing domestic markets (Siguaw & Honeycutt, 1993). The merged goal of market-oriented channel members is the satisfaction of customer needs. This focus on customer needs has been highly touted as the dominant contributing factor in the successful turnaround of Caterpillar (Fites, 1996); furthermore, Arthur Anderson & Company (1995) has advocated adoption of a market orientation for the wholesaling industry. Our study highlights the importance and benefits of both parties in the channel dyad seeking to fulfill customer needs. A mutually held market orientation allows channel members to better serve shifting market needs within the context of strategic partners pursuing the same goals. Conversely, firms failing to establish alliances maintain adversarial relationships (Spekman, 1988), which continue to promote the individual interests of each firm (Bucklin, 1966; El-Ansary, 1975).

Fites (1996) notes that the factor that really makes the relationship work is not contractual agreements or techniques but mutual trust. To create trusting channel relationships, firms should adopt market-oriented behaviors. Our research clearly indicates that market orientation has a positive and significant effect on the level of trust in the dyadic relationship and thereby indirectly influences cooperation and commitment. Market-oriented behaviors serve as a means of initializing feelings of trust in the early stages of the relationship and as a method of maintaining high levels of trust in the latter stages of the association. The impact of market orientation on trust is especially important given that trust and commitment have been identified as key mediating variables in the relationship marketing process (Morgan & Hunt, 1994) and because "[p]ractitioners are placing more emphasis on using relational norms and attitudes such as trust and commitment to maintain continuity rather than the use of authoritative control mechanisms or vertical integration" (Weitz & Jap, 1995, p. 317). Consequently, the practice of market-oriented behaviors is a critical means of building and reinforcing trust in the channel relationship to keep channels intact and to reduce channel tensions.

Market orientation also has a positive direct and indirect effect on channel performance. Because better performance is the ultimate goal of business, a strong market orientation appears to be a critical element for all firms. Firms wanting to adopt a market orientation, and that have this orientation acknowledged by other channel members, must actively and publicly acquire and use information in day-to-day operations to achieve long-term customer satisfaction through superior organizational performance. In other words, the firms must continuously be seen by other channel members to collect or generate information and overtly react based on that information. A note of caution regarding the adoption of a market orientation is warranted, however. The activities and behaviors associated with a market orientation necessitate the commitment of resources (Kohli & Jaworski, 1990); therefore, a firm should ascertain that the benefits of better channel relationships and the corresponding increase in performance will more than offset the costs related to market-oriented actions. On the basis of this information, practitioners may elect to position their companies at varying degrees along the market-orientation continuum; thus, some firms may choose to adopt only a limited set of market-oriented behaviors, where the marginal cost of market orientation equals the marginal revenue generated from enhanced channel performance.

Our study indicated that trust has a significant effect on cooperation. This finding suggests that channel members must be cooperative with one another in the relationship before channel members are willing to commit to the relationship. After all, commitment to a relationship occurs when two channel members are determined to maintain an enduring and stable relationship with one another (Moorman et al., 1992; Morgan & Hunt, 1994), with both parties willing to take risks in the relationship (Gundlach & Murphy, 1993) and to make short-term sacrifices to sustain the relationship if necessary (Dwyer et al., 1987). Anderson and Weitz (1992) emphasize the importance of stability for commitment and a virtual pledge for continuity in the relationship. Channel relationships may periodically encounter problems, such as missed deadlines for delivery, but the intent of the parties is to sustain the relationship over the long term. This desire for a sustained and enduring relationship would be dubious if the channel members are uncooperative.

Our findings also indicate that members that are committed to maintaining their channel relationship will outperform other channel structures whose members lack a basic foundation of commitment. This study also found that increased performance directly increases the level of market orientation that the firm pursues. As organizations recognize the benefits directly and indirectly derived from a market orientation, they may escalate market-oriented actions to yield even greater rewards in terms of strengthened channel bonds and financial gains.

These findings indicate that companies should strive to increase communication and associate with channel members that have similar values to increase trust and commitment in the dyadic relationship. Relationship termination costs significantly affected commitment, which may suggest that commitment to the relationship might be solidified by channel members investing heavily in each other's business. Both suppliers and distributors may be well served to require idiosyncratic investments that would make it difficult to terminate the relationship (Williamson, 1983).

Limitations of the Study and Suggestions for Future Research

Although the findings from this study are significant to channel relationship research, they are based on cross-sectional data that do not fully capture the dynamics of change and connectedness between the parties in the relationship. Future research efforts should focus on long-term characteristics and effects of channel relationships; as Kohli and Jaworski (1990, p. 16) note, "[a] change in orientation takes place slowly." Indeed, Lichtenthal and Wilson (1992) identify some of the reasons why market orientation is a time-consuming process: "[I]n the short or intermediate run, capital equipment commitments, limits of technology, financing constraints, the need to retrain labor, and even established union rules prohibit rapid adjustment of the product-service benefit bundle the firm offers" (p. 205). Kohli and Jaworski (1990) found that firms seeking a greater market orientation planned to complete the process during a period of 4 years. Data collected during this 4-year period would provide valuable insight into the effects of various levels of market-oriented behaviors.

Future research should also investigate the appropriate method to be used to calculate true "dyadic" scores from respondents in different organizations. This study used the aggregation approach suggested by Kumar et al. (1994). Others, however, have noted limitations in this method and in the latent-trait approach that was proposed but rejected by Kumar et al. (1994). As pointed out by Weitz and Jap (1995), the problems associated with how to combine scores from two organizations into a true dyadic score have the potential to severely "impede empirical research on channel relationships" (p. 317). Perhaps the long stream of research that has been conducted relative to the use of multiple informants within an organization can be used to develop an appropriate methodology for the combination of information from informants in different organizations.

Future research should more carefully examine the market orientation construct and measures of the construct. First, possible antecedents of market orientation, such as organizational culture and values, and outcome measures other than those specified in this research should be examined. Second, a measure of actual or true market orientation in a relationship should be refined. Although the MARKOR scale measures self-reported market orientation, in a dyadic relationship the self-perceived level of market orientation of one dyad member may not necessarily agree with perceptions of the other dyad member. For the purposes of this study, we measured market orientation using the MARKOR scale (Jaworski & Kohli, 1993) and adjusted the results using the Customer Orientation scale (Deshpandé, Farley, & Webster, 1993) in an effort to measure "true" market orientation. A less cumbersome scale would allow each channel member to periodically measure its level of market orientation as perceived by the other party and make adjustments as needed. As each party defines the suitable level of market orientation within the dyad, the degree of trust, cooperation, commitment, and performance will rise or fall in a corresponding fashion.

Finally, as previously noted, the responses of the supplier and distributor groups were significantly different on most constructs of interest to this study. The effects of these different perceptions on channel performance should be investigated. Furthermore, studies that seek to determine the steps necessary for altering the perceptions of channel partners would be invaluable to practitioners seeking to enhance channel relationships. For example, what specific requirements are essential for generating equivalent levels of commitment or trust for both parties in the dyad? Similarly, what levels and modes of communication are necessary to create the perception that the supplier provides more than adequate information? As our model indicates, increasing perceived levels of these key constructs will only serve to heighten performance.

Appendix 11.A: Scale Development and Properties

There are potential methodological problems associated with using data collected from two firms involved in a dyadic relationship (Weitz & Jap, 1995). Primarily, the problem lies in how one goes about using both scores to represent the "dyadic score." This problem is similar to the issues associated with combining scores collected from multiple informants within the same organization. According to Kumar et al. (1994), there are primarily two methods that can be used to combine these scores—the "aggregation" approach and the "latent trait" approach. The aggregation approach pools the responses from each respondent and creates a dyadic score by averaging the responses to each construct. The latent trait approach treats the two responses as indicators of a latent construct that can be modeled using structural equation techniques. On the basis of arguments presented by Kumar et al. (1994) and of the use of this approach in other studies (Anderson & Weitz, 1992; Kaufman & Stern, 1988), we chose to use the aggregation approach. As pointed out by Kumar et al. (1994), this approach reduces random error but not necessarily systematic error. If one assumes, however, as have others (Anderson, 1987; Anderson & Narus, 1990; Marsh & Bailey, 1991), that informant bias factors are uncorrelated, then systematic error may also be less. Accordingly, all measures were determined by averaging the responses to each item in a particular scale.

The model presented in Figure 11.1 proposes that there are five primary constructs and five mediating constructs. The measurement of each of these will be discussed in turn in the subsequent sections. With the exception of one of the market orientation scales and the relationship termination costs scale, all scales exhibited unidimensionality evidenced by the following criteria: (a) high item intercorrelations, (b) high item-total correlations, and (c) a factor analysis that indicated the presence of a single factor with all factor loadings >.4 and having the theoretically correct sign. Internal consistency was assessed by calculating the Cronbach's alpha and comparing the results to the widely accepted criteria established by Nunnally (1978).

Market Orientation (DYADMO). As discussed previously, this study conceptualizes dyadic market orientation to be composed of the actual market orientation exhibited by the suppliers and distributors as well as the perceptions each has of the other party's level of market orientation. The actual market orientation was measured using the MARKOR scale first reported by Jaworski and Kohli (1993). Perceptions of the other party's market orientation were measured using the Customer Orientation scale developed by Deshpandé et al. (1993).

Jaworski and Kohli (1993) presented a comprehensive study designed to validate the MARKOR scale. They proposed that market orientation is a function of (a) the extent to which a firm generates intelligence about the market, (b) the dissemination of that information throughout the firm, and (c) the extent to which an organization responds based on the information gathered and disseminated. After initially developing a 32-item scale, their subsequent analysis resulted in a 20-item scale in which the intelligence dissemination and responsiveness components were collapsed into a single factor. This 20-item scale was used in the current analysis.

Our initial analysis of the inter-item and item-total correlations indicated that 3 of the 20 items did not exhibit a high degree of correlation with the other items. The item-total correlations for the three items were .31, .39, and .29. In addition, the average correlations of the three items with the other items in the scale were .18, .21, and .17, respectively. On the basis of this evidence, these three items were deleted from the scale. An exploratory factor analysis of the remaining 17 items indicated a three-factor solution. Loadings for the first factor, however, were quite high (between .68 and .44), and a screen test of the eigenvalues indicated a break between the first and second factor, with the first eigenvalue being more than twice as large as the second (5.26 vs. 2.12). On the basis of this analysis and consistent with Jaworski and Kohli (1993), the 17 items were used as a unidimensional scale. The Cronbach's alpha value of .86 indicated a high degree of internal consistency.

The scale developed by Deshpandé et al. (1993) was used to measure one party's perceptions of the extent to which the other party exhibited market-oriented behaviors. The scale also had a high degree of internal consistency as indicated by the Cronbach's alpha level of .86.

For each respondent, the average score for the MARKOR scale was added to the average score for the customer orientation scale to develop the score for the market orientation of the dyad. Accordingly, higher scores indicate higher levels of dyadic market orientation.

Trust (DYADTRST). Trust was measured using an 18-item scale first presented by Ganesan (1994). In addition to being unidimensional, the scale exhibited a Cronbach's alpha level of .95, which indicates a high degree of internal consistency.

Cooperation (DYADCOOP). Cooperation was assessed using a scale developed by Cannon (1992). The scale is composed of six items that require respondents to indicate the extent to which the items accurately/inaccurately describe their experience with the specified trading partner. The Cronbach alpha for the scale was a very acceptable .83.

Commitment (DYADCOMT). A seven-item scale developed by Morgan and Hunt (1994) was used to measure commitment. The Cronbach's alpha level of .90 indicates a high degree of internal consistency.

Performance (DYADPERF). Two different types of performance data were collected. First, respondents were asked to provide a number of actual "objective" financial measures (e.g., annual dollar sales volume, change in market share, change in sales, and return on assets). Although it would appear that objective financial measures are the preferred way to measure organizational performance, several studies have questioned the use of these measures (Govindarajan, 1988; Naman & Slevin, 1993; Sandberg & Hofer, 1987; Sapienza, Smith, & Gannon, 1988). Essentially, these researchers argue that oftentimes respondents are unwilling to provide objective performance data; if they do, it may not be representative of true organizational performance or may not be consistent with data provided by other firms. Accordingly, a measure developed by Naman and Slevin (1993) was also used to evaluate organizational performance. The measure called for respondents to indicate their degree of satisfaction with seven items (e.g., cash flow, gross profit margin, and return on investment) using a response scale anchored by strongly dissatisfied (1) and strongly satisfied (7). Naman and Slevin (1993) argue that in addition to overcoming the problems mentioned previously, this scale (a) provides the ability to measure the true multidimensional nature of organizational performance rather than relying on single measures and (b) allows the assessment of intermethod reliability. The reliability of the scale was assessed by calculating the Cronbach's alpha, which was a very high .92. Only the subjective measure was used in the subsequent analysis because the large number of returned questionnaires with missing objective financial data prohibited the effective use of this information.

Communication (DYADCOMM). This construct was measured using a six-item scale developed by Anderson and Weitz (1992). In addition to meeting the previously mentioned tests for unidimensionality, the scale had a Cronbach's alpha level of .82.

Relationship Benefits (DYADBENF). The relationship benefits variable was adapted from a measure presented by Anderson and Weitz (1992) and was designed to provide an assessment of the types of nonfinancial benefits accruing to both firms involved in a dyadic relationship. In addition to being unidimensional based on the criteria presented earlier, the measure, which consists of five items, had an associated Cronbach's alpha level of .75.

Relationship Termination Costs (DYADCOST). The construct known as relationship termination costs was measured using a 12-item scale adapted from Anderson and Weitz (1992). The inter-item correlations for the scale items were all highly significant and in the appropriate direction (i.e., positive). The item-total correlations were also high, and there was no appreciable increase in reliability based on the deletion of any single item. The factor analysis, however, indicated a three-factor solution. Closer inspection indicated that although three factors were extracted, the loadings on the first factor were all high (.67-.40) and in the theoretically correct direction. In addition, a screen test indicated a significant break between the first and second eigenvalue (5.30 vs. 1.31). Finally, there were only three cross-loadings that exceeded .4: two on the second factor and one on the third factor. Given this evidence, and the fact that the scale was designed by Anderson and Weitz (1992) to be unidimensional, we decided to use all the items in the scale. The Cronbach's alpha level of .88 indicated a high degree of internal consistency.

Shared Values (DYADVALU). A five-item scale first presented by Hunt et al. (1989) was used to measure shared values. Both suppliers and distributors were asked to respond to each of the five items based on the degree to which they agreed or disagreed with the statement as it pertained to their own firm. In addition, the suppliers and distributors responded to the five items based on how they (the responding firm) believed the other party in the dyadic relationship would agree or disagree with the statements concerning their own firm (the responding firm). Thus, each item resulted in two scores—one indicating the degree to which the statement reflected the perceptions of the responding firm and one indicating the extent to which the responding firm felt the other firm in the dyadic relationship would agree or disagree with the statement concerning the responding firm.

The score for the scale was created by first calculating the absolute value of the difference between the two scores. Because this resulted in lower scores indicating a higher degree of agreement, the "difference" scores were reversed so that higher values represented a situation in which the responding firm believed that there were no differences between its values and those of the other firm involved in the dyadic relationship. The difficulty in assessing the psychometric properties of scales based on difference scores has been discussed by Iacobucci, Grayson, and Ostrom (1994), whose discussion is relative to the SERVQUAL scale (Zeithaml, Parasuraman, & Berry, 1990). As Iacobucci et al. point out, difference score-based constructs have been proven in some cases to be unreliable even if the component scales are quite reliable. In addition to assessing service quality, however, difference scores have a long history of use in the organizational theory literature. Accordingly, we decided to use the scale in this research.

Relationship Duration (DYADDUR). This construct was measured by a single item that simply asked each respondent to indicate the length of time the business relationship had endured between the two firms.

References

Achrol, R. (1991). Evolution of the marketing organization: New forms for turbulent environments. *Journal of Marketing, 55*(4), 77-93.

And now, the post-industrial corporation. (1986, March 3). *Business Week, 65,* 64-71.

Anderson, E., & Weitz, B. (1992, February). The use of pledges to build and sustain commitment in distribution channels. *Journal of Marketing Research, 29,* 18-34.

Anderson, J. C. (1987, April). An approach for confirmatory measurement and structural equation modeling of organizational properties. *Management Science, 33,* 525-541.

Anderson, J. C., Håkansson, H., & Johanson, J. (1994). Dyadic business relationships within a network context. *Journal of Marketing, 58*(4), 1-15.

Anderson, J. C., & Narus, J. A. (1990). A model of distributor firm and manufacturer firm working partnerships. *Journal of Marketing, 54*(1), 42-58.

Angle, H. L., & Lawson, M. B. (1993). Changes in affective and continuance commitment in times of relocation. *Journal of Business Research, 26,* 3-15.

Arthur Anderson & Company. (1995). *Facing the forces of change: Transforming your business with best practices.* Washington, DC: Distribution Research & Education Foundation.

Baker, T. L., & Hawes, J. M. (1993). The relationship between strategy and structure within channel dyad. *Journal of Marketing Channels, 2*(4), 83-97.

Barksdale, H. C., & Darden, B. (1971). Marketers' attitudes toward the marketing concept. *Journal of Marketing, 35*(4), 29-36.

Becker, C. S. (1987). Friendship between women: A phenomenological study of best friends. *Journal of Phenomenological Psychology, 18,* 59-72.

Bell, M. L., & Emory, C. W. (1971). The faltering marketing concept. *Journal of Marketing, 35*(4), 37-42.

Buchanan, L. (1992, February). Vertical trade relationships: The role of dependence and symmetry in attaining organizational goals. *Journal of Marketing Research, 29,* 65-75.

Bucklin, L. P. (1966). *A theory of distribution channel structure.* Berkeley: University of California, Institute of Business and Economic Research.

Cadogan, J. W., & Diamantopoulos, A. (1995, March). Narver & Slater, Kohli & Jaworski and the market orientation construct: Integration and internationalization. *Journal of Strategic Marketing, 3,* 41-60.

Cannon, J. P. (1992). *A taxonomy of buyer-seller relationships in business markets.* Unpublished doctoral dissertation, University of North Carolina at Chapel Hill.

Carnevale, D. G., & Wechsler, B. (1992, February). Trust in the public sector: Individual and organizational determinants. *Administration & Society, 23,* 471-494.

Cook, J., & Wall, T. (1980). New work attitude measures of trust, organizational commitment and personal need nonfulfillment. *Journal of Occupational Psychology, 53,* 39-52.

Day, G. S. (1994). The capabilities of market-driven organizations. *Journal of Marketing, 58*(4), 37-52.

Day, G. S., & Wensley, R. (1983). Marketing theory with a strategic orientation. *Journal of Marketing, 47*(4), 79-89.

Deshpandé, R., Farley, J. U., & Webster, F. E., Jr. (1993). Corporate culture, customer orientation, and innovativeness in Japanese firms: A quadrad analysis. *Journal of Marketing, 57*(1), 23-37. (See also Chapter 4)

Deutsch, M. (1960). The effect of motivational orientation on trust and suspicion. *Human Relations, 13,* 123-139.

Diamantopoulos, A., & Hart, S. (1993). Linking market orientation and company performance: Preliminary evidence on Kohli and Jaworski's framework. *Journal of Strategic Marketing, 1*(2), 93-121.

Dreher, A. (1993). Marketing orientation: How to grasp the phenomenon. In J. Chias & J. Sureda (Eds.), *Marketing for the new Europe: Dealing with complexity* (pp. 375-393). Barcelona: European Marketing Academy.

Dwyer, F. R., Schurr, P. H., & Oh, S. (1987). Developing buyer-seller relationships. *Journal of Marketing, 51*(2), 11-27.

El-Ansary, A. (1975, Summer). Determinants of power-dependence in the distribution channel. *Journal of Retailing, 51*, 59-74, 94.

Fites, D. V. (1996, March/April). Make your dealers your partners. *Harvard Business Review, 74*, 84-95.

Frazier, G. L., & Antia, K. D. (1995, Fall). Exchange relationships and interfirm power in channels of distribution. *Journal of the Academy of Marketing Science, 23*, 321-326.

Ganesan, S. (1994). Determinants of long-term orientation in buyer-seller relationships. *Journal of Marketing, 58*(2), 1-19.

Garfinkel, H. (1964). Studies of routine grounds of everyday activities. *Social Problems, 11*, 225-250.

Gladstein, D. L. (1984, December). Groups in context: A model of task group effectiveness. *Administrative Science Quarterly, 29*, 499-517.

Golembiewski, R. T., & McConkie, M. L. (1975). The centrality of interpersonal trust in group processes. In C. L. Cooper (Ed.), *Theories of group processes* (pp. 131-185). New York: John Wiley.

Govindarajan, V. (1988). A contingency approach to strategy implementation at the business unit level: Integrating administrative mechanisms with strategy. *Academy of Management Journal, 31*(4), 828-853.

Gundlach, G. T., & Murphy, P. E. (1993). Ethical and legal foundations of relational marketing exchange. *Journal of Marketing, 57*(4), 35-46.

Heide, J. B., & John, G. (1988). The role of dependence balancing in safe guarding transaction-specific assets in conventional channels. *Journal of Marketing, 52*(1), 20-35.

Heide, J. B., & Stump, R. L. (1995). Performance implications of buyer-seller relationships in industrial markets. *Journal of Business Research, 32*, 57-66.

Hickson, D. J., Hinnings, C. R., Lee, C. A., Schneck, R. E., & Pennings, J. M. (1971, June). A strategic contingencies theory of intraorganizational power. *Administrative Science Quarterly, 16*, 216-229.

Houston, F. S. (1986). The marketing concept: What it is and what it is not. *Journal of Marketing, 50*(2), 81-87.

Hrebiniak, L. G. (1971). *A multivariate analysis of professional and organizational commitment orientations among teachers and nurses.* Unpublished doctoral dissertation, State University of New York at Buffalo.

Hunt, S. D., Wood, V. R., & Chonko, L. B. (1989). Corporate ethical values and organizational commitment in marketing. *Journal of Marketing, 53*(3), 79-90.

Iacobucci, D., Grayson, K., & Ostrom, A. (1994). The calculus of service quality and customer satisfaction: Theoretical and empirical differentiation and integration. In T. Swartz, D. E. Bowen, & S. W. Brown (Eds.), *Advances in services marketing and management: Research and practice* (pp. 23-52). Greenwich, CT: JAI.

Jaworski, B. J., & Kohli, A. K. (1993). Market orientation: Antecedents and consequences. *Journal of Marketing, 57*(3), 53-70. (See also Chapter 5)

Kaufman, P. J., & Stern, L. W. (1988). Relational exchange norms, perceptions of unfairness, and retained hostility in commercial litigation. *Journal of Conflict Resolution, 32*(3), 534-552.

Kelley, H. H. (1983). Love and commitment. In H. H. Kelley et al. (Eds.), *Close relationships* (pp. 265-314). New York: Freeman.

King, R. L. (1965). The marketing concept. In G. Schwartz (Ed.), *Science in marketing* (pp. 70-97). New York: John Wiley.

Kohli, A. K., & Jaworski, B. J. (1990). Market orientation: The construct, research propositions, and managerial implications. *Journal of Marketing, 54*(2), 1-18. (See also Chapter 2)

Kohli, A. K., Jaworski, B. J., & Kumar, A. (1993, November). MARKOR: A measure of market orientation. *Journal of Marketing Research, 30,* 467-477.

Kumar, N., Hibbard, J. D., & Stern, L. W. (1994). *The nature and consequences of marketing channel intermediary commitment* (Report No. 94-115). Cambridge, MA: Marketing Science Institute.

Kumar, N., Scheer, L. K., & Steenkamp, J.-B. E. M. (1995, February). The effects of supplier fairness on vulnerable resellers. *Journal of Marketing Research, 32,* 54-65.

Lichtenthal, J. D., & Wilson, D. T. (1992). Becoming market oriented. *Journal of Business Research, 24,* 191-207.

Loomis, J. (1959). Communication, the development of trust, and cooperative behavior. *Human Relations, 12,* 305-315.

Luhman, N. (1979). *Trust and power.* London: Wiley.

Lusch, R. F., & Laczniak, G. R. (1987, Fall). The evolving marketing concept, competitive intensity and organizational performance. *Journal of the Academy of Marketing Science, 15,* 1-11.

Macneil, I. (1978). Contracts: Adjustment of long-term economic relations under classical, neo-classical, and relational contract law. *Northwestern Law Review, 72,* 854-906.

Marsh, H. W., & Bailey, M. (1991). Confirmatory factor analyses of multitrait-multimethod data: A comparison of alternative models. *Applied Psychological Measurement, 15,* 47-70.

McNamara, C. P. (1972). The present status of the marketing concept. *Journal of Marketing, 36*(1), 50-57.

Mellinger, G. D. (1956). Interpersonal trust as a factor in communication. *Journal of Abnormal Social Psychology, 52,* 304-309.

Moorman, C., Zaltman, G., & Deshpandé, R. (1992, August). Relationships between providers and users of market research: The dynamics of trust within and between organizations. *Journal of Marketing Research, 29,* 314-328.

Morgan, R. M., & Hunt, S. D. (1994). The commitment-trust theory of relationship marketing. *Journal of Marketing, 58*(3), 20-38.

Naman, J. L., & Slevin, D. P. (1993, February). Entrepreneurship and the concept of fit: A model and empirical tests. *Strategic Management Journal, 14,* 137-153.

Narver, J. C., & Slater, S. F. (1990). The effect of a market orientation on business profitability. *Journal of Marketing, 54*(4), 20-35. (See also Chapter 3)

Neilson, C. C., & Wilson, E. J. (1994). Interorganizational cooperation in buyer-seller relationships. In J. Sheth & A. Parvatiyar (Eds.), *Relationship marketing: Theory, methods and applications* (pp. 2-10). 1994 Research Conference Proceedings, Center for Relationship Marketing, Roberto C. Goizueta Business School, Emory University, Atlanta.

Nevin, J. R. (1995, Fall). Relationship marketing and distribution channels: Exploring fundamental issues. *Journal of the Academy of Marketing Science, 24,* 327-334.

Nunnally, J. C. (1978). *Psychometric theory.* New York: McGraw-Hill.

Porter, L. W., Steers, R. M., Mowday, R. T., & Boulian, P. V. (1974). Organizational commitment, job satisfaction, and turnover among psychiatric technicians. *Journal of Applied Psychology, 59*(5), 603-609.

Pruitt, D. G. (1981). *Negotiation behavior.* New York: Academic Press.

Rotter, J. B. (1967). A new scale for the measurement of interpersonal trust. *Journal of Personality, 35,* 651-665.

Ruekert, R. W. (1992). Developing a market orientation: An organizational strategy perspective. *International Journal of Research in Marketing, 9,* 225-245.

Samter, W., & Burleson, B. (1984, May 26). When you're down and troubled . . . have you got a friend? Effects of cognitive and motivational factors on spontaneous comforting in a quasi-natural situation. *Annual International Communication Association Proceedings, 213-217.*

Sandberg, W. R., & Hofer, C. W. (1987). Improving new venture performance: The role of strategy, industry structure, and the entrepreneur. *Journal of Business Venturing, 2,* 5-28.

Sapienza, H. J., Smith, K. G., & Gannon, M. J. (1988). Using subjective evaluations of organizational performance in small business research. *American Journal of Small Business, 12*(3), 45-53.

Selnes, F., & Wesenberg, P. (1993). Organizational processes in becoming more market-oriented. In R. Varadarajan & B. Jaworski (Eds.), *Marketing theory and applications* (Vol. 4, pp. 22-31). Chicago: American Marketing Association.

Shapiro, B. P. (1988, November/December). What the hell is "market oriented"? *Harvard Business Review, 66,* 119-125.

Shapiro, D. L., Sheppard, B. H., & Cheraskin, L. (1992, October). Business on a handshake. *Negotiation Journal, 365-377.*

Siguaw, J. A., Brown, G., & Widing, R. E., II. (1994, February). The influence of the market orientation of the firm on sales force behavior and attitudes. *Journal of Marketing Research, 31,* 106-116.

Siguaw, J. A., & Honeycutt, E. D. (1993). Flexible manufacturing and the organization's marketing practices. *Journal of Strategic Marketing, 1,* 231-245.

Skinner, S. J., Gassenheimer, J. B., & Kelley, S. W. (1992). Cooperation in supplier-dealer relations. *Journal of Retailing, 68*(2), 174-193.

Slater, S. F., & Narver, J. C. (1994). Does competitive environment moderate the market orientation-performance relationship? *Journal of Marketing, 58*(1), 46-55. (See also Chapter 6)

Slater, S. F., Narver, J. C., & Aaby, N.-E. (1994). The strategic profile of a market-oriented business. In R. Achrol & A. Mitchell (Eds.), *Enhancing knowledge development in marketing* (pp. 11-12). American Marketing Association.

Spekman, R. E. (1988, July/August). Strategic supplier selection: Understanding long-term buyer relationship. *Business Horizons, 31,* 75-81.

Stern, L. W., & El-Ansary, A. (1990). *Marketing channels.* Englewood Cliffs, NJ: Prentice Hall.

Varadarajan, P. R., & Cunningham, M. H. (1995, Fall). Strategic alliance: A synthesis of conceptual foundations. *Journal of the Academy of Marketing Science, 23,* 282-296.

Webster, F. E. (1988, May/June). Rediscovering the marketing concept. *Business Horizons, 31,* 29-39.

Webster, F. E. (1992). The changing role of marketing in the corporation. *Journal of Marketing, 56*(4), 1-17.

Weitz, B. A., & Jap, S. D. (1995, Fall). Relationship marketing in distribution channels. *Journal of the Academy of Marketing Science, 23,* 305-320.

Williamson, O. (1983, September). Credible commitment: Using hostages to support exchange. *American Economic Review, 73,* 519-540.

Wilson, D. T. (1995, Fall). An integrated model of buyer-seller relationships. *Journal of the Academy of Marketing Science, 23,* 335-345.

Zeithaml, V. A., Parasuraman, A., & Berry, L. L. (1990). *Delivering quality service: Balancing customer perceptions and expectations.* New York: Free Press.

Additional Reading

Eddy, W. B. (1981). *Public organization behavior and development.* Cambridge, MA: Winthrop.

Morgan, R. M., & Morgan, N. A. (1991). An exploratory study of market orientation in the U.K. consulting engineering profession. *International Journal of Advertising, 10*(4), 333-347.

Webster, C. (1993). Refinement of the marketing culture scale and the relationship between marketing culture and profitability of a service firm. *Journal of Business Research, 26,* 111-131.

Zand, D. E. (1972). Trust and managerial problem solving. *Administrative Science Quarterly, 17,* 229-239.

Appendix: Publication History

Chapter 2 was originally released by MSI as Report #90-113. A later version was published in 1990 as "Market Orientation: The Construct, Research Propositions, and Managerial Implications," Ajay K. Kohli and Bernard J. Jaworski, *Journal of Marketing 54*(2), 1-18.

Chapter 3 was originally released by MSI as Report #89-120. A later version was published in 1990 as "The Effect of a Market Orientation on Business Profitability," John C. Narver and Stanley F. Slater, *Journal of Marketing 54*(4), 20-35.

Chapter 4 was originally released by MSI as Report # 92-100. A later version was published in 1993 as "Corporate Culture, Customer Orientation, and Innovativeness in Japanese Firms: A Quadrad Analysis," Rohit Deshpandé, John U. Farley, and Frederick E. Webster, Jr., *Journal of Marketing 57*(1), 23-37.

Chapter 5 was originally released by MSI as Report #92-104. A later version was published in 1993 as "Market Orientation: Antecedents and Consequences," Bernard J. Jaworski and Ajay K. Kohli, *Journal of Marketing 57*(3), 53-70.

Chapter 6 was originally released by MSI as Report # 92-118. A later version was published in 1994 as "Does the Competitive Environment

Moderate the Market Orientation-Performance Relationship?" Stanley F. Slater and John C. Narver, *Journal of Marketing 58*(1), 46-55.

Chapter 7 was originally released by MSI as Report #95-102. A later version was published in 1996 as "A Longitudinal Study of the Impact of Market Structure, Firm Structure, Strategy, and Market Orientation Culture on Dimensions of Small-Firm Performance," Alfred M. Pelham and David T. Wilson, *Journal of the Academy of Marketing Science 24*(1), 27-43.

Chapter 8 was originally released by MSI as Report No. 93-121.

Chapter 9 was originally released by MSI as Report No. 96-125. A later version was published in 1998 as "Measuring Market Orientation: Generalization and Synthesis," Rohit Deshpandé and John Farley, *Journal of Market-Focused Management 2*(3), 213-232.

Chapter 10 was originally released by MSI as Report No. 94-103. A later version was published in 1995 as "Market Orientation and the Learning Organization," Stanley F. Slater and John C. Narver, *Journal of Marketing 59*(3), 63-74.

Chapter 11 was originally released by MSI as Report No. 97-103. A later version was published in 1998 as "Effects of Supplier Market Orientation on Distributor Market Orientation and the Channel Relationship: The Distributor Perspective," Judy A. Siguaw, Penny M. Simpson, and Thomas L. Baker, *Journal of Marketing 62*(3), 99-111.

Author Index

Subject Index

Adaptive learning, 240, 241, 245
Adhocracy cultures, 83, 85, 95, 97-98
Allaire, Paul, 254
Analog Devices, 255-256, 257

Banc One, 253
Bell Atlantic, 252
Buyer power, 63, 66, 142, 143-144
    for commodity businesses, 68
    measures, 149
    relationship to market orientation, 159
    relationship to performance, 149, 156

Canon, 98, 251, 257
Center for Entrepreneurship, Eastern
    Michigan University, 176
Centralization, 28-29, 109, 110, 119, 122, 125
    in learning organizations, 254
    in small firms, 174
    measuring, 116, 129, 177, 188
Channel relationships:
    benefits, 272, 279, 284-285, 296
    commitment in, 272, 275, 276, 277,
        279-280, 285-286, 288, 291, 295
    communication in, 272, 278, 284, 296
    competitive advantage of, 289

cooperation in, 272, 274-275, 277, 279,
    284-286, 291, 295
duration, 272, 279-280, 285, 288-289, 297
dyadic research, 271, 280-286, 293-297
future research directions, 291-293
influence of market orientation, 268, 269,
    271-273, 285-286
limitations of study, 291-292
management of, 289-291
market orientation of partners, 273,
    276-278, 285, 286-291
perceptions of partner's market
    orientation, 273, 281, 292
performance of participants, 272,
    276-277, 278, 285-286, 288, 290, 295
shared values, 272, 279, 284, 285, 297
termination costs, 272, 279-280, 285, 291,
    296-297
trust in, 272, 273-275, 278, 279, 284, 290,
    291, 295
Clan cultures, 83-85, 95, 97-98
Coca-Cola, 242
Commitment:
    cooperation and, 275
    in channel relationships, 272, 277,
        279-280, 285-286, 288
    influence on performance, 276, 291
    measures, 295

About the Authors

Thomas L. Baker is Associate Professor of Marketing in the Department of Management and Marketing, Cameron School of Business, at the University of North Carolina at Wilmington. His research interests include inter- and intraorganizational relationships, cooperation and competition, and services marketing.

Rohit Deshpandé is Executive Director at the Marketing Science Institute and the Sebastion Kresge Professor of Marketing at Harvard Business School. His primary research interests are in global marketing strategy implementation.

John U. Farley is Henkel Professor of Marketing at the Chinese European International Business School in Shanghai; C.V. Starr Distinguished Research Fellow in International Business, Amos Tuck School, at Dartmouth College; and Ira A. Lipman Professor Emeritus of Marketing, The Wharton School, at the University of Pennsylvania. His research interests include marketing and business strategies in world markets and development and application of management science techniques to problems related to global marketing and strategy.

Robert L. Jacobson is Evert McCabe Distinguished Professor of Marketing and Transportation and Chairman of the Department of Marketing and International Business, School of Business Administration, at the University of Washington. His teaching and research interests include marketing strategy, marketing management, entrepreneurial management, and econometrics.

Bernard J. Jaworski is the Jeanne and David Tappan Marketing Fellow and Professor of Marketing at the University of Southern California. His research focuses on building and implementing market-driven organizations, the effects of marketing communications on customers, building strong brands, and directing and managing the sales force.

Ajay K. Kohli is the Sam Barshop Centennial Professor of Marketing Administration at the University of Texas at Austin. His research interests include market orientation and sales management.

John C. Narver is Professor in the Department of Marketing and International Business, School of Business Administration, at the University of Washington. His research and teaching interests include the effects and creation of customer-focused organizations, marketing strategy, and pricing.

Alfred M. Pelham is Assistant Professor of Marketing at Grand Valley State University. His research interests include small business management, market orientation, and consultative selling and sales management.

Judy A. Siguaw is Associate Professor of Marketing at Cornell University. Her research focuses on channel relationships, market orientation, and sales and sales management.

Penny M. Simpson is Associate Professor of Marketing and the David D. Morgan Professor of Marketing at Northwestern State University of Louisiana. Her research interests include channel of distribution and relationship marketing and advertising effectiveness and ethics.

Stanley F. Slater is Professor and Director of the Business Administration Program at the University of Washington, Bothell. His current research and writing are concerned with marketing strategy implementation and the processes of organizational learning.

Frederick E. Webster, Jr. is Charles Henry Jones Third Century Professor of Management, Amos Tuck School, at Dartmouth College. Currently, his research focuses on marketing organization.

David T. Wilson is Alvin H. Clemens Professor of Entrepreneurial Studies at Pennsylvania State University. His research interests include strategic alliances and relationships and marketing value creation.